Sandra L. Kearse-Stockton

# 480 Codorus Street Book II

### Trials and Tribulations

*by*

Sandra L. Kearse-Stockton

Sandra L. Kearse-Stockton

Copyright 2021 Sandra L. Kearse-Stockton,
All rights reserved.
last revised August 25, 2021

No part of this book may be reproduced in any form or by any electronic or mechanical means including information storage and retrieval systems, without permission in writing from the author. The only exception is by a reviewer, who may quote short excerpts in a review.

# Dedication

This book is dedicated to awesome girlfriends, Retired USA Colonel Sharon Singleton, Retired USA Lieutenant Colonel Ruth Anne Minor, Denise Middleton-Brown, Family Nurse Practitioner, Karla Graham, Social Worker, Access Housing, Inc., and Portia Owens-Perry, who have forever supported me in all of my endeavors. A special dedication to my husband Aaron Edward Stockton whom I love so dearly and to my children, Kimmy Jo Kearse, Kevin Scott Kearse Sr, Karmentrina Schevelle Kearse and Keenan Wynn Kearse Sr (may he rest in peace), Tracey Smallwood (my niece), and the late Joann Borders, who was my very best girlfriend who gave me so much guidance during my young years and throughout her life. She was a big part of my life. I hope that I live in their hearts for all eternity as well as in the hearts of all the generations to follow in my blood line. This book is also dedicated to all of the women and men with or without children trying to survive life as we know it in this world today.

Sandra L. Kearse-Stockton

## **A Special Thanks to Friends of My Children from Andrews Air Force Base**

Debra Warner, Julie Cannon-Holley, Stephanie Marshall-Smoot

## **A Very Special Thanks to Granddaughter Sandra-Alexis Schevelle Rodriguez**

<u>For coordinating my wardrobe and applying my makeup for live appearances.</u>

<u>I thank wholeheartedly all of the family and friends who have stepped up to support me in my writing endeavors.</u>

## LIVING IN TURMOIL

Dying to Live

Suffocating to Breathe

Nothing in the World

To put my mind at ease.

Struggling for Right,

Toying with Wrong,

Longing for a Time

And a World long Gone.

Thoughts nipping at my Heels,

Memories pulling at my Mind,

Lost souls Whispering

"You are running out of time."

Bodies torn apart,

Organs functioning no More,

Right side and Left side,

My brain is at War.

Thirsting for Knowledge,

Drowning with Achievements,

Lords of the Jungle,

Lousing their sick Sense.

# Foreword

## A Great Storyteller

What makes a great storyteller? Is it just vision? Is it the ability to see not just what's in front of you but the periphery where the real story lies? Sandra makes us wonder if seeing around corners is a superpower. To understand what exists in the margins is one thing, but the artistry is in how you tell the story.

W.E.B. Dubois once said, "The Artist's struggle for integrity...the poets [meaning all artists] are finally the only people who know the truth about us."

Sandra Stockton is a Poet; she knows the truth about us. The truth about us was made manifest in her life. She shared that truth in her first work, *480 Codorus Street*. There she laid bare her life, and in so doing she told us about ours. Out of the trauma, the pain, and the sorrow, joy happens. Codorus Street is as American as apple pie. We walked those streets with her. We realized that happiness lives in each of us, and it is our job to let it flourish.

How does the Poet complete a work? Sandra used word imagery the same way a visual artist paints a collage. *480 Codorus Street* is her collage. She shared a life complete with all that living in society's margins brings.

At the end of *480 Codorus Street,* Lt. Colonel Sandra Stockton tempts us with what's coming. She made it clear that this was the first of three books. She introduced us to Aaron, the cutie pie who comes into her life. She promised us that she would make it clear who Aaron was and who Ace is.

What Sandra brought and what Lt. Colonel Stockton brings is clarity. She makes W.E.B. Dubois' depiction of an artist as a poet a fact.

In *480 Codorus Street,* we learned about Sandra now we learn who Lt. Colonel Sandra L. Stockton is. We have had the pleasure of seeing her over time, yet *Codorus Street* proved how little we really knew about her. It whets the appetite knowing how much more there is to know.

The one thing we are sure of is her love for self and her love for others. That love she shares with all of us who live in the margins.

Criminal District Court Judge Calvin Johnson (ret)
New Orleans, USA

# Introduction

Everything that you read here is from my memories, from my perspective only. Although my siblings Mary Elizabeth, Mabel Lee, Dorothy Mae (rest in peace), Lugenia, Bonita Faith, and Clifford Earl (rest in peace) have experienced many of the same things that I have experienced, their perspective might be very different from mine. We were all cut from the same cloth, but we are all different. Everyone starts from somewhere. I started out at 480 Codorus Street, one of seven children born to William Junior Smallwood and Dorothy Mae Jackson-Smallwood, may they both rest in peace. I was meant to be where I am at today. It was decided before I was born. A great storyteller I am of my past and the past of my ancestors.

I was born Sandra Lee Smallwood in York, Pennsylvania on June of 1949 in the southwest section of a York City neighborhood that stood by the Codorus Creek. Codorus Street was demolished in the 1960s. It is now covered mostly by the Martin Luther King Jr. Park. Codorus Street neighborhood was a close-knit, predominately Black part of York County. I remember a neighborhood where color did not matter. Neighbors helped each other. The world is so vast now, to the point that some do not even know their neighbors or even want to know their neighbors.

Work on this book, *480 Codorus Street*, started many, many years ago when I was a very young adult. I was very good at sharing my life stories with my immediate family and friends. I wanted to share my life experiences and shed some light on my life as I knew it and how my experiences could benefit others. My life story and family history are memories I want to share primarily with my children so that they may pass my story on to their children and that my story may blossom into a generational historical gift for them. It actually lays out for them the manner in which I have lived, the values I live by, and surviving unpredictability as it showed itself to me time and time again. I share my hidden scars because I have held them in for so many years. I feel emotionally free.

I pray that anyone who reads and shares my story will embrace it as a gift as that is my hope. One should always treat another as they wish to be treated, and remember: Honestly is always the best policy. If you live by these principles, you should have a meaningful life. It is my time to shine, and my books will be one of my most challenging tests of my time and life span. My life is a masterpiece, it is full of color, and I know the Holy Spirit walks with me and my family. I wake up every day and make sure to praise God and thank Him for my colorful life. The good and the not so good parts is what created me. If I should pass on from this earth today or tomorrow, I have truly lived and appreciated all that God has given to me.

# Chapter One: My Next Move

Summer 1972, there was a lot going on. My brother Bucky's daughter Tameca was born. Lord, was she going to be spoiled just like her dad was? Being the only boy and the baby had gotten him a lot of perks. Mom never brought up the fact that while Bucky and my play brother Wayne used to babysit for me that they were doing more than babysitting. Bucky was her baby; he could do no wrong. Mom babysat Tameca for her mom and Bucky. That allowed for me and all of my sisters to see and have her at our houses quite a bit. Tameca looked just like my baby brother. He would father only one child ever.

Summer was coming to an end, and my boyfriend Aaron had not telephoned me. It had been two weeks now. It was all good. I told him that with or without him I would find a father for my children and a husband for me. I did not have time for feeling sorry for myself or my relationships. I had to prepare my kids for the new school year, which started in two weeks.

The Jerry Lewis Labor Day Telethon was quickly approaching, and my daughter Kimmy Jo was bugging me about helping her and her siblings to get the yard decorated for her penny carnival. The telethon would send us the kits to make the penny games. They would blow up balloons and I would tie them on the yard gate and on the clothesline. All of the neighborhood kids would come and pitch pennies into boxes that we made. They all knew about Kimmy Jo's penny carnival. Kimmy Jo would faithfully watch the Jerry Lewis Telethon every year, and every year we all had to help her. I would look out of the window and watch her, Karmentrina, Kevin, Keenan, and her friend Debbie Mitchell, a next-door neighbor, running the show. They had so much fun.

I was tired, but it was worth it to see them so involved and happy. I never remember sending the pennies anywhere.

Karmentrina now reminds me that Kimmy would count out pennies for them to go to Eddie's corner store for ice cream and candy. Business-minded Kimmy Jo, that's my girl.

Mom was sewing the girls' school uniforms, letting out hems and cuffs for the boys. I had worked out a budget to get new special shoes for Kimmy Jo and Kevin with their fallen arches. Lord knows them Stride Rite shoes were so damn expensive. I could hardly think about school, but I had to.

It darn sure was not my kids' fault that Aaron had not called me. I was just so aggressive. Maybe I'd scared him off with such serious expectations. After all, we had only known each other for six or seven months. I was about to lose my funking mind thinking about this handsome, single military man. Lord knows he had choices. Yep, I must have been crazy. I decided that I would go sit and talk with Mom about the whole situation. She always knew the right thing to say to settle me down.

A few days later I went to visit Mom and laid it all out for her. I knew I could not talk to Mary because she always said he was too young for me. The rest of my sisters were too young to give me advice. They were always coming to me for advice.

Mom told me to just "hold my horses" and give the boy time to think about it. If it was meant to be it would happen. Mom took the opportunity to tell me that I should think hard about getting married right now because once I remarried, I would lose my Social Security survivor benefits. I told Mom that I never gave that any thought, nor did I ever know of such a penalty.

I told Mom that I just wanted to get out of York, Pennsylvania for good. I did not know how I was going to do it, but I was, with or without Aaron Stockton. So, Mom, as sure as you are my mother, it would happen. Believe in me, my children will have another father, and I will have another husband. A man who will love and take care of us.

After the long talk with Mom, I decided to just be patient, something that I have never been. I was going to be as patient as I was able to be and know that things would work out for me.

Just when I was getting ready to walk back down to my house at Codorus Street Projects, Mom looked at me and asked, "Sandra, have you told that boy that you could not have any more children?"

I hesitated for a few moments and said no, I did not.

"Sandra, you have to tell him."

"Mom, I will when he tells me he wants to marry me."

"Is that fair, Sandra?"

"Mom, life is not fair; you taught me that."

When I left Mom's house, I knew I would have to deal with more emotions. Should I tell him? Should I not tell him? It was obvious that I had to tell him, but what would be the right time? Damn it, I did not ask for her input on that.

# Chapter Two: You Are Drowning Me

The next morning, I awakened feeling pretty good. The kids were already downstairs eating cereal and waiting for me to come down to the kitchen. When I got downstairs and passed the pantry, the door was open. I walked in, and all I could smell was vanilla. I'm like *What the hell? Why is this damn pantry smelling like vanilla?*

Keenan Wynn and baby girl Karmentrina chimed in, and in unison said, "It was Kevin, Mom. He was eating the cake icing out of the can."

I yelled, "Kevin Scott, get that paddle. I done told you about coming in this pantry and stealing food. Boy, you are not starving. Come here, Kevin Scott."

He entered the pantry with the paddle, and his face looked so sad; maybe he was starving. I just could not beat his butt that morning. I told him that the next time I baked a cake he was not getting any icing on his slice. Between tears and snot running down his little face, he said, "Okay, Mommy, I'm sorry."

I sent him to wash his face and blow his nose. I proceeded to the kitchen and told them it was hair washing day and to clean up the kitchen so we could get done. The girls started opening their hair. I heard Kevin saying that he hated getting his hair washed because I always tried to drown him.

I said, "I heard that, Kevin, and just for that, I am going to drown you this morning, and whoever does not like it can get drowned with you."

He started crying, and Tracey said, "Shut up, Kevin. You know Mom is not going to drown you. If you would not jerk your head out of the sink and get water all over the floor, Mom could get done faster. You always have to start crying and acting up."

The girls and Keenan never were afraid to get their hair washed. I told Tracey and Kimmy Jo that they were first because it took me hours to plat or braid Karmentrina's hair; she was always crying and grabbing the comb, making me crack her hands with it so I could get done. Her hair was so thick, she was born with an afro. I would tell her to suck her thumb and shut up before I had to get the paddle. There were no switches in our yard.

I had so much to get done that day. I was hanging that night with Renee and Mom at the Legion. It was supposed to be a live band. I was not going to be idle, just waiting for Aaron to call me. Shit, I had to keep up appearances just in case this situation I was in did not pan out.

I do not know where Karmentrina and Kevin inherited their hair from—Lord knows! Kimmy Jo and Keenan had the fine hair. Lucky them. Breakfast done, hair done, and I was ready to get out of this house.

I had planned to call Mr. Bill last night for a ride but forgot. So I called him, and he said no problem. He came to pick us up to go shopping for school shoes for Karmentrina and Keenan Wynn and underwear and socks for all of them. Lord knows I was tired of repairing their old worn-out socks. Mr. Bill never charged me anything, just wanted a few bottles of pickled pig feet.

I was worn out when we returned home. As soon as we got in the door, the kids were asking for a snack. I sat down in the kitchen and took my flipflops off. Then I went to heat water for tea. The kids wanted to go outside in the yard to play, but I told them they had to put away all of their things from our shopping and then eat something before they went out.

Keenan Wynn did not want to go in the back yard; he wanted to play in the front yard with his imaginary friend, the big green man. I would be so glad when he stopped believing that the big green man existed. I tried explaining to him that it was just make believe, and he cried so much.

Mom told me to just let him believe it. He would outgrow it. *I hope so, Mom, because people are going to start to think my baby is crazy, talking to some big green man in the yard.* I used to listen to him out there having his two-way conversations and thinking maybe he was talking to someone that I could not see. He eventually did stop referring to his imaginary friend. I was more than happy about that.

It was getting late, and I had to get ready to go out. I was broke as all get-out, but I was going out. I went over to Joann's house to borrow twenty dollars. She always helped me out. Later when I walked back to my house, I called Mom and told her to tell Bucky and Wayne I needed them to babysit. They always agreed.

It was about seven p.m., and Mr. Bill was bringing Mom by to pick me up. Renee was meeting us at the Legion. I did not wear makeup, but I always put a fake mole on my face. Well, I just made my little tiny one bigger and sexier. I sent Karmentrina to find my eyebrow pencil from the bathroom and some matches to melt the tip a little. That helped me to put my eyeliner on more easily. I would put a touch on my thin brows.

In the meantime, Bucky Branch stopped by to see if Aaron was coming down for the weekend. I knew what he wanted. I told him I had not heard from him recently. He wanted to know why. I told him that I probably scared him off, but I wasn't too worried. I still had options.

He said, "Who?"

*Not you, Bucky Branch, little playboy, no way in this life.* We can only be friends. It was about eight fifteen p.m., and Mr. Bill was blowing the horn. Bucky and Wayne were with them. I walked to the car with a little flirtatious walk in my yellow hotpants set and new sandals to match and sporting my new afro haircut.

Mom looked at me and said, "I know that is not what you are wearing and where is your bra?"

"Mom, this is the style nowadays."

She said, "Okay, Sandra, see how you like it when you are old and fat with titties bigger than footballs hanging from your chest. You should wear a bra all the time and even sleep in one to keep from getting such large breasts. See how cute you will feel then."

"Mom, what matters is now, right now."

Mom said, "Okay, smart-ass."

The Legion was not crowded when we arrived. I paid for me and Mom's way in, three dollars and fifty cents each. We found good seats close to the stage—flirting distance. Mom bought the first drink for us. Renee rolled in soon after we did, but she soon disappeared to somewhere telling me she would catch me tomorrow.

The place filled up quickly, and the band was popping. About nine thirty p.m., a man came to our table and told me my sister Mary was at the entry door and wanted to see me. I knew what she wanted: me to pay her way in. She always did that and never paid me back.

I followed the man out to the entry door and told her that she never paid me back and she said, "But I always get free drinks for us."

I responded, "That is true." I paid the three dollars and fifty cents to the guy sitting by the door, and he let her enter.

The joint was jumping. Mary had our drinks coming to our table like she said she would. It was time for the band to take another twenty-minute break. It was my chance to flirt with the lead guitar player close up now.

I told Mom I was going to the bathroom, and she said, "Take your drink with you."

I was like, "Why? You are sitting here with Mary."

She said, "What did I teach you about bars and drinks? Keep it with you at all times unless you are finished with it."

I picked it up and drank it down. It was watered-down rum and Coke. They never gave you good drinks. I never cared because I was not a drinker. I could sip on the same rum and Coke for hours, but in that same period of time Mom and Mary could clear five time as many drinks. Mom was drinking VO liquor on the rocks with a water chaser. I do not know how she could drink that VO. It tasted horrible. I sipped her drink and damn near choked to death.

I cornered the guitar player in the hallway back by the bathrooms, and he gave me his name and phone number. We talked for a few minutes, then it was time for him to go back to the stage.

When I returned to our table, Mom said, "I am not slow, Sandra."

I said, "What?"

Mary chimed in and said, "What is his name and what is his number?"

"I do not know what you guys are talking about."

It was getting late, and I was getting ready to call Mr. Bill to come for us, but Mary said she would get us a ride. We decided to hang for a little while longer. The band stopped at one o'clock in the morning. We had about one and half hours left to party.

They called last call for alcohol, and Mary's friend bought us another round of drinks. Just then, one of Mr. Bill's friends came over to our table and told Mom that one of her daughters was outside arguing with some man. Mary and I looked at each other and left the table, telling Mom to just wait; we would be back.

We went to the entry hallway and had the man at the door stamp our hands so we could get back in. We went outside and saw Mabel arguing with her boyfriend, Elmer.

We walked over to them, and she said, "I got this; this mother fucker isn't crazy."

With that being said, Mary and I went back into the Legion and told Mom what was going on, and she said, "Oh, Mabel, I'm not worried about her then."

The room soon started to clear out, and Mary was securing our ride. She was now sitting at the bar and got up and came over to us and said, "Let's go."

I glanced at the guitar player packing up his equipment. He winked at me, and Mary said, "I saw that, Sandra."

# Chapter Three: Do Not Let the Left Hand Know What the Right Hand Is Up To

It was Saturday morning, and I was so tired. I heard the kids downstairs watching cartoons. Kevin came up to tell me we had no more cereal. I had to get up and get the kids in the kitchen for breakfast. Fried eggs this morning, all out of cereal. They had to do their chores before they could go outside to play.

After they had breakfast and cleaned up their rooms, I let them go outside in the back yard. They stayed out there for a couple of hours, then they were bored. I decided we would walk up to Mom's house for a short visit. They always loved going to Nanny's house. She might not be feeling it after hanging out last night with me and Mary.

She was her normal self when we got there and was cooking for supper. We stayed for about an hour and walked back down to our house. We walked through the back door, and I could see the mailman was at the front door.

Kimmy Jo damn near broke her neck getting to the door to get the mail. She was reading the envelopes. She yelled, "Mom, here is a letter from your Air Force boyfriend."

I almost hated that her ass could read—so damn nosy, she read everything. I sat down with my tea and opened the letter. He did not mention marriage, but he said in a short note, "Sandra, here is some money to help you with school clothing and school supplies for the children."

That was a surprise but one I needed because I had no idea where I was going to get Kimmy Jo's confirmation dress from. I had already purchased Kimmy Jo's and Kevin's shoes from Stride Rite. Although I was grateful for the three hundred dollars, he did not mention marriage, and that pissed me off. I was not even playing with his high yellow ass. Although it was so hard waiting to see him in person, I had chosen not to call him. He might be playing hard to get, or he might feel like I was trapping him into making a decision he would not be able to live with. Shit, let me keep it real. If it were the other way around, and a man wanted me to marry him and raise his four children, I do not think so!

I decided to call the guitar player and see what was up with him. We talked for a while, and he invited me to come to Coatesville the following Saturday to see him in the Elks Lodge. I told him I would try to make it there. I hung up the phone and said to myself, *See you Saturday, Dennis. Now I am going to have to find a ride and someone to go with me.* I hooked up with Julia, Renee, and one of her friends with a car.

The next Saturday, we rolled into Coatesville, Pennsylvania to the Elks Lodge. It was a two-story building with a very small room. It was packed, and it seemed like a lot of faces were familiar to me. We were having a hard time finding seats. The bartender had someone bring in some chairs for us. I decided that I would go to the bathroom before I got comfortable.

When I entered the bathroom, I ran smack into Mom, and she said, "What are you doing here?"

I asked her the same thing, and she said that she came on a bus trip with the York, Pennsylvania Elks Lodge. We both laughed. I asked Mom if she remembered the guitar player from the Legion a week ago, and she said, "I knew your sneaky ass was up to something."

"Mom, I have to keep my options open. After all, I am a performer as well as he is. Our groups may be able to hook up one day."

Mom said, "Sandra, I was not born yesterday."

*Of course not, Mom. I am so much like you.*

Me and my girls had so much fun that evening into the early morning. The show was coming to a close, and Julia was ready to leave. I told her to give me a few minutes. The people on the bus from York cleared out. The place was just about empty. I told Dennis I had to leave now, and he said he could take me home if I had waited for him. I did not think that was such a great idea, for I barely knew his name.

He asked for my phone number, and I started to share it but I was thinking about Aaron. What if he called me with the words I needed to hear? I did not want any man knowing my phone number or my address until I knew what my next move was going to be. Hummm!

It was a quiet ride home. Everyone fell asleep except the driver and me. I never go to sleep when someone is driving me. I was wondering if Aaron phoned me while I was hanging out.

I thought the struggle of holding on to my four children as a widowed 19-year-old mother was next to impossible. But here I was at twenty-two years of age and still holding on to my kids without a husband or father for them. I had to keep it real. If Aaron did not respond, then I would continue with my struggles to find a husband and a father for my children. It might not be today or tomorrow, but it would not be forever. Like they say, Rome was not built in a day.

# Chapter Four: Marriage Proposal

It was the end of September 1972, and the kids had been back to school for almost a month. The days were long and lonely when the kids were at school. But it was a different story in the evening. After dinner, it was always time for learning. I always took the time to work on math and teaching them how to write each other's names. Karmentrina's name was difficult for her to learn, so I used the Mickey Mouse jingle to help her. M – I -C -K -E -Y MOUSE - KAR – MEN – TRINA – MICKEY MOUSE. That worked out so well so I used songs and games to help them to learn and memorize.

I had to spend a lot more time with Kevin, for his attention span was difficult to hold. But let *The Three Stooges* come on the television, and he would not move. There were no daily phone calls from Aaron now. I wanted to call him, but I did not want him to think I was hard up for him. After so many days, I decided I would call him.

I made a telephone call to Aaron's job at Andrews Air Force Base, and a clerk answered and told me that Airman Stockton was on leave. I was mad as all get-out. On leave and did not tell me. I picked up the phone and called Doug, who worked with and shared a room in the barracks with Aaron. He told me everything was good. Just chill. There his ass went with that chill bullshit.

Doug must have called him because Aaron called me about nine p.m. when the kids were already in bed. I was so happy to hear from him but worried about what he was going to say.

The first thing out of his mouth was, "When do you want to get married?" I was thinking *What the F...?* I almost stopped breathing. I was quiet. He said, "Are you there, Sandra?"

"I am here." I was so happy, beyond words. "Why did you take so long to call me?"

Aaron said that he wanted to tell his family who were all in different states about us. Three brothers and two sisters and his mother. He was the youngest of his siblings and his mom's baby, and he did not want to do anything before he spoke with them.

He told me that his brother George was so upset and asked him if he were crazy, marrying a bitch in the projects with four kids in the ghetto. He reminded me that the reason I went into the military was to do better than our mom did. Aaron told me that he reminded his brother George that they too once lived in the projects with their mom in Roanoke when they were kids. He told George that I was the one who would share his dreams. A family, a big house, and to travel the world. He said he made it clear to George that I was the one. "I am going to live that life with Sandra and her four children."

His sister Kaye was the only sibling who was okay with it, and he said his mother in North Carolina told him that if it made him happy, then she would be happy too. He said that as long as his mom was okay with it, no one else mattered. His older brother Michael was stationed in Thailand and voiced concerns but he told Aaron it was his choice.

We talked for hours that night. He told me he would see me on the weekend, two days from then.

Now as happy as I was, I still had to tell him that I could not have any more children. That would surely change his mind. At least I knew that I was a good catch. I could hardly sleep that night and vowed not to tell anyone about the proposal for it might have backfired.

I had to tell someone. I called my best girlfriend Joann and told her. She was so happy for me and told me to come over tomorrow. I called my girl Renee Ware (rest in peace) and told her. She said, "Girlfriend, you got this, hang tight."

I also called two of my sisters, Candace and Portia, for I knew they could keep it to themselves. Neither of them lived in York. I would walk to Mom's house the next day and tell her before all of my big-mouth sisters and brother all found out.

The next morning, I walked over to Joann's house, and we talked and laughed for about an hour. Then she threw a curve ball at me and said, "Sandi, do you love Aaron?" I stared at her and she said, "You do not, do you?"

I said, "I will never tell; I am out of here, girlfriend. I have to go now, Joann. Talk to you later."

I do not know why she had to ask that question. I guess she knew the real Sandra! Why did it matter? Many years ago, marriages were arranged, and many worked out. So I guess one could say I arranged this situation. Whether it worked out or not, I was going to be out of York, Pennsylvania with my kids. I would fake it until I made it.

I went home, collected my kids, and walked to Mom's house to tell her. She was cool but wanted to know if I'd told him about not being able to have any more kids. That made me cut my visit short. She kept bringing that shit up. Mom always had a way of getting to me. She was right. I was dreading that moment but I had to tell him. It was a nice sunny and very warm day. Perfect day to feel good. So I was going to try and stay positive.

Two days later, Saturday morning, I woke up and had so many mixed emotions about being married. I really had no experience with marriage. I'd only lived with Joseph a couple of months before he was murdered, and that was in Mom's house with Mabel, Mr. Bill, and my three children.

I did not really believe Aaron wanted to marry me. It was now early afternoon, and Aaron was walking in the door. The kids were so excited to see him, as they always were. I think it was because they were expecting gifts.

After the kids hung around with him for a while, I told him I wanted to talk with him alone. I told the kids to watch cartoons until we were finished talking. We went upstairs to my bedroom, and I told him that I changed my mind and did not want to get married, and he questioned me as to why. I told him that I felt that I pushed him into his decision, because he took so long to contact me.

He looked at me and said, "Really, Sandra, when are we getting married?"

Aaron told me he was hesitant because for the two years before he enlisted into the Air Force, he was living with his sister Kaye and helping her with her five children. He wanted to go to see her in Pittsburg and talk with her in person. He knew that when he married me, he would not be able to financially help her any longer, and she was okay with his decision. "So you see, Sandra, I am a responsible man, I had things to work out first."

I told him that he could continue to financially support his sister and her children as long as he needed to. That we would be okay with our monies together. Thoughts were running all through my head because I still had to tell him that I would not be able to have any children for him. In my brain I was thinking, *Lord Jesus, I have to tell him.*

He said, "What is wrong? I thought you wanted to get married, so what is the problem?"

I just blurted it out and said to him, "I had a tubal ligation, and I cannot have any more children."

He said, "That is what is bothering you?" He came close, hugged me, and said, "Do you think we can afford to have more children? You have four children and a niece hanging on to you." He said many men marry women with children and never have children of their own.

"Do not worry about the Stockton name. My brothers will have sons. I am good. I love you and your children, and I will be the man you have been looking for in your life. Give me that chance. I promise you I will be there until the end."

I said, "We have only known each other for such a short time."

He said, "Do you want to just go together for a year or so? If you wait, I may get impatient." He laughed.

I answered, "No, let's get married."

He said, "Set the date."

I would tell the children in the morning with Aaron. He was leaving tomorrow, but he said he would come back every weekend that he was able to, depending on his work schedule.

So it was really going to happen for me and my kids. Leaving York, yeah! It could not come soon enough. I could not wait to go and let my mom know that I told Aaron I could not have any more children. She would be happy for me, I was sure.

# Chapter Five: Negotiations Taking Place

Morning came quicker than I could anticipate. I could hardly believe that Aaron was going to marry me. I had to find a way to convince Kimmy Jo, because she wanted Bruce to be my husband.

Kimmy Jo was so intelligent; she read everything in sight. It is hard being a teen mom. At some point a teen is a child raising a child. I would have to meet her at her level for her to understand what was about to happen.

In our immediate family, I always gave the kids a vote on family situations if at all possible. All four of them went into the pantry, their favorite meeting place to discuss the possibility of my marriage to Aaron. They were in the pantry for about ten minutes. They walked out into the living room and babygirl, the one who has always been the vocal leader of the group, blurted out, "Mom it is three to one. Kimmy Jo does not want Aaron to be your husband."

Aaron looked at me as if he wanted to go over to her, and I said to everyone that Kimmy Jo and I were going into the pantry and have our own meeting.

I asked Kimmy Jo why she did not want Aaron to be my husband, and she looked at me with tears in her eyes and said, "He might take you away somewhere."

I told her that would never happen because I loved her and her sister and brothers more than anyone in the world. I told her that he would help our family to be a whole family like we once were when her dad Joseph was alive.

She said, "What if somebody kills him, Mom? We will be sad again."

I told her that if I were to marry Bruce the same thing could happen. Bruce already had kids, and Aaron did not. He wanted to have kids, and he said he wanted all of them to be his kids.

Kimmy asked why he could not go and get his own kids. I told her he did not know anyone else he could get kids from. She was warming up a little.

I said, "We will get married on a special day."

She said, "What day?"

I told her, "Your birthday, Kimmy Jo, February twenty-fourth. Every year it will be very special because we will have a party for your birthday and a party for my anniversary."

She wanted to know what an anniversary was, and I told her it was like a birthday party. We would have a party on that day every year to celebrate all the years that Aaron and I were married. I told her we would have two cakes, one for her and one for us.

She said it would be okay if we get married on her birthday like I told her. She left to go and tell her sister and brothers about the plan.

They were all so very happy that I'd found a dad for them and a husband for me. Karmentrina wanted to know if she could tell her friends she was getting a new dad. I told her of course she could.

I had had so much freedom in the past two years. Did I really want to give it up? Parties, flirting, and seeing Bruce on the down-low. Something I was so good at. Bruce was always on my mind; after all, he was the man I truly loved more than any other man in my life. I just could not deal with his baby's mom calling and begging all the damn time for diapers and formula, shit, too damn much. Got on my darn nerves.

My girls and I used to go to the clubs just to see who we could pull. I knew I was going to have to make some changes but hopefully not too many. For starters, I would have to let the "do drop in crew" know that things were going to change.

Definitely out of town trips on the weekend would have to stop. The singing group was out because I did plan to follow Aaron to wherever he was going. I would miss being on the stage. Maybe I would be able to find a group wherever we were going and begin to sing again. Whatever, I would miss my friends in the projects, especially Joanne and Peggy.

I knew my kids would miss their friends, Mom, and all of their aunts, uncles, and cousins. We would come back to visit whenever we were able to. There were so many thoughts running around in my head. I had to put my thoughts to rest for a minute and figure out how we were going to get married. We would need money. I would need a dress, and my kids would need clothing for the wedding. So much to do.

# Chapter Six: Money Does Not Grow on Trees

Who would have thought that planning a wedding would take so much work? I decided that we needed to look at rings. So during the time when the kids were in school, I started to shop for rings. Aaron told me to pick out what I wanted and to let him know the cost. I found a nice set for six hundred and twenty-five dollars at a small downtown jewelry store on East Market Street.

Soon after I found the rings I called and told him about them, and he said no problem, he would take care of it when he came home Saturday. He arrived early on the weekend, and we went downtown for him to see the rings. He liked them. The jeweler told him to come back by the counter to be fitted, and he did.

Aaron asked for the bill, and the jeweler told him there was a balance of seventy-five dollars. I told him that the three hundred dollars that he had sent me for school clothes and supplies came in handy as well as the money from the grant I received from Hurricane Agnes. I spent just enough to get living room furniture which I purchased used from the Salvation Army and had it reupholstered in dark brown and red velvet. Everyone who came to my house thought it was beautiful, thanks to Pokey's husband, Rock Mitchell, who upholstered the furniture for me. Aaron paid the balance, and I was to pick them up the following week.

When we returned home from getting our rings, Renee was at the house with Wayne Bailey. She had been shopping and told me she brought Kimmy Jo everything she needed for confirmation: white dress, hat, and shoes. I did not know how she knew her size so well, but she told me that was her craft. That's my girl!

We sat in the kitchen and talked for a while, mostly about the upcoming wedding. Aaron decided to walk up to the corner Bar, Eddie's, while we started verbally throwing out ideas.

I told them I wanted an African wedding, and Wayne said, "You will need African dancers. I will take care of that." Wayne was president, choreographer, and dancer in the Lincoln University African American Dance ensemble group at Lincoln University, a historically Black university near Oxford, Pennsylvania. Wayne said they would do it for gas money and food. He said he would provide three drummers and nine dancers, including himself.

Wow, I did not expect all of that. I readily agreed. Then we started talking about where we could have the reception. We had no real ideas, but I knew that I needed to work on that quickly. I decided it was getting late, and my kids were probably hungry, especially Kevin. He was always saying he was hungry. Boy probably had a tapeworm.

Wayne decided he would make soup and sandwiches for them, and that was just fine with me. I was not feeling making anything. I told them I was going to walk up to the bar and see what Aaron was up to. I invited Renee, and we left through the back door.

Wayne yelled out the door, "Nobody wants your Air Force man," and we all laughed.

We stayed at the bar for about a half hour because Wayne had somewhere to go, and Aaron was leaving in the early morning.

While we were there, Smickle Wright walked in and looked dead at me. He said, "Hey," and I returned the salutation and then went on to introduce him to Aaron. They shook hands, and Smickle said to Aaron, "You got the prize."

We said our goodbyes and left the bar. Aaron said, "Who was that?"

I told him, "The guy who claims to be Keenan's dad. He was with me when I carried him. I think I told you about that when Keenan was hit by a car in front of the house not too long ago."

Aaron said, "Oh yeah."

Sunday morning when Aaron left to go back to the Air Force base, he told me to take it easy; things would work out. The taxi blew the horn outside, and he left.

Early Monday morning after I walked my kids to school, I decided to work on my wedding plans during the school days when I was home alone. I started checking on establishments where I could have the reception. There was nothing we could afford. A friend told me to check with the YMCA because Kimmy Jo and Kevin Scott had memberships there, so I did.

After searching for a few weeks, they agreed to rent a large room to me, a large bare room. No big deal. I grew up with a mom who knew how to survive on a dime. The cost was two hundred and twenty-five dollars, and we had to be out by ten o'clock p.m. I knew that would work. I would set up groups of family and friends to help me to pull off this wedding. I had so many ideas.

My kids had to be a part of this. My girl Renee and my sister Portia must play a part in it. I had many nieces and nephews, and some of them would have to be included. We would need dresses, African dresses. I would not be able to afford to buy material and have the dresses made. I must start thinking creatively and spend little money. I would have to get the dresses for all of the flower girls because the children I wanted to be in the wedding party did not have parents with extra money, and most were single moms like me.

I figured out that caftan dresses would be our best bet. I wanted to be married in sky blue, a godly color. Renee and Portia would have to buy their own, and they could pick the color they wanted to wear. I knew they would be okay with that.

I started going to discount stores to look for dresses for the flower girls. That was all I was able to think about that time. I was feeling mentally overwhelmed.

Late during the week, Aaron called me to ask me if I would consider getting married in a Catholic church.

I asked him, "What would I have to do?" because I am not Catholic and I wanted to get married in my church, Church of God and Christ. He said to me that he thought I was Catholic since my children went to Catholic school. I told him no, I just thought they would get a better education in the Catholic school system.

He told me he'd spoken with the Catholic priest on Andrews Air Force Base and was told I would have to convert to be Catholic if I was not a Catholic or the Catholic Church would not recognize our marriage. I told him that I would have to think about that.

After we ended the phone call, I called my church to see if I could get a date for our wedding. I was already ignoring Aaron. If he thought I was converting to Catholicism, he had another thought coming. Another roadblock that had to be knocked down and quickly.

I had only five months until Saturday, February twenty-fourth, our wedding day and Kimmy Jo's eighth birthday. Lord knows I would never forget that bargain I made with her.

I had to stop and catch my breath. I had to get prepared for Kimmy Jo's confirmation, which was in two weeks. She had all of the clothing that she needed, so that was not an issue, thanks to Renee. I had to check to see what the kids and I were going to wear for the event. I was allowed to invite a few people, so I invited Mom and Mr. Bill to go along with us.

It would be some time before confirmations came up for the other kids. I would get started back on wedding stuff after Kimmy Jo's confirmation. That would give me some breathing room before I would tell Aaron we were not having a Catholic wedding. Getting married in a Catholic Church was just too much. Confirmation classes, marriage counseling—I did not think so.

I was sure he would be okay with it. At least I hoped so. I would let him know why I did not want to convert to Catholicism this weekend. I would also ask him who his best man was going to be since Doug would be overseas during the time of the wedding.

# Chapter Seven: Time Stops for No One

Finally, confirmation was here. It was on a weeknight, so Aaron could not attend. All went well. Kimmy Jo looked so cute in her white dress, shoes, and veil over her eyeglasses. My daughter was growing up so fast right in front of my eyes as were her siblings. Now a little girl, tomorrow a grown woman. Wow!

While we were listening to the program, I could not help but wonder how Aaron would react when I told him I did not want to convert to Catholicism just to get married in a Catholic church. I had already convinced myself that he would be okay with it.

The program was soon over, and there were snacks for the guests. I had to keep an eye on Kevin, for he would have helped himself to all of the snacks if he could get away with it. I sure hoped that boy did not have worms. I would address it at his next clinic appointment.

Mr. Bill dropped us off just before bedtime, then he and Mom went home. I told the kids it was time for bed, to get their pajamas on and brush their teeth. Keenan called downstairs to tell me we did not have any toothpaste. I knew that I had been supposed to pick some up, but I'd forgotten.

I yelled back to him, "You all have to use soap. Rinse the bar of soap off first before you run your toothbrush over it."

Keenan yelled to me, "Mom, Kimmy Jo said something smart."

I yelled back, "Lucky for her I did not hear her. Get the hell done and go to bed right now. I ain't playing with you all. Don't forget to say your prayers."

Multiple voices: "Okay, Mommy."

It got quiet upstairs. I went up to see if all were sleeping, and they were. I decided to make some tea and watch Perry Mason. I loved that show; it was one of my favorites. Now I could watch television in my room with the color television Aaron had gifted to me last spring. It was a little, round color television hanging from the ceiling. I thought I had it going on.

I fell asleep with the television on, like I always did. When I woke up, the TV was all snowy and buzzing. I got up and woke the kids up, for it was a school day.

Morning hustle before school was always a lot to do if we did not prepare before going to bed the night before. There had been no time last night, for we'd arrived home late after the program. There was only one bathroom, and everyone always had to go to the bathroom at the same time. I always had to help them along. I would go in there and wet the face cloth with cold water and wiped everyone's face with that cold water. They hated that, but I remembered when Nanny in Columbia washed our faces with cold water. It most certainly moved things along.

Finally, everyone was dressed and in the kitchen, sitting in their seats. I fixed the cereal bowls, and everyone ate. Of course, Kevin wanted an extra bowl, and I gave it to him.

Keenan looked at his brother and said, "Kevin, you are not starving."

I said, "Shut up, Keenan Wynn," and he said, "Mom, that's what you said." I knew he heard that straight from my mouth.

"Keenan, only a mom is allowed to say that to her kids."

He said, "Okay, Mom."

I told the kids to get ready to go so we would not be late.

The day went so fast, it was darn near two o'clock, time for me to go to pick up Keenan from McKinley-Cookes Child development center, Karmentrina from Holy Child, and then go to meet Kimmy Jo and Kevin from Saint Patrick's around the corner. We would stop on Penn Park for the kids to play for a while, like Mom used to take me and my sisters there to play on the swings and the merry-go-round. Wow! Seemed like such a long time ago.

It was getting close to four o'clock, time for us to start walking home across College Avenue Bridge. They were getting baked beans and hot dogs for supper. I was not feeling cooking anything that would take a lot of time. I could not wait for their baths and bedtime this evening. Playing in the park tired me out more than them. I would let them watch television and stay up until eight-thirty p.m.

They usually agreed on what to watch. *The Three Stooges* and *The Little Rascals* were their favorites. There were not too many choices back in those days.

I still had to tell Aaron about my thoughts on the Catholic wedding. If he did not call me this evening, after the kids were in bed, I would call him. I needed to deal with that issue as soon as possible.

The clock read eight-thirty p.m., time for the little ones to go to bed. School tomorrow. No sooner were they settled than the telephone rang. I answered it and it was Aaron.

He said, "Hey, babe, how is everything?"

I answered, "Everything is good!" I told him that I was not feeling getting married in a Catholic church and I went on to ask him if he understood why. He responded that he understood and wanted to know if we could raise the children as Catholics, and I said yes, we could, for they had been exposed to Catholicism most of their lives.

He said, "Well, then, it is settled."

Aaron asked me to tell him about the wedding plans. I told him that I was just thinking things out on paper for the time being and that I had some money saved up for us to use, but it would not cover a honeymoon. I wanted us to go to Jamaica. It looked so pretty in the magazine. I had met with a triple A travel agent and they said a week's stay with airfare and meals would be about fifteen hundred dollars. Aaron told me that would be okay, not to worry; he had it covered. I told him that was great and that I would put a down payment on it this week. As usual, we talked for a very long time, and he told me he could not come up for the weekend for he had duty. I did not want to hear that, but it was what it was. We ended the phone call soon and then said good night to each other. I guess we were kind of engaged.

I decided since Aaron was not coming up that weekend I would hang out with Renee and her sister Wanda at the Legion. They were having a disc jockey. Not as good as a live band, but still, it was something to do.

Saturday came quickly, and I summoned Bucky and Wayne to babysit for me. They loved babysitting for me. Spoiled-ass brothers, Bucky and my play brother Wayne, thinking that I did not know they were sneaking girls in when my kids were in bed. Hopefully they wouldn't make any babies. Lord knows that would not be a good thing.

We walked to the Legion that night. I invited Peggy, but she did not want to go. When we got there, it was the same old crowd, talking the same old bullshit. That is why I needed to get the hell out of York, Pennsylvania and sooner rather than later.

We found a seat at the bar, which was just okay, for we would see all who came through the front entry door. No sooner were we settled than I saw Bruce Wright come in. He was looking so good. He made his way into the crowd, not looking my way at all.

I knew he could not ignore me; I could play the game; after all, I invented the game. I stayed on my bar stool most of the evening, and soon Bruce made his way to where I was sitting with Renee and Wanda. He asked us what we were drinking and told the barmaid to set us up with drinks.

He stood by me for a while, long enough to ask me to go with him to his place. I told him that I could not, and he responded in my ear, "I know you are supposed to be getting married, but you are not married yet."

Bad girl Sandra showed up, and I agreed to go with him. I told my girls that I was leaving, and they knew with who. I started to have second thoughts when I stepped into his car, but I went anyway, just for old times' sake.

He took me home about four o'clock in the morning. I made my way quietly into my back door. Everyone was still asleep. My brothers were asleep on the living room floor. I stepped over them and crept up to my room, where Karmentrina was asleep in my bed. If it was not her, it would be Tracey when she would be at the house with us. I do not know why they had to find refuge in my room.

# Chapter Eight: At the Crossroads

I should have felt as guilty as hell the next morning, but I did not. That was not good. I just am not an emotional person when it comes to men. I guess William taught me that. I knew I still felt some kind of way for Bruce, and he knew it as well.

If I was going to get married to Aaron, then I had to get the hell out of York as soon as we got married and could make that happen. I did not need my kids being caught up in the middle of stuff that I do not have any business doing. I did not care about people talking about me; that had happened so many times before. I did not want my kids to be hurt by people running their damn mouths in the street about me because the projects are a Peyton Place.

When you live in a very small city like York, Pennsylvania, it is more than likely that you will be talked about in a gossip circle at one time or another. That is how it was. Everyone just loved to have something to talk about. When I was being slick-ass Sandra, I figured if they were going to talk about me, I should give them something to gossip about; after all, gossip should be juicy.

It was the end of October, and I needed to get focused again on this wedding. I went to visit the Reverend Arthur Matthews, the pastor at Emmanuel Church of God and Christ. I needed to ask him if he would marry Aaron and me. He agreed, and it did not matter that Aaron was Catholic. He wanted to meet him, and I had to set that up.

It was getting close to Aaron's birthday in two weeks: Wednesday, November first. I wished it was on a weekend; however, we would figure it out. I went to visit him the Saturday after his birthday. He had a hotel room for us for two nights across from Andrews Air Force Base. He was off on Monday and had made an arrangement to get me to the

Greyhound bus terminal to catch my bus back to York. After I settled in our room, we went out to get something to eat in the area.

The next day he took me shopping at the Base Exchange (BX) and the commissary, where he ordered a birthday cake with a number one on it. I did not think anything of it, but I knew he was more than a year old.

It was a big cake, and I asked him why so big, and he said, "You can take the rest to our *kids*."

I caught that and said, "Our *kids*!"

He said, "Yes, our *kids*."

We had too much stuff to carry across the highway to the hotel, so he called his boy Paige, who came and gave us a ride across the road. When we got there with all of our stuff, we put it inside of our hotel room and then walked down to Jiffy Subs for something to eat. It was close to the hotel and in walking distance, and the road we had to cross was not too wide.

I was ready to be inside where it was warm. It was so cold outside. We ate our subs and fries and had some wine that Aaron had purchased earlier. We were ready to cut a slice of cake, and I stopped him to give him the birthday cards the kids made for him. He seemed so happy and said he would hang them up in his room in the barracks. Everyone's card said *Happy birthday, Daddy* except Kimmy Jo. Her card said *Happy birthday to mom's boyfriend*.

He said, "Three out of four is good."

We laughed and ate our cake. We decided to get in bed and watch television. I went into the bathroom to put on my nightgown and came back in the room. There were two candles lit and incense burning. He was already under the covers with just his underwear on. I knew what he wanted.

In the morning, he said, "Thanks for the birthday present." We walked up to the McDonalds and had breakfast, and Aaron told me that Paige was coming for us at noon to take us to

Crystal City Mall. It was a very large mall, much bigger than Landover Mall, where he always took me shopping when I came down to Maryland. Just like clockwork, Paige was there on time: twelve noon. I had been introduced to him several months ago when he'd visited my house in York with Aaron.

When we arrived at the mall, I was in awe. I had never seen a mall so big. We were in there like forever. We saw a movie while we were there. The big-screen saga of Priest, *Superfly*, was playing. This was a time when the big screens were showing Black tough men and women. It was a movie not to miss.

After the movie, we left to go home. When we went outside, we forgot where the car was parked. I never saw so many automobiles. We were walking and walking and walking. I was so fucking mad. I did not have a car and did not think I should be responsible for locating it. Aaron and Paige looked like stupid and stupider looking for that damn car. They both looked uncomfortable and were walking with a little limp. I was happy and saying to myself, *That is what the fuck you both get trying to look like Superfly and wearing them damn platform shoes.*

I was not slow. When he said we were going to the mall, I knew that meant walking. I had on flat shoes just for that reason. Dorothy did not raise any dumb children.

It was closing time, and people were filing out in droves. Cars were leaving at a quick pace. After the lot was almost empty, Paige saw his car and yelled, "There it is, Ace."

That car looked as if it was ten miles away from us. I gave Aaron a look that he was not feeling. He looked at Paige, and Paige told him to stay put; he would go and get the car.

I learned a lesson that night. If I ever go to a mall with anyone, especially them two Air Force dummies, I am going to write down where the car is parked. What made it so bad was we were parked under a light. We probably walked past it more than once.

I was so glad when we got to the hotel room, and I was hoping Aaron did not invite Paige to come in. Great, he did not. The first thing we did was to take off our shoes. He asked to rub my feet with lotion. I kind of softened up a little. We had some wine and discussed the movie. He pulled out a joint from his overnight bag and lit it up.

He asked me if I wanted a drag, and I said, "You know I do not know how to smoke." The last time I'd tried to smoke a cigarette was when I was twelve years old and living in Lancaster, Pennsylvania with my mom and siblings. Mary tried to teach me how to smoke. It did not go well. I almost choked to death. I slept well that night, and I do not have to say why.

I woke up early from the hotel wakeup call at five o'clock. Aaron had duty and was going to come back and pick me up later with Paige. My bus was scheduled to leave at twelve-fifteen that afternoon. It was right on time. We said our goodbyes, and I stepped onto the bus.

He yelled, "See you on Thanksgiving Day, babe."

I wanted to be home before my kids were let out of school. I knew Mom was probably tired of them by now. They would be happy to see that I was picking them up.

I was so glad when I finally got to them and walked home over that long College Avenue Bridge. Carrying that small suitcase and the rest of Aaron's birthday cake was enough.

Needless to say, when we arrived home and got to the cake, it was kind of mashed up. The number one was still mashed on the cake.

Keenan said, "Mom, is your boyfriend just one year old?"

Kimmy Jo chimed in and said, "No, silly, he is a man. Only little kids can be one year old."

Keenan wanted to know why it was only a number one on the cake, and I said to them all, "Just shut up and eat the damn cake."

They were happy and ate it anyways. Kevin said he would eat anyone's cake who did not want theirs. I told Kevin that he could have more tomorrow because everyone was eating their own cake.

# Chapter Nine: Family Ties

It was just three weeks until Thanksgiving Day was here and about twelve weeks until our wedding day. I had to get to work on finalizing our wedding plans. I did not want any craziness. I made a list of everyone I wanted in my wedding: seven flower girls, Gloria Banks, Kathryn Little, Sharon Little, Wendy Bracey of Baltimore, Tracey and my girls Karmentrina and Kimmy Jo, Portia for my maid of honor, ring bearer was Bernard Smallwood, my nephew, eight bridesmaids, to include Mabel, Lorna Clerk, Norma Mitchell, Renee Ware, Margaret Williams, Maxine Banks, Mary Branch, and my sister-in-law from my first marriage, Esther Kearse, three ushers, Darryl "Boo" Wright (rest in peace), Barrion E. Banks (rest in peace) and Wayne Allen Wilson, my play brother. Clifford (Bucky) would give me away. Although I would invite my dad to the wedding, there was no way William Junior Smallwood was going to walk me down that church aisle. The music we would walk down the aisle on would be selected by both of us.

This wedding was kind of growing. I still needed someone to sing a solo, if I could get it done for little or no money. The next plan would be to hit the discount stores for clothes and shoes, because Lord knows that money was tight. I knew that Franklin Discount Stores and the Super Shoe store would most likely be my best bet for getting deals. I called and got all of the flower girls' sizes so I could make sure they all had the same dress or similar.

That Friday evening, Renee and I went to Franklin Discounts and found a dress that I liked for the flower girls, and they were only nine dollars and ninety-nine cents each. I knew I could afford that price. We found everyone's size. I put them on layaway with a fifty-dollar deposit. The balance was twenty dollars and some change. That was easy. I saw shoes at Super Shoes, and they were ten dollars a pair. Black patent leather, probably fake leather, but they would work. I told all of the parents about the cost of the shoes and told them if they could not afford it to just make sure their child had on black shoes. All agreed.

Thanksgiving was tomorrow, and I had to go to Mom's house to help her to get ready for dinner. I was wondering when Aaron would show up. He had not called me today.

I got the gang together, and we walked to Mom's house. It was so darn cold. I put Vaseline on their little faces to keep the cold air from chafing their skin. I bundled them all up with coats, scarfs, and their gloves. The cold wind was killing Keenan Wynn, and I had to put him on my back. By the time we arrived there, they were all freezing, and so was I.

She said there were enough leftovers in the icebox to feed the kids. *Yeah! That's what I am talking about.* We were going to need a ride back, so I hoped Mr. Bill was home. It was iffy if he would be. He would be off tomorrow and Friday, so that meant he most likely had been paid today. He was good at going to the local bar and paying for drinks for everybody. Mom used to get so mad. He would work all week and not drink a drop of alcohol, but on Friday he made up for what he did not drink during the week.

Mom told me I did not have to bring anything since I was going to help her, but I took rolls because everyone loved bread, and I would be able to afford that. I was happy about that, for I did not want to cook anything. She told me to *Peel the onions and don't try to get out of it because all of your sisters always say they can't peel the onions.*

I hated peeling onions. My eyes would burn and tear up something awful. Mr. Bill was home watching television, and I asked him as soon as I got in the door if he would give us a ride back home. He responded yeah. Not much talk, but it was all good. We had a ride.

I found some leftover spaghetti in the icebox and took out a saucepan and heated enough for me and the kids. Mom was peeling the cooked potatoes for the potato salad, and I had to peel the onions—that bowl had so many onions.

I asked Mom why she needed so many onions, and she said for the potato salad, macaroni salad, dressing, and the greens. So, with that, I pulled up a chair by the table, sat down, and started peeling the onions, and of course my eyes were burning and tearing so much I could hardly see. Mom told me to take the onions over to the sink and run the cold water over them as I peeled and cut them. I was thinking, *Lord Jesus there has to be a better way.*

Dottie Mae (rest in peace) stopped by, half-ass drunk, and Mom asked where she had been.

Dottie Mae responded, "Why?"

Mom said, "Don't be getting smart, Midget. You going to make me come over there and slap your drunk ass. I told you about being out by yourself when you have been drinking."

Dottie Mae told Mom that she'd only walked from around the corner and that she could take care of herself. Mom said around the corner was too far. It was dark outside, and anything could have happened to her. Dottie Mae parked herself in a living room chair and fell asleep. Mom told Mr. Bill to throw a quilt that was on the sofa over her. She would most likely be there until tomorrow morning wondering how she got there. The kids and I all laughed.

Just then Bonita came over; she lived next door. I told her that Mom wanted her to help with peeling the onions. She looked at me and said, "I know you are lying, Sandi."

I responded, "Why would I lie? Anyways are you going to help me or not?"

She came over to the sink and started to help me, saying she was only staying over for a little while because Barrion was home with the kids, and he had somewhere to go. *Yeah, most likely the corner bar where Dottie Mae just came from.* The bar would most likely be crowded because tomorrow was a holiday. Long weekend for most.

My kids were getting bored, and Keenan wanted to know if he could go over to Aunt Bonita's house and play with his cousin

Sean. I allowed it. I would collect him when we were leaving to go back home. Bonita told Mom she only came over to borrow some sugar, and Mom asked her what she was going to put the sugar in. Bonita told her she would borrow a cup and bring it back tomorrow.

Mom said, "Oh no, you won't. You girls are always borrowing and not returning things like you say you will." She stopped what she was doing and took a small paper brown bag from a kitchen cabinet and poured some sugar into it and gave it to Bonita and told her, "You can keep the bag, little girl."

Bonita responded to Mom, "You know roaches live in them old brown bags." I laughed my ass off at that one. Mom was right on time.

I stayed about an hour later, then told Mr. Bill I was ready to go. We got our coats on, and I sent Kimmy over to get Keenan. Mom told Mr. Bill not to forget his way back when he dropped us off. I did not laugh at that one. Mom's face looked quite serious. When we got home, the kitchen light was on, and I know I did not leave it on. We went through the back yard like we always do. Our backyard was on the street side. I heard the radio paying inside.

I went to put the key in the keyhole, and the door opened. It was Aaron. I was very happy, as were the kids, to see him.

He said, "I wanted to surprise you."

I said, "You most certainly did that."

# Chapter Ten: Thanksgiving Dinner at Mom's House

I was excited about going to Thanksgiving dinner with the family this year because Aaron would be present. Lord knows I hoped there were no sibling arguments this year. I did not want him to see any craziness from my sisters. Bucky was never in an argument; he was the baby boy and the only boy in our family. He just did not side with anyone, saying; "I'm not in it."

Somebody was always mad about something. Somebody said something about somebody's child or somebody's child hit somebody else's child. Somebody rolled their eyes at someone else. Stupid stuff! That would not include my Keenan, for he only used his teeth for a weapon. I hoped none of the kids provoked him when I was not around because they would be bitten. Karmentrina was still carrying the bite marks on her chest Keenan had given her a couple of years before.

The children were up and ready for breakfast and baths. They could not wait to get dressed to attend dinner at their nanny's house. We wanted to get there by three o'clock p.m. In the meantime we watched the Macy's New York City annual Thanksgiving parade. Aaron was asking if Mr. Bill watched football. I told him I did not know but he could check when we got to Mom's house.

When we showed up at Mom's house, big mouth Pokey was already there, and Bonita looked out of her front door as we were arriving.

Sean was next to her yelling to Keenan, "Hi, Keenan, I am coming over to Nanny's house to play with you and Bubbles." We went inside the house and took off our coats. Keenan and Kevin threw their coats on the floor.

I yelled at them, "You better pick them coats up and bring them to me to hang up in the closet, right now."

While I was doing that, Aaron went over to the couch, greeted and shook Mr. Bill's hand. He spoke to my sisters on his way to the living room. He then walked through the house to the kitchen and pulled a pint of VO liquor from his pocket and gave it to Mom.

Mom was in the kitchen. It was not hard to see everyone from wherever you were sitting or standing in Mom's house, for it was a shotgun house. You could look straight through the house from one end to the other.

Mom could see Mary on the front porch and said, "Sandra, open the door for Mary and the kids."

Bucky and Wayne came downstairs and sat in the living room with Aaron and Mr. Bill. It seemed like Dottie Mae and Mabel were the only ones missing. They soon showed up about the same time. Mabel's boyfriend Elmer drove her to Mom's house.

I asked her why he did not come in, and she said, "It is a long story, girl."

Everything was going well, and Mom and Mary had set up all the food in the kitchen. There were tables set up for the little kids, the dining room table, and a card table set up for the adults. The guys were going to sit in the living room. Mom fixed Mr. Bill's plate and told all of the girls to fix their kids' plates.

That seemed like it took forever, all of the girls trying to fit into Mom's kitchen at the same time. Finally, we all had our plates, and we said grace. Mom added a few words for us. Mom told us that friends may come and go but family should always be around and support each other. I was thinking to myself that we all did need to stop the petty arguments that we got into.

She continued with, "I will be here for all of you until the man above punches my ticket. I hope he has some VO there for me."

The kids were at their table wondering why a man was going to punch Nanny's ticket. All the grownups laughed. I quickly made up a story for them.

We began eating. Mom had baked turkey with stuffing, ham, sweet potatoes, collard greens, homemade biscuits, mashed potatoes, and gravy. When I saw the biscuits, I was a little pissed. I would be taking my rolls back home with me, for I knew my sisters would try to take off with them. There was also baked apple pie and sweet potato pie.

Aaron seemed comfortable in the living room with the guys "shooting the breeze." I had so much food on my plate and knew I had better squeeze it all in, for I always told my children that it would be a sin to throw food away because people in foreign countries were starving. Why did I ever teach them that? Probably because Mom taught it to me when I was a little girl.

This is one time that I had wished that Kevin would have asked me for my food. We were all stuffed. I had to stand up and walk around a little bit so I could fit the rest of my food into my stomach. Mom settled down and pulled out her pint of VO and said, "Thank you, soon-to-be son-in-law."

The house got quiet. Mary pulled out a bottle of liquor from her pocketbook. It looked like a shopping bag. Mr. Bill retrieved two beers for himself and Aaron from the kitchen icebox. Mom turned on her record player and started playing blues and reminiscing about the good old days. Dottie Mae asked Mom for a shot glass of her VO. Mom told her okay but not to drink it all; that VO needed to last her for a while.

Soon after Dottie Mae's drink, she was ready to go home and started to walk toward the front door. Mom stopped her and said, "Dottie Mae, I told you about walking the streets in the dark. Just wait for a few minutes. Bill will drive you home."

Mr. Bill got up and asked Aaron to ride along with him to take Dottie Mae to her house. They left and returned about twenty minutes later. Dottie Mae lived very close to Mom, as did Bonita, next door. The rest of us stayed for quite some time.

Elmer came to pick up Mabel and her crew. Mary's husband Clabber came to pick her up, and Mr. Bill took me, Aaron, and my kids home as well as Pokey. Thank goodness everything went well. I did not need my family scaring Aaron away.

# Chapter Eleven: Christmas at 351 Stone Avenue

It was Sunday, December twenty-fourth, 1972, Christmas Eve. I had a lot to get done. I promised the kids I would make banana pudding and Jell-O with fruit cocktail in it. The kids loved when I baked cakes and cookies. They always wanted to help and get the spoon and bowel to lick the sweet mix and the icing. It would not take long, but I just had to fit it in, and I did.

Aaron was home until January first, 1973, roughly two months before our wedding. We all decorated our Christmas tree. The kid's toys were in Mom's attic, and nothing better be missing when I went to get them. This would be our first Christmas with Aaron. He decided to spend the holidays with us. It was going to feel strange not having Bruce around. It was time for me to move on for real.

I had all of the kids' toys and clothes in Mom's attic, and Aaron brought two big boxes with him for the kids. He said they could open them on Christmas morning. The children all went to bed after leaving out milk and cookies for Santa Claus.

Renee was at the house. She stayed while Aaron and I walked up to Mom's house to get the toys. There was nothing missing from my stuff. Mr. Bill gave us a ride back to the projects.

When we arrived back at the house, we took out all of the toys that had to be put together. Renee and I were in charge of wrapping all presents that had to be wrapped. In the boxes that Aaron brought to the house were little toy soldiers and mini military cars and trucks for the boys, dolls for the girls, paper doll cut out books for the girls as well as big coloring books for them all. I glanced over at Aaron; he looked all involved with putting the bikes together. He took his shirt off for it was so hot in the house. We could not control the heat in the projects. I kept watching him and noticed that he was still working on the same little tricycle that I'd bought for Keenan. He kept saying pieces were missing. I kept thinking to myself that he was going to need some help. I did not want to hurt his feelings; however, I did not want my kids disappointed and wondering why Santa Claus did not put their toys together. I went into the kitchen and phoned Barrion and asked him to come and help Aaron. He agreed to come after he put Sean's bike together. I told Aaron that Barrion was coming down to help him and he said, "Okay."

He came about midnight high as a kite. I wondered if the job was going to get done properly. Aaron pulled out a joint and lit it up. He took a drag and passed it to Barrion. Renee and I had finished wrapping the gifts in the kitchen. In about an hour, the boy's bikes and trucks were put together. The girl's dolls and a doll house were displayed nicely. Christmas was saved.

The first thing in the morning, Karmentrina and Keenan were at my door knocking and asking if they could go downstairs. I told them to get dressed, brush their teeth and I would be out of my room in a few minutes. When I came out of my room, all of the kids were dressed. We went down to the kitchen, and on the way, they saw that the cookies and milk were gone. They were so excited and they wanted to open one Christmas present, but I said no. The girls wanted to play with the dolls and the doll house and I told them that breakfast came first. They almost swallowed their cereal and milk down in one swallow. They were done so fast, washed off their area on the kitchen table and were in the living room with very big eyes.

They gathered all of their own gifts and found a spot for them. It was always fun watching them opening their gifts at Christmas time, but this Christmas day would be special because the man I was going to marry was with us, their soon-to-be father. I always remembered when my mom did not have enough money to buy me and my siblings gifts at Christmas time. I felt so blessed for me and my children.

The living room was a total disaster, wrappings all over the place. I told Kimmy Jo to go into the pantry to get some large brown paper bags to dispose of the trash. She came back with four bags and told everyone to clean up their own areas. I was thinking look at my daughter handling her business. My brothers stopped by to hang out for a while sporting their new sneakers and sweat suits. They were both so spoiled by Mom.

It was January the first and time for Aaron to leave for the base. His bus was to leave at two o'clock p.m. He would take a taxicab to the greyhound bus terminal. Aaron told me to let him know if I needed any money for the wedding. And I told him everything was all taken care of. I needed to get cranking on the wedding plans because the day was quickly approaching, and I needed everything to be next to perfect.

# Chapter Twelve: Wedding Jitters

All of the dresses for the flower girls and bridesmaids were paid off. I hoped that all would have their black shoes. My baby blue floor length caftan dress was in layaway. Aaron told me that he'd found a black, blue and white dashikis top with a hat to match. The boys were wearing black pants and shoes with dashikis, any color they choose, since it was going to be an African wedding with multiple colors. The rings and Young Men's Christian Association (YMCA) cost were paid in full. Mom had told me that the food planning was in motion and to not worry about it. She organized with family and friends what was needed to feed the wedding party and all of the guests. I would not have to worry about liquor for it was not permitted in the building. Good old Mom, Dot, always came through. That was another thing off of my plate.

The honeymoon was also paid in full. The only cost now would be on our wedding day, a cash gift donation to the minister and the church. The wedding time was planned for six o'clock in the evening. The reception would follow immediately after the wedding ceremony at the YMCA at seven o'clock p.m. I would have to buy some inexpensive candles to light up the aisle that we would walk down, for the church lights would be dimmed for our candlelight wedding.

I invited more than one hundred guests to attend the wedding ceremony. Most of the invitations I would hand deliver in person. Half of them hung out at my house anyways, so that would be an easy task. I still needed to go and have a conversation with Bruce's mom, Ms. Ninsey. I always loved her and knew she cared about me and my kids. I had to tell her why I chose to marry Aaron, and it had to be soon. Bruce and I had our talks about my decision, and even though he did not agree with me, he respected my decision.

The very next day while the kids were in school, I went to see Ms. Ninsey. She and I talked for a very long time, and after I explained to her why I was going to marry Aaron, she told me she understood why I had made my decision.

She said, "You are a mom, Lou, as I am, I do understand." I invited her to my wedding, and I hoped that she would attend. I felt good about our interaction. I did not know if I would have acted the same way if I were in her shoes. Now that I had that out of the way, I could move on and not worry about what she thought of me. I will always love Ms. Ninsey.

# Chapter Thirteen: Surprise, Surprise, Surprise

Oh, my goodness gracious! I forgot to tell Aaron that he needed to come to York on a weekday so we could go and apply for our marriage license. The wedding was only four weeks away. I called him that evening, and he agreed to come up the following Monday. We were surely cutting it close. That would be three weeks away from our planned wedding day. Lord Jesus! How did I forget that? I was married before and I knew we needed a marriage license. Dammit!

Aaron showed up on Monday while the kids were in school. I met him at the greyhound bus terminal, and we walked to the York city court house, which was only a few blocks away. We needed to complete everything and be on time to pick up the kids from school. We maneuvered our way to the office where marriage licenses were obtained. There was an older white man sitting at a desk behind a glass partition. He stood up and walked over to the window and asked if he could help us.

I responded to him saying that we were there to apply for a marriage license. He said, "No problem" and gave us the application. He told us to fill out the paperwork and return it to him once completed. We took a seat. We were the only ones in the area filling out paperwork.

I completed my part of the paperwork first, and Aaron would finish his part a few minutes later. I looked at him and said, "Are you ready to do this? You may change your mind if you want to, I would certainly understand."

Aaron looked back at me and said, "No, babe. Let's do this."

We walked up to the window and the man saw us and he walked over toward us. He requested our identification cards and then said, "Let me take a look."

Aaron used his military identification card and his birth certificate, and I used my driver's license and birth certificate. He took the papers to his desk to go over them and then he returned rather quickly and said to us, "You will not be getting a marriage license today."

I said, "Why not?"

The man looked at Aaron and said, "You must be twenty-one to get a marriage license in the state of Pennsylvania."

I looked at him like, if my looks could kill, he would have dropped dead right there in the spot where he was standing. The man went on to say that we could get married, but Aaron would need a co-signer.

I said to thank you to the clerk, and we left the building. I was so angry with him and I asked him just how many fucking Air Force identification cards he had. I hate to say it, but Mary Elizabeth was right, but if I could help it, she would never get this information until after we were married.

Aaron tried to hold my hand, but I snatched it away from him and said to him to walk home to the house and that I would pick up the kids alone.

He said, "No! I want to go with you."

I told him that was not a very good idea. Aaron asked me if I loved him and I angrily said to him just what does love have to do with this? He had the nerve to say to me that our intimacy was real love, and I responded, "So good sex means you can lie to me? Good sex I can get anywhere, but it is not about good sex. It is about a truthful relationship. You lied about your age, and you had a fake military identification card that you showed me when we met. Where did you get that from?" I answered it myself. "Oh yeah, you and Doug work in the personnel section at Andrews Air Force Base."

If I thought I could have gotten away with it, I would have punched him right in the face in that courthouse. After all, he was a trained military man, and his reflexes might have reacted before his brain did. That would have not been good, for there most certainly would not have been any damn wedding. I told him we could talk when I got home with the kids. If he had gone with me, I might have pushed him over the College Avenue Bridge. Lord knows I did not want to kill him in front of my kids. "You have a door key, Aaron, so go ahead," I said. "I will be home after I pick up the kids."

While I was walking to the schools, all I could think of was if Mary knew this information, she would have a ball with it. I knew time was limited and his siblings did not live in the area. Only one of his siblings was okay with us getting married. Maybe he would ask her to sign for us. If he was not able to get a co-signer, we would have to wait until he turned twenty-one in November and then push the wedding to February twenty-fourth, 1974. Dammit, I was so pissed off.

Aaron had leave for two days, but when I walked into the house, I told him that I needed to not be around him for two whole days. He called the bus terminal and got a reservation for eleven o'clock that evening. The kids were disappointed when I told them that Aaron had to go back to the base. I was thinking about so many things. How would I live this situation down and all the money I'd spent from my flood stimulus money? Dammit to hell, I was so fucking mad. I had to talk to someone about all of this. I wanted to talk with Joanne, but I knew she was going to give me a long rational point of view.

When Joanne met Aaron, she said to me, "Girlfriend, you got a keeper."

So my best bet was Renee because she would listen to me cuss and cuss with me. Renee spent the night with me. We drank a couple bottles of Boones Farm wine, and I felt much better the next day.

I knew Aaron would call me today and I wondered what kind of bullshit he was going to tell me. The phone rang while the kids were eating breakfast and getting ready for school. I told him to call me back in a couple of hours because the kids would not be at home. He called me back as I asked him to.

I said hello and he said, "Babe, I am sorry. Don't worry; my sister Kaye has agreed to come to York to sign for me. She would come to York on Friday, and I would meet her at the bus terminal for I would be there Thursday night if you say I can come."

I agreed, and he did show up Thursday evening about six o'clock p.m. As usual, the kids were glad to see him. I tried to act happy, but inside I was not feeling Aaron Edward Paul Stockton and his Catholic ass. When the children went to bed, we retired to my room to talk. He pulled out a pack of Kool cigarettes, took one out of the pack, and lit it with a cigarette lighter that I brought for him when I was at Landover mall with him some time ago.

He started out by saying he did not want me to feel like I could not trust him. I put my pajamas on and sat on the bed. I asked him if there were any more surprises because I did not need any more damn surprises. He was sitting by the dresser smoking his cigarette, and he said, "Yes, there are some things I must share with you."

I said, "What?"

He said, "First of all, I was living with a girl and her two kids in an apartment at Berry Farms Projects in South East Washington, DC."

I interrupted him to ask if they were his children and he said, "No, I have no children. I am there out of convenience. I deal drugs and could not store my product in the barracks. I paid all of her rent and gave her money as needed."

I said, "Were you sleeping with her, and if so, how long?"

He responded, "Since a year before I met you."

I responded, "Since the summer you have been with me and my kids most weekends. So when did you stop seeing her or are you still seeing her?"

"I broke up with her in November the week you came for my birthday."

"I guess you are saying you have not seen her since November?"

"Yes!"

I could not help myself; the words just flew out of my mouth. "You yellow motherfucker, how could you? How can I ever trust you?"

He said, "You can trust me because I am asking you to. I love you and want only you. You have my word. I am the man who will be there for you and our children forever. I promise you that."

Now I wished I had gone further with the guitar player Dennis and Bruce when I hooked up with them a couple of months ago. He continued with telling me his truths and said once he decided to ask me to marry him, no other woman mattered to him.

I asked him, "What about her two children?"

He said, "I knew it would most like affect her kids, but I will not see her or them again. I promise you that."

The next thing he went on to tell me was that he'd had girlfriends in Pittsburgh for the past two years, but he'd cut them off back in the summer for he knew that was not what he wanted. He had copies of the breakup letters he'd sent to all five of the girls in Pittsburgh. In all of the letters, which were all the same, he said, "Accept this friendship ring as our friendship only."

I said, "Okay, playboy, is there anything else I need to know? Get your truths out in the open." I was thinking to myself, *I do not care what he had done to this point, he is not messing up my chances to get the hell out of York, Pennsylvania.*

Now he was sitting in the chair chain smoking and choking my ass with all of the smoke. I got up and cracked the window to help to clear it out. It was getting late, and I asked him if he was going to share my bed. He damn near fell over the chair standing up to get his clothes off. Inside my head I was laughing my ass off and thinking, *Aaron Edward Stockton, you ain't got shit on me.*

The next day, all went as planned. We got the kids off to school and then ate breakfast at Woolworth Five and Dime store on Market Street. Kaye's bus was not supposed to arrive until eleven thirty a.m. We ate and then walked down the street to the Bon Ton Department store to look around and pass the time.

About ten forty-five a.m. we walked to the bus terminal to meet Kaye. It would be my first-time meeting anyone in Aaron's family. I was a little nervous. We arrived at the terminal; the bus was on time. We stood there while the bus was unloading, and Kaye finally walked out of the bus. She was beautiful, fair skinned, with long beautiful hair. She waved and called, "Hey, Ace" and walked over to us.

She was carrying an overnight bag. I guess she was planning on spending the night with us. Aaron introduced us, and she hugged me. We then walked to the court house to get our marriage license. We already had our paperwork from last week already completed.

The same clerk was at the desk and said to us, "Do you have a co-signer" and Aaron replied, "Yes, I do."

Kaye had legal papers showing she was his guardian in the state of Pennsylvania. Whew, glad that was over without any more glitches. I did not give a damn if Mary was right about his age or not. We were getting married in two weeks.

We walked back to my house all talking about the wedding. I hit it off with her right away. When we walked into the house through the back door, Kaye commented on the black and silver kitchen, and she loved my living room furniture that I had reupholstered from the Salvation Army.

Aaron left us alone while he went to pick up the kids from their schools. She told me a lot about their family.

"I see you brought an overnight bag so I assumed you were going to spend the night with us," I said.

She said, "Yes."

I showed her to my room, for Aaron and I would sleep downstairs on the floor with quilts. She told me that Aaron had told her so much about me and that he loved me and my kids. She went on to say that he did not care who did or did not agree with him, for he was the one marrying me.

"I can tell you that he will be good to you and your kids," she said. "He is my mommas' baby, and he always stepped up for me, our mother, and my five kids. He always worked a part-time job while he was in high school and living with me. He was an honor roll student in high school and received an all-expense paid scholarship to Carnegie Mellon University in downtown Pittsburgh for math. Soon after he received the letter and all of the family was aware, he decided that he did not want to go to college. Momma wanted him to go because none of us had college degrees. So when Aaron asked me to sign for him to join the Air Force, I did not hesitate, for I knew he was a mature young adult and that two of our brothers Michael and Louis were already in the Air Force."

Aaron retuned home with the kids, and they were excited to meet their soon-to-be aunt Kaye. I got them settled at the kitchen table to do homework. Of course, Kevin always said he had no homework. I always had to threaten him about getting his homework done.

Usually once I would get the paddle, his homework situation magically changed. Kevin said, "Oh yeah, Mom I have a little bit of homework to do."

"Great! Let's get done so we can all eat dinner."

After we all ate dinner, we went into the living room and watched television until it was time for the kids to go to bed. I escorted them up to their rooms. When I returned, Aaron and Kaye were smoking a joint, drinking wine, and listening to music on the radio. They were talking about life in Pittsburgh when they were growing up.

They stayed up like forever. I fell asleep on the sofa. Aaron soon woke me up and had made our beds on the floor with the quilts. He said Kaye was asleep in my room. The next day Kaye went back to Pittsburgh, and Aaron stayed on until Sunday. That Saturday night I kept the marriage paperwork in the Bible. It was official, and I did not want it getting lost somehow.

# Chapter Fourteen: Our Wedding Day

After months of planning, the wedding was now upon us. From the ceremony to the reception, everything was organized. I was praying that nothing would go wrong, and the frustrating part was that it is very difficult to predict what might or might not happen ahead of time. I tried very hard to think about the "what ifs," and I thought I prepared ahead of time for issues that might happen ahead of the wedding day.

I hoped everyone would show up as planned. Not having one of the wedding party participants or the dancers show up on my wedding day would be catastrophic. I had no worries about anyone getting drunk because no alcoholic beverages were permitted in the building. We did have liquor at the house for folks if they stopped by. That saved us a lot of money.

I thought that the best way to avoid a catastrophe would be to handle things myself. I knew that if something went wrong, my mom, sisters, Renee, and my maid of honor would save the day. No one in my family would like seeing my plans fall apart because most of them were in the ceremony, so I knew they would do whatever had to be done to save the day.

It was the day before the wedding, and everybody was at my house. Aaron was supposed to arrive in the evening. The day before I'd gone over everything with the wedding party and called the bakery to check on the cake, which would be delivered to the YMCA by four o'clock p.m. I'd picked up my blue caftan dress on Monday, so that was taken care of in enough time. Aaron told me that he and Paige had their dashiki shirts and would pick up one for Bucky.

I needed someone at the church with me to make sure everything was in place. My girlfriends and my sisters would help me to decorate in the morning. Everyone who was in the wedding party had their clothing. Wayne's group of dancers and drummers from Lincoln University were to arrive on Saturday afternoon. The DJ I'd hired the week before was on board. There was supposed to be no bad weather, just cold at 27 degrees Fahrenheit, no issues there. Hair and makeup no issue. Renee was to do my hair, and I already had the afro puffs that I was going to wear. The only makeup I would use consisted of an eyebrow pencil for eye lining and making my face mole larger and lipstick.

This was going to be the wedding of my dreams, for I'd never had a real wedding. Not like my first marriage to Joseph, going to a preacher's house in Baltimore, Maryland, saying a few words and I do, then signing some papers.

It was wedding day, and Aaron had arrived the night before as he was supposed to and hung out at the corner bar with his brother George, who was down from Pittsburgh, and his brother-in-law Larry Brown from Virginia. It was four-thirty in the evening, and all of the wedding party was present at the church. We went over how everyone would walk in. We practiced to music by Billy Paul, "Let's Stay Together," a selection that Aaron wanted us to use.

The flowers were in place and guest were filing in most steadily. The ushers, Barrion Banks, Darryl Wright, and Wayne Wilson seated everyone without any incidents. Guests were signing the guest book and talking. The church had standing room only. I thought it was time for me to go to my dressing area and put on my dress. I would soon come out and start mingling with our guests.

It was getting close to six o'clock p.m., and everyone was there except Aaron. I started to panic a little bit, thinking he might have backed out of the wedding.

Just then, Bucky asked, "Who was supposed to pick him up from your house? Because I stopped by your house and he told me you had a ride for him."

I responded, "Dammit, I forgot to set up his ride."

Bucky said not to worry; he would go to get him. That was going to take about thirty minutes. Renee told the pastor about what was going on and then made an announcement to the guests, and everyone started chatting again.

In the meantime, Bruce walked in with his mom. We greeted each other with hugs. I was happy to see them, especially Ms. Ninsey. That moment let me know that they were both okay with my decision.

I kept looking at the church clock. It seemed like it was going so slow. Just then Bucky and Aaron walked in. Aaron looked at me and said, "You are so beautiful."

I looked at him and said, "I like your matching hat."

The wedding party and I were very happy to see them. I instructed Aaron to go to the front of the church with the pastor and to also have the DJ to start the record and play it until the entire wedding party was in their final places. The lights went low for our candlelight wedding ceremony, and the wedding party started the program. My bouquet was of blue and white pom poms. The ring bearer, Bernard, started walking out, the flower girls followed, the bridesmaids, and then Portia, my maid of honor and Paige, Aaron's best man. Doug was his best man of choice; however, he was out of the country on a military assignment. Aaron's parents were not present but his oldest sister, Helena, represented them. I was nervous, and I could tell Aaron was also. We wrote our own vows and read them during the ceremony.

The ceremony was over about seven-thirty. All had gone wonderfully. Everyone was told that we were going straight to the reception. When we arrived, the room was full. I knew that I'd only invited about one hundred and twelve people—where in the hell did all the people come from? Family and guests were everywhere. The gift table was running over with gifts. Karmentrina and Keenan were running around and telling everyone they had a new dad. Kimmy Jo and Kevin were busy hanging around with their cousins. Mom and my sisters took care of getting people organized to eat.

We toasted with apple cider champagne. After everyone was fed, it was showtime with the dancers. They were fantastic. Everyone enjoyed them. Wayne and his dancers made my reception something to talk about. After the dancers performed, we decided it was time to cut the cake. We kept the top layer for our first anniversary. We were going to open gifts, but there was too many and no time for it. We made an announcement to thank everyone for their gifts and sharing our wedding memories with us. We were supposed to be out by ten o'clock; however, we ran over by an hour, but the man in charge said not to worry. He was so kind.

Guests started to clear out. Our family members with cars helped to transport all of our gifts to our house at three fifty-one Stone Avenue. Sounds strange, our house and not my house. His brother George and his sister Helena and her husband followed us to our house. Kaye was spending the night. Packing all of the gifts into the house was a task. There was limited space downstairs: a kitchen, living room, and a pantry. It seemed like all of my close friends and family members decided to come to the house. We were squeezed in there like sardines in a can.

Aaron wanted to open gifts, and even though I did not want to, I complied, and we opened several gifts. My feet were killing me, and all I wanted to do was take my shoes off and go to bed. Aaron and I took the kids upstairs and got them settled, they were exhausted. I told Aaron to go downstairs and tell Kaye she would be sleeping in our room.

He said, "Where are we sleeping?" and I said, "I will be on the couch, and you will be on the floor. We have many quilts and blankets."

He said, "This is our marriage night, and we are supposed to sleep together."

I told him I did not think so because I was still angry with him about the girl at Berry Farms Projects in Washington, DC. He said to me, "I thought you said you forgave me?"

"I did! My mouth told you that I did but my heart did not."

We went back down stairs and entertained for some time. Liquor was no problem; bottles were all on the kitchen table. We decided it was time for everyone to leave. After everyone cleared out, Aaron continued to try to get me to sleep with him, saying, "We are married now; you have to sleep with me."

I told him that we were sleeping together in the living room, but I would be on the couch, and he would be on the floor. He finally knew I was serious. He went into the kitchen to smoke a cigarette and fix himself a drink. He yelled from the kitchen, "Am I going to be on sex punishment when we go on our honeymoon next week?"

I yelled back, "Maybe."

# Chapter Fifteen: The Jamaican Honeymoon

February twenty-seven, we were on a plane to Montego Bay, Jamaica, where we would stay for seven days at an all-inclusive resort. I felt okay with the kids staying back at home with Mom and my sisters. That was the second plane ride that I had ever been on. This flight was a lot farther than flying to Chicago. I was a bit nervous, but Aaron took it in stride, for he had flown many times since joining the Air Force.

It was a five hour and forty-minute flight with one stop, and I hoped that we would get there safely. During the flight, we were offered lunch in little tiny trays. When we were finished eating, Aaron asked for seconds, and I felt embarrassed until I saw another passenger ask for seconds. I figured it must be permitted. The plane hit a little turbulence a few times, and that scared the heck out of me. Aaron held my hand and told me it would be okay, and it was.

I was happy when we arrived and disembarked from the plane. We went to collect our luggage and then get our transportation to the resort. When we stepped outside of the terminal, it was so very hot but beautiful. I never saw such beauty. After all, I had only ever been to York, Columbia, Lancaster, PA, Baltimore, MD and Chicago, Illinois. This felt like heaven.

We made it to the resort, and the concierge greeted us in the lobby. Guests were walking around with drinks, and Aaron asked the concierge how he could get one. Inside I was thinking to myself, *What have I gotten myself into?*

A waiter was summoned, and we ordered a drink. That was the first time I had a Bahama Mama. It was so good. After tasting that drink, I asked for a few more. I was glad big mouth asked about the drinks.

They explained to us our meal plan and how to get taxi transportation to wherever we wanted to go. Then we were escorted to our room by the bellman. He told us his name and said that if we needed anything to let him know; he worked the day shift. Just then the maid walked in and introduced herself. She was an older lady and seemed very kind. The room was clean and neat. There were nets over the bed for mosquitos. The maid told us that she would clean our room every day in the afternoon and to let the front desk know if we needed anything done in our room.

Aaron was dying to get outside and wanted us to just go somewhere. Outside of the resort, there were a string of small table vendors selling clothing, statues, beads, raisin bread, and everything you could imagine. I brought a loaf of raisin bread. I was reluctant at first because there were flies everywhere but not on the wrapping of the bread. Aaron wanted some cookies, and I told him not to because flies were everywhere. He said he would wash them down with some liquor when we got back to the resort.

I said, "Lord Jesus, you are not in the field, you do not have to do flies." I opened the loaf of raisin bread and broke off a small piece. It was so good. I knew where I was going in the morning for breakfast. Raisin bread and Bahama Mamas. That would work for me. We soon headed back across the road to the resort, and there were so many taxi drivers asking us if we needed a ride. Aaron started approaching different drivers to try to get a deal on the cost for us to go downtown and back. He finally decided on a driver by the name of Luis, who drove us to an area where there were many people out and about. I guess you would not call it downtown or in town as we know it to be from home. He took us to a spot and told us that was where he would pick us up again. We knew he would come back for us because he told Aaron that we did not have to pay him until he returned for us.

We stayed for about two hours, and just like he'd said, he returned for us right on time. Once we arrived back at the resort, he and Aaron had a few drinks. They discussed what he would charge us to be our driver for the week. I saw Aaron give him some money, but I did not know how much. I knew how much money I had, but I did not know what he had.

When we retired to our room, Aaron told me he gave Luis two hundred dollars in US currency. My quick response was, "Are you crazy? We do not even know that man. Do you know how to get in touch with him?"

I asked him if we could afford it, and he responded, "I got this, babe, no worries."

I said, "I hope he comes back tomorrow."

It was just about time for the evening meal at our resort, so we hustled over to the dining area to eat. There was so much food: fruit, vegetables, desserts. You name it, they had it. We ate like it was our last meal. After dinner, we sat outside next to the pool listening to Jamaican music by a local band and of course killing Bahama Mamas. Of course, Aaron was drinking whatever they offered him. He had to try so many different ones. I told him to stop before he got drunk. His response was not to worry because they barely had any liquor in them.

We eventually quit drinking and made our way to our room. I walked, and he stumbled to our room. As soon as we walked in, Aaron asked me if he was still on sex restriction.

I told him, "No, just get undressed and get in bed." I went into the bathroom, and when I came out, Aaron was passed out, spread out over the whole bed sideways and snoring something awful.

I knew that was not going to work for me. I started elbowing him to move over, but that did not work. I put a pillow on the floor and pushed him off of the bed right onto the floor and covered him up. Finally, I went to sleep.

The next morning, he woke up and asked me how he got on the floor. I told him not to ask me because I was in the bed before he was. We got ourselves together and went to breakfast, and again, there was so much food.

We hung around by the pool that morning until lunch time. I told Aaron I was not hungry, and he said he too was not hungry. I was killing the Bahama Mamas, and all that liquid filled me up even more. I do not know how Aaron was putting away all the drinks he had; he was sampling all different kinds of drinks again.

By the time the evening rolled around, everyone who worked in the resort knew Aaron's name. I told Aaron that I was going to go to the concierge and talk with him to see if we could get off the meal plan and get a refund for all of the meals. There was no way we could stay around for three meals a day, and it was just too much food. After talking with him, we were able to get a refund. Later they gave us the money for the canceled meals. The refund was in Jamaican money. We had no problem spending it.

Early that evening, Luis came to the resort, and I bet Aaron was some kind of relieved. He asked us where we wanted to go, and I responded that we wanted to see how real people lived, not what they showed the tourists.

He said, "No problem. I will take you to meet my family and friends, and then we will go from there." That evening he took us to a Jamaican bar and restaurant where the music was jumping and the crowd was feeling it, dancing reggae all over the floor. He told us the owner was a good friend of his. We ate, drank, and danced. Everyone was so friendly. They were feeding us rice and peas with cod fish. I tried most and was okay with it, but the fish heads I could not do. They brought out boiled bananas and fried dumplings. They just kept on bringing more food.

It was getting late, and the air was cool. The windows were open as well as the doors. I guess that was how they cooled off at night. I was ready to go, so Aaron told Luis we were ready to leave. We arrived late, and Aaron wanted to sit by the pool. I opted out and went to our room. I do not know what time he returned to our room, for I was asleep.

The next day was day three, and I was tired. Luis came by, but I did not want to go out that early. He asked Aaron to hang out with him on a few runs and they would come back for me around lunch time. I agreed; I felt safe at the resort. Well, let me tell you, it was hours before I saw either one of them.

Luis showed up about two o'clock and Aaron was not with him. I was a little concerned, but Luis told me he was fine and that he was there to take me to where Aaron was. We went to the bar where we'd hung out the evening before.

I walked into the bar, and Aaron was dancing with two Jamaican women, one of whom had no teeth. The reggae music was blasting. Aaron looked up and saw me and said, "Babe, your breakfast is on the bar."

Mind you, it was after two o'clock in the afternoon. His ass was half-ass drunk. Luckily there was a police officer in the bar because I was going to kill him. They were doing the limbo, and he was hollering, "Look at me, babe."

I took a seat at the bar, where my cold breakfast was fried bananas and pineapples. I was darn hungry, so I ate the food, but I was thinking to myself, *Boy you are in big trouble.* In only three days, he was off the reservation.

Luis took us back to the resort and told us he would come to pick us up later, but I told him we were going to pass but to pick us up in the morning. He agreed. Aaron wanted to sit by the pool, and I did not. He kept asking me to sit by the pool, but I could not swim, and if he became drunk, and I fell in, we would both drown with his drunk ass trying to save me. I don't think so.

I told him, "Let's go to our room."

He told me he would come later. I said okay. When I got back to the room, the maid was cleaning it. I struck up a conversation with her, and she was admiring Aaron's bottles of cologne on the dresser. She started to tell me about her son and her husband and that she wished they could afford such colognes, and I felt that she deserved to have some cologne for her son and her husband. Working as a maid cleaning up behind adults when you can't afford to get a bottle of cologne for the both of them was sad.

So I took it upon myself to give her all of Aaron's cologne on the dresser as well as his deodorant. He could use mine if he needed some. That would fix his ass for leaving me here at the resort waiting for him for hours and hungry too. I bet the next time he would think about it, dancing with them Jamaican women. The one with no teeth was hanging all over him. He was just laughing and telling me to come over and join them. I kept thinking about the two women and him dancing.

When he eventually came to the room, I would not let him come in. I told him to go sleep with the toothless Jamaican woman at the bar. He kept banging on the door like a crazy man, so I finally did let him in. I gave him a pillow and told him he got the floor. He pleaded so damn much that I let him get into the bed, but I told him to stay on his side and that I was not playing. He did not miss his cologne until the morning when he got up to take his shower.

Day four. Aaron woke up early and complained of a headache. I wanted to laugh and said, "You should not have been drinking all that liquor last night. Are you a closet alcoholic or what? Tell me now."

He went in to take a shower. He went to the dresser to get his deodorant and noticed that all of his cologne bottles and deodorant were missing. He was getting so agitated and saying, "That damn maid must have stolen my stuff. They were my expensive ones. I am going right down to that front desk and report her."

I was thinking if he found out what I did he might snap out like William used to do when I was a little girl. I hoped not because it would not be pretty because ain't no man going to be beating on me like William used to beat up on Dot. I don't think so. I told him to wait a minute.

He said, "Why?"

I told him that I gave it all to the maid for her son and her husband because she could never afford to buy it for them. She was so grateful. Aaron wanted to know what I gave the maid that belonged to me and I told him that I did not have anything to give her.

He was feeling that I was still angry with him. He looked at me and said, "Sandra, can we start over?" He paused and said, "Hello, my name is Aaron. What is your name?"

I told him, "My name is Sandra Lee Stockton, your wife, and you better start treating me like your wife, or else. Don't leave my ass in this room while you partying with other women."

He apologized and said that he was so very sorry, and was he back on sex restriction?

I said no with a very serious face, like *Do not try me, Mr. Stockton*. We went to bed as friends that night.

Day five. Luis came for us very early in the morning. He took us on a tour of Montego Bay, which happened to be the second largest city in Jamaica after Kingston, the capital. We walked along the beaches and watched people swimming and dancing to Jamaican music. Luis rented an umbrella for us, and he and Aaron went swimming.

I did not partake in swimming, for I had a fear of drowning since I was a little girl when I went fishing with William, my dad. He put a pair of his rubber boots on me, and we walked into the water. He went ahead, and I followed. I lost one of his boots, and he tried to make me go in the water and find it. I was just a little girl, and the water was up to my butt. I panicked and froze. Mom walked thru the water to get me and she found the boot. I have been afraid ever since. I probably will never learn to swim.

We stayed on the beach for hours, and then finally Luis said to us, "Let's go. I will take you to meet my father and his wife." He turned in the umbrella, and we collected our things and left the beach.

It was quite a ride to his father's house in the countryside. It was a beautiful house with a screened-in porch and pineapple trees in the front yard. We parked in the front yard, and a woman was sitting on the porch. She was young with a dark complexion, beautiful with long, pretty hair. Luis told us it was his stepmother.

His father came from the front door to greet Luis and us. Luis kind of told him all about us in a few words. His father introduced us to his wife. We all joined his stepmother on the front porch. I struck up a conversation about the pineapple trees. "Must be nice you can get free pineapples anytime you want to."

His father laughed. He then went into the house and came out with a large machete. He went over and cut down some pineapples and split them open for us to try. They were delicious. We stayed for dinner and enjoyed a fine Jamaican meal. Peas, rice, fried bananas, and fried fish with the heads attached. I could not get past the fish heads with the little beady eyes staring in my face. Of course, Aaron dug right in like he was native Jamaican.

Later, after dinner, we sat on the porch, and they drank Jamaican beer and I drank pineapple juice. We stayed until the late hours, and then Luis drove us back to the resort. It was a very long ride. I fell asleep, but I must have felt the car stop, for I woke up and we were at the resort. Luis told us that he would pick us up the next day to go to the country to meet more of his family and friends.

Day Six. Beautiful morning and no rain. We were lucky we did not get rain at all thus far. Luis picked us up about eleven in the morning and said we were going to his cousin's house. He asked us if we liked pork chops, and we both responded yes, of course.

We rode quite a ways through the country side and arrived at our destination. We had to get out of the car and walk up a very steep dirt hill to his cousin's house. It was so hot, and the sun was beaming down on us. I was wondering how far we had to walk up that hill. There were no trees in sight. I finally saw a small house, and so did Aaron. Luis said we were almost there.

We soon arrived at a wooden one-story block house with a tin roof. We noticed several other small houses as we got closer to the house we were going to. Luis told us that it was a squatter settlement, and the rent was cheap, like seventy-five dollars a month. I was thinking wow, living in the projects in America was like a castle to this.

After all that traveling and climbing that hill, I had to pee really badly. I asked Luis where the bathroom was, and he pointed me to an area in back of the house and told me I could go anywhere in that area. I looked at Aaron, and he said, "Come on, babe, I will go with you."

Now I had to hike up another damn hill to pee. Thank God I did not have to do anything else because he did not offer me any toilet paper. Aaron took the time to pee while we were up there. When we walked back down to the house, Luis showed us outside where water and soap was for us to wash our hands.

We went inside the house, where there were four rooms. Several guys were cooking meat on a wood stove in the back of the house. I guess that was the kitchen area. We sat on some wooden chairs that were in the front part of the house, the room where we entered. There were several people in there playing dominoes. It was interesting to watch. Everyone was nice to us. The aroma from the kitchen was smelling so good.

Luis came, and we followed him into the kitchen to get some food when it was ready. When we entered the kitchen, there was a man with a machete chopping meat off of a huge pig that hung from the ceiling. They had roasted it outside and brought it into the kitchen for all to share.

Luis looked at us and said, "You will love these pork chops. This is as fresh as you can get." Dinner was fresh pork chops, rice and beans. It was delicious, and of course greedy ass had to ask for more.

After dinner, they were drinking Jamaican run, and I whispered to Aaron, "You better not have more than three drinks. I am watching you and counting."

He did well. I guess he did not want to sleep on the floor at the resort that night.

We had to walk back down the hill to the car with flashlights, but that was not the worst. The drive back to the resort was like an old horror movie. They had no streetlights or pavements. I don't know how they knew what side of the road to drive on. Luis dropped us off and asked what time we wanted to be picked up in the morning. We told him to come over tomorrow evening and hang out with us, for tomorrow would be our last day in Montego Bay. He agreed. We were both tired and both did not waste any time getting ready for bed.

Day Seven. We woke up late and got ourselves together to walk down to the markets to get something to eat and to buy gifts for our kids and some friends and family members. Our first stop was for the raisin bread and cheese; it was so good. We broke off some of the bread and ate it with some of the cheese. We would eat more of that if we got too hungry while out shopping at the markets. There were so many knickknacks, shirts, dresses, and other stuff with *Jamaica* printed on them.

We were out there for a long time and finally decided we had enough to carry home with us, so we returned to the resort. We took our stuff to our room and then went to sit outside to relax and have drinks. After all, they were free. We stayed out there for a couple of hours, and I told Aaron I was going to take a nap.

I asked him if I could trust him to be alone out there and he laughed and said, "Babe, you forgave me, remember? I'm good."

I responded, "You better be, Aaron." It was around six p.m. when I woke up, and Aaron was still outside. Luis was with him. I guess he did not want to wake me up when Luis arrived. We ordered dinner by the pool and stayed out there for hours, just enjoying the atmosphere and the local resort band. They were really good, and they killed Bob Marley, one of my favorites.

Tomorrow we would be leaving. I almost hated that we were going to leave, but I missed my kids so much. It had been years since I was away from my kids for more than a week, back in Philadelphia. The Chicago trip was only a few days. Compared to that, this was very long.

We cut the night short and said our goodbyes to Luis. We gave him our phone number in the United States, and he gave us his number. We told him that if he ever came to the US and was in the vicinity of York, Pennsylvania, he could visit with us. We also told him to thank his parents and family for hosting us while we were in their homes. We really did enjoy ourselves.

We went back to the room and packed up all of our belongings. Our ride to the airport was scheduled for ten o'clock in the morning. We had to be there early enough to go through customs and to shop at the duty-free store. We needed to finish spending our Jamaican currency from the refund on our dining program.

Day Eight. We had a wake-up call at seven o'clock in the morning. Aaron had the bellman come for our luggage. He went downstairs with him, for he wanted to tip some of the employees. He refused to tip the maid, for he felt that his cologne and deodorant was enough of a tip for her. So when he left the room, I left her a tip in US dollars, which converted to more in her money.

The resort shuttle was on time for our transportation to the airport. The shuttle was full; there were many guests leaving Jamaica that day. We arrived in record time. We headed for customs and were told we could not take the open food with us. So we went and found a seat and ate the rest of our raisin bread and cheese. I was definitely going to miss that; it was always so good.

We finished and went through customs without any glitches. We headed to the duty-free store to buy some things. Aaron purchased two liters of rum, and I wanted to buy bangles. He convinced me to get two liters of rum for him because it was much cheaper in Jamaica but we could only take two liters each.

He said, "You will travel many places with me, and I am sure you will find bangles better than these."

I agreed, for they looked as if they would not last very long. He could not believe how cheap cigarettes were, and he wanted to buy five cartons, but he was only permitted to buy two.

It seemed like Aaron was getting the best of what he wanted, and I was getting nothing. Oh well, such is married life. Now I was feeling some kind of way for giving the maid all of his cologne and deodorant. I apologized before we got on the plane, and he said no worries he would buy more because they were pretty cheap at the base exchange store (BX).

The airline announcer was calling seat numbers to board the plane. We were seated in the middle of the plane, and I had a window seat like I had on the way here. I asked Aaron if he wanted to sit by the window and he said, "No, I'm good."

I was happy because Aaron was smoking on the plane, and if the other person did next to him it would have been horrible sitting between them. No sooner than the stewardess gave the safety briefing on the plane, someone was coming around with drinks. Soda and coffee was free, but liquor had a cost. I told Aaron he better not order any liquor. He said okay and pulled out a miniature from his carry-on and made his own drink.

I was thinking to myself, *Lord Jesus, I hope he is not an alcoholic.* About two hours into the flight, they were coming around with lunch.

Aaron whispered to me, "Babe, is it okay if I ask for seconds because you know we really did not have a full breakfast."

I told him I did not care because I was hungry as well. I might need seconds myself.

We arrived at the Harrisburg Airport safely and disembarked the plane without any issues. We made our way to the baggage carousel. There were so many people there waiting for their luggage. It seemed like forever before any luggage started to come out. We had two big suitcases to carry. Aaron waited for them to come out while I sat with our carry-on bags close by.

We hoped that Mr. Bill and Bucky would be outside waiting for us because I told them before we left the time we were supposed to arrive back at home. We collected our luggage and made our way outside. It was a struggle carrying all of our belongings. Wearing our winter coats helped to lighten the load. It was 40 degrees Fahrenheit. We were sure missing that Jamaican heat right about now.

Carrying our suitcases was a task; suitcases did not have wheels back then. We found a spot outside of the terminal where travelers were to be picked up. It was so cold. Aaron started walking and looking for them. He spotted Bucky and summoned him over to help carry our luggage to the car where Mr. Bill was waiting. To my surprise, they were on time. I was so glad to be going home to see my kids and I was sure Mom was about tired of them.

# Chapter Sixteen: The Honeymoon Is Over

Wow! what a honeymoon. We really did not know each other—at all. A new chapter for Sandra. I was now a military wife with benefits. Check mate! I got what I wanted: a husband for me and a father for my four children. After that honeymoon, I just hoped that I would not end up killing his ass.

He was on leave for two more weeks, and there was much to discuss. We walked the kids to their schools, and they had so many questions. Babygirl wanted to know if she could tell her teacher she had a new dad, and we told her of course. Kevin wanted to know if their last name would now be Stockton, since that was my new last name. I told him not yet. I did not want to answer those kinds of questions.

We visited each school office to add Aaron on to their school records so that he would be able to pick them up without me. After we returned back home from taking the kids to school, we worked on necessary paperwork. Aaron had paperwork with him for us to complete so that the kids and I would be able to get our military identification cards. That would allow us to enter the installation as well as get care at the military hospital, clinics, and all facilities on base.

He also completed paperwork assigning me as his beneficiary on his service group life insurance. I signed the form as was required. I told him I would put his name on my insurance policy along with my kids and remove my mother. Aaron also filled out paperwork for an allotment for me and the kids. He told me he would make arrangements for me to bring the kids to Maryland to get their identification cards. He had paperwork adding me to his Andrews Air Force Base credit union checking account and said he would get a membership card for me later. I took the opportunity to remind him that I wanted to move away from York, and he said he would take care of that also. He said he would put our family's name on the waiting list and that it could take from six months to a year to get housing. He was entitled to housing since he now had dependents. Housing was hard to get and we would not be able to afford off base housing based on the cost in that area.

I told him that we would stay at the Codorus Street projects for now because I was settled in. The kids and I had a good routine with good support systems in place. In the meantime, Aaron would look for Catholic schools located in the area by Andrews Air Force Base for the kids to attend.

We went to Mom's house when we completed the paperwork so she could make sure it was in order. After she reviewed everything, she said it looked good to her. We decided it was time to take that hike over the College Avenue Bridge to collect our kids. We were headed toward the front door, and Mom called to me, "Sandra, did you tell the people in the office at the projects that you got married?"

No, I did not, but you could believe I would take care of that after Aaron left for the base. I was sure they already knew; a letter was no doubt on the way to 351 Stone Avenue. Damn nosy-ass neighbors I had. Always minding someone else's business. I knew they would raise the rent. We made our way out of the door, and as soon as Mom stepped back into her front door, I told Aaron that she always managed to remind her daughters to do the right thing. Dot was just too darn honest. Always thinking somebody was going to jail.

We walked across that bridge to get the kids, and it was so cold and windy. We made our rounds, and Kimmy Jo and Kevin were last to get picked up. Aaron insisted on us getting a cab. So we went to the front office to use the phone and called a cab. He told me it was too cold for the kids to be walking back and forth across that bridge in the wintertime.

I said, "Mr. Stockton, the kids and I have survived too many days to count walking back and forth across the Codorus Street Bridge in the cold winters. I was not able to afford a taxi to and from school for the kids. Now if you want to increase my allotment to cover taxi fares, please do."

He looked at me and said, "I guess if you bundle them up enough, it will be okay."

I responded that we always bundled up warmly. That night Aaron told me he would give me a break and take the kids to and from the school while he was on leave and cook dinner every night. I knew he could cook breakfast, but I did not know about dinner.

The next morning, I woke the kids up and got them ready for school. Hot oatmeal and toast for breakfast. After they ate, I started cleaning the table and then walked through the living room and put the morning news on. I yelled to Aaron in the kitchen, "Babe, don't forget to bundle them up. Make sure they have their gloves and put scarfs around their face and neck."

Kimmy Jo yelled, "Mom, we put Vaseline on our faces already."

*See you when you get back, Aaron. I am looking forward to what we will have for dinner.* He returned home and told me everything went okay.

He picked up the kids after school, and he said everything went well. When the kids were settled and went into the kitchen to do their homework, he walked into the pantry to look to see what he would make for dinner. I was thinking to myself, *This is going to be good.*

He came out of the pantry with two boxes of Kraft macaroni and cheese and two cans of peas. I asked what he was going to do about meat, and he said, "Just wait and see."

He looked in the freezer and took out a pack of smoked sausage. Well, he cut up the sausage into small pieces and fried it with onion. That with the peas and Kraft macaroni and cheese turned out okay. He told me that I could help him tomorrow if I wanted to. I responded of course I would love to.

That was a good move for him. Two weeks was winding down. It had felt good this past ten days with Aaron and the kids. He helped them with their homework and cleaning around the house was a good touch also. It seemed like he just could not sit still.

It is the last night that Aaron would be on leave. The kids did not want him to leave, but he had to. They had much to say: *When are you coming back? Are we going to move with you? Can our cousins come with us?*

I stepped in and told the kids that we would go with Aaron soon, and we would live with him, but right now he had to get ready to go back to his job tomorrow. The next morning, Aaron took a taxicab to the Greyhound bus terminal. I was sad to see him leave. I actually liked the guy.

# Chapter Seventeen: Base Confinement

We had only been married for about two months when Aaron called me early on a Monday morning from the base and told me he'd gotten busted and was on base confinement.

I asked him just what that meant. Had he gotten caught with drugs on him? I knew he sold marijuana but not much about anything else.

He said that early Sunday morning, one of his friends assigned with the military police called him and told him that the Office of Special Investigations (OSI) was going to stop him at the gate when he returned to the base and take him to search his room. He told me they'd gotten a tip that there were drugs. "I called my boys and told them to get rid of the drugs in my room because they had a key to my room and my closet," he said. "I told them they could have all of the marijuana and pills, just remove it from my room. Sunday evening the (OSI) did stop me at the gate and escorted me to the barracks for a room inspection. They had to cut the lock off of my door because I did not have a key."

They found miscellaneous drug related articles and equipment in his barracks room when they searched it. Although there were no drugs to be found, the drug dogs alerted them that drugs had been there in quite a few places. However, the barracks manager knew that he had not stayed in the barracks for a week, so they did not incarcerate him.

Aaron told me he had to see the base commander in one week and that his JAG officer (judge advocate general) told him that it would be wise for me to be with him. I asked him if it would be in a court room and he said no, just the base commanders' office. Not a damn soul was going to hear this information about my drug dealing military husband. *Lord Jesus, what have I gotten into?*

I worked it out with Bonita to watch my kids for a day because I had to go to Andrews Air Force Base to complete paperwork. That was the story that I gave her. The following week I took a bus to Washington, DC, and Aaron and one of his friends picked me up. Someone I did not know.

I was so nervous, and Aaron's face looked puzzled. As I always do, I was thinking to myself, *I have not even got my military identification cards yet and he is about to get his ass kicked out of the military service. Some choice I made!* The money was good, and I enjoyed all of the gifts for me and the kids, but it was not a good move. I should have encouraged him to stop dealing drugs a long time ago. I felt that no matter which way things went, the drug dealing business was over. I was to blame too because I had no problem spending the money.

When we entered the room, there were several men in uniforms. I did not know who was who or what rank they were. It was all Greek to me. His squadron commander, first sergeant and civilian supervisor were present and all spoke highly of Aaron and pleaded for leniency.

The base commander than looked at both of us and said, "I understand that you both recently were married and you have four children. Is that correct?"

We both answered, "Yes, sir" at the same time like I was in the military too.

The base commander looked at Aaron and said, "I am not going to recommend a bad conduct discharge (BCD). I am going to keep you in the military, but you will give me two stripes and three months' pay and base confinement is lifted."

He asked Aaron if he thought that was fair, and Aaron said, "Yes, sir."

He said, "So many here have spoken highly of you, and I feel after hearing them that you deserve a chance. Do not make me regret my decision."

It was all over quickly, and I needed to get back home. Aaron wanted me to spend the night, but his face was the last thing I wanted to see in the morning. I took the opportunity to ask him if he was done dealing drugs. He gave me a solemn look. I was just as guilty as if I had been rolling up them nickel bags for spending all that money. I knew in my heart he did not make the kind of money we were spending. But it felt good, even though it was wrong. "We have now paid the price, we are done, are we not Aaron?"

He looked directly into my eyes and said, "We are done with that life, Sandra."

I made it home at a decent time and picked up the kids from Bonita's house. Renee and Wanda stopped by for a while. We watched television for a few hours and then they left. I did not share any information with them, for I was trusting no one with that. When they left, I started to think about money because I did not know what Aaron's paycheck would look like now. I knew I was in good shape with my pension, my secretarial job, and the funds from my rental property in Philadelphia, which I still owned. Thank goodness the project rental office did not know about that. Whatever it was, it would have to work out.

The next day when the mail was delivered, I noticed a letter from the department of Social Security. I knew they were telling me my new monthly amount for the kids. To my surprise, the amount was the same as before we married. It now only listed the names of the kids and not my name. So I guess there was no need for Mom to worry about my pension being cut.

The next day, the mail carrier had another letter from the Social Security office. Now what did they want? I opened the letter and started to read and saw that my kids' survival benefits were being decreased because another child's mother had made a claim for benefits. The letter said I could contest it, but I knew better because I knew the child belonged to Joseph Kearse as my children did. Now my money was looking a little smaller, but I knew Aaron and I would get past all of the challenges that we had been going through lately. What else was going to happen?

# Chapter Eighteen: You Are Leaving Me?

It was now the middle of April 1973, and Aaron would be home for Easter weekend. Friday, April twentieth, he showed up and had money for us to go shopping for the kids. I stopped him and asked it the money was drug money, because I was not playing with him about dealing. He told me to relax; it was money he already had stashed before he got busted.

I had already purchased clothing for the kids but wanted to make Easter baskets for them. So we went and bought all of the fixings for the baskets. He boiled and painted Easter eggs with the kids that evening. It seemed like he had more fun than they did. It was near eleven p.m. when they got to bed.

That night Aaron told me that he had to leave Andrews Air Force Base in June. I asked him where he was going, and he told me that he and all of the guys who were involved in the drug ring had all received orders to Thailand.

I said, "Where in the heck is that?"

He said, "I know you have heard of Vietnam! It is very close to Vietnam."

"Why can't we go with you?"

He explained that it was a solo short tour of duty. He reminded me that his brother Michael was stationed there at Bangkok Royal Thai Air Force Base. I asked him if he would be close to where his brother was. He told me he would be stationed at Takhli Royal Thai Air Force Base, a little ways from him. Maybe two to three hours' driving time.

I preceded to ask Aaron what day he would be leaving in June, and he responded, "I will let you know soon."

I was so hurt and had many mixed feelings about all of that information. He told me he was going to try to work his assignment so he could return back to Andrews AFB. It was starting to feel like we really were not married at all. At least I did not feel married. I was feeling some kind of way for that weekend. I was wondering if he had set this all up and asked to go to Thailand. After all, Doug was in Thailand, his friend Whatley, Cruz, and his brother were all in Thailand at different Air Force Bases. I wondered! There is always something that I have to accept and or deal with. I told Aaron that we would tell the kids next month. I had to decide how I would tell them.

Easter weekend went well. The kids loved their baskets, and they were dressed to impress for Sunday school on Easter morning. They would meet up with all their cousins at Mom's house later on. That was the place to be on holidays.

The days were passing by so fast. I decided to tell the kids about our temporary separation from Aaron. I did not want them to feel betrayed by him or to feel they would never see him again. I just went for it after dinner one evening. I told them that Aaron's job was sending him far away to do a special job for America. Babygirl wanted to know why they had to ask her dad to go. Kevin wanted to know if it would be like when their dad Joseph was killed, if he would never come back, and Kimmy Jo told them that it was going to be for a long time but he would not be dead.

Mom said, "He is coming back in one year."

Keenan said, "Mom, is a year a lot of days?"

I smiled and told him yes but we would keep track of the days on a calendar. I took the wall calendar down and showed them how we would cross off every day when he left; that way we would know what day he would be coming back home.

Kimmy Jo said, "Now you can marry Bruce, Mommy."

I responded, "I cannot. I can only be married to one person at a time. I could get in trouble with the cops if I marry Bruce."

Kimmy Jo said, "Mom, don't tell the cops."

Lord of mercy, this child was only eight years old and already scheming. I later informed my family about the overseas tour coming up. Well, I knew we would not be leaving York, Pennsylvania any time soon. Had I gone from bad to worse? I had not had a chance to even feel married yet. We still had more time to spend with Aaron, for he would not be leaving until August first, four months away. He was on leave for thirty days prior to leaving us. He brought all of his belongings to 351 Stone Avenue that he would not be taking overseas with him. He had so much stuff. I convinced him to help me pack all of it in boxes until he returned back home. He told me not to worry about money, for he would be living in the barracks, and meals were free. He would only need the essentials, and he would increase my allotment while he was away.

Time just flew by; we had a going away cookout in the projects at our house a week before he left. It was an early event, for I wanted the kids to be there as well to say goodbye to their new dad. Everyone and their brother came to the party. His friend Paige also came up, my sister Portia and Kathy also surprised me and showed up. All of the potheads looking for marijuana, but Aaron was out of the business.

I hoped like hell that he did not pull out any marijuana after what we had been through. That would have given me another opportunity to kill him on the spot. All of my sisters and their men stopped by as well as my girlfriends. Joanne and Mom helped me with the food. We had plenty. I sent Bucky Branch and my brother Bucky to the liquor store to buy beer. If they wanted anything stronger, they had to buy it. All cleared out at a reasonable time.

# Chapter Nineteen: Just Like It Used to Be!

It had been three weeks since Aaron left for Thailand. I was not sure if I missed him or not, for we never lived together for any substantial amount of time. I tried not to dwell on it too much; besides, the annual Jerry Lewis telethon for Jerry's Kids was back, and Kimmy Jo was hyped up for her annual penny carnival. That surely would take my mind off of him for a little while.

Kimmy Jo had her siblings and her little friend Debbie from next door hyped up. I guess they were thinking about how much ice cream they could buy with the pennies. Even though I sent for the telethon kit for Kimmy Jo every year, I do not remember her giving me any pennies to mail to the telethon fund. She now had included her half-brother Jay, who lived adjacent to us in the projects, in her plans. All of the kids loved him and called him their big brother. I was happy that they were building a relationship with him. His mother and I were okay with it. As soon as the telethon was over, it would be time to start school.

School would start in two weeks, and the kids were ready. Kevin is repeating the first grade. After a conference with his teacher, I decided to hold him back, for his grades were on the borderline of failure. I did not want him to be passed to the second grade, for his struggle would have been too much academically. Kimmy Jo would be in third grade. Karmentrina would join them at Saint Patrick's in full day kindergarten. Keenan would remain at McKinley-Cookes Child Development Center. All of my kids started their education journey at the McKinley-Cookes Child Development Center. I remember how hard it was getting Kevin through the program. He would have tantrums and throw chairs and yell at the teachers when he did not get his way. I think that something was going on mentally for him. After seeing his father murdered, he never seemed to be the same. When Kevin was born, he had to remain in the hospital for about a week after my discharge. He was born with jaundice and did not respond well on his Apgar test at one and five minutes. Mom was worried about him.

I felt it necessary for them to get a good start, and I knew they would get it at McKinley-Cookes Child Development Center. They learned so much there, like setting the table, how to pass the food to the next person when they put something on their plate from the bowl, pushing their chairs in after they were done eating, and wiping off the table. I stayed involved in the program for as long as my children attended. I always advocated for children and mothers in the struggle from a young age until now.

Two of his cousins would be there with him, Bubbles and Sean. Time was moving slow, or so it seemed. I was working full time and taking care of the kids. It kept me busy, but I had not been hanging out with friends, even though many still stopped by all the time.

Aaron wrote letters and sent cards and little gifts frequently to me and the kids. They loved when they get letters from him, as did I. But it was not like seeing him there in person. We barely had a chance to get to know each other. In one letter he told me he was going to move off base, but he said not to worry, that it would not affect the money that he was sending to me and the kids. Several airmen had the opportunity to move off of the base because of the return of soldiers from Vietnam, which made for a shortage of rooms in the barracks. Plus, he told me that he would be getting additional money to live off the base. He had earned his two stripes back and was now an E4, Sergeant. I was happy about that. I could not help thinking that maybe he was living with someone else. I swore that if he was, I'd better not ever find out about it.

The weather was getting colder now, and I did not plan on staying in the house all the time and missing out on night life. I made a deal with myself, that the next time I was invited out, I would be going. November the first was coming up, Aaron's twenty-first birthday. Maybe I should go out and celebrate for him. Why not? I was sure he would be celebrating over there, and I wondered with whom. I knew he told me that all of his boys were stationed at different installations and his brother was two hours away from him by car.

It did not take long before I was living just like I had before I met Aaron, hanging out, clubbing and just being me. I ran into one of my old flames at the corner bar one evening. He ordered a drink for me, saying, "Do you still drink rum and Coke?"

I nodded yes! He told me there was going to be a live band at the Legion that night and wanted to know if I was going. I told him that I would think about it and maybe I would go. I left the bar soon after, and he was still there. I walked a few blocks to Bonita's house to see if she would babysit for me, and she said it would not be a problem.

I walked across the College Avenue Bridge alone in the dark to the Legion that evening. It was crowded, as it always was when there was a live band. I kind of knew everyone who was there. I found a seat with some friends and made myself comfortable. Yes, Bruce was there, and of course we connected. I left the Legion with him, and the rest is history. It felt like we never broke up.

I walked around York with my head up, like I did not care what the hell people thought about me. As far as I was concerned, it was none of their business. Of course, Joanne warned me that it was a dangerous choice that I was making, and I knew she was right. But I'd never stopped loving Bruce, and I did not know if I ever could. My house was back to being the drop-in spot, and all of my crew knew what was up with me. They dared not talk to me about it.

Mom was different; she spoke her mind and told me so. She said to me, "Your dream was to marry and move away from York. You may have messed that dream up now, Sandra."

I had no words for Mom, for she spoke the truth. I ran into Georgette one day, a friend, and she said to me, "May I ask you a question?" I responded yes. "Aren't you worried about what will happen when your husband comes home and hears about you and Bruce?"

I told her no I was not. No one had to answer for me, only me. She said, "I wish I was bold like you." I told her it was not about being bold at all.

The days went quickly and love letters with poems for me and letters for the kids came often. One time he wrote that he had barracks duty and was outside looking at the moon and was wondering if it was the same moon I was looking at. So sweet! In another letter he told me he was very sick with hepatitis and that his skin and eyes had turned yellow, but he was getting better. I started to worry somewhat about him over there.

The kids were doing well in their schools and asked often when their dad would come home. I told them that Aaron would write and let us know when he would be coming home. Time was moving so fast, winter, spring and now summer was approaching.

I had to cut things off with Bruce. It would be difficult, but it was something I had to do before Aaron returned back to the States. He did not want to cut it off and told me to get a divorce and leave York with him. In the back of my mind, I was thinking about his baby's mom always calling and begging for Pampers, formula and etc. I would not be able to deal with that.

It was now August, and Aaron should be home any day, but he never sent a letter letting me know when he would arrive in country or what day he would arrive in York. The kids had marked off all of the days on the calendar and wondered what day he would return. On Tuesday, August the twentieth, there was a knock on the door, and it was Aaron. I was surprised to see him standing there in the flesh. I asked him how he got home and he told me Doug picked him up from Dover Air Force Base in Delaware earlier that day and gave him a ride home.

He was so skinny. I asked him why, and he said, "Babe, Thailand is the drug capital of the world."

I said, "What does that mean?"

He said that we would talk later. He picked up his duffle bag and entered the house. I called the kids from the living room to tell them that their dad was home. They were so excited. He went up to our room, and the kids and I kind of smothered him until it was time for them to go to bed.

That night was my opportunity to drop the bombshell about my hanging out, but I chose not to. I did not know what I was waiting for. I asked him to tell me about the drug capital of the world and what it had to do with him being so skinny. He told me he was addicted to opium/hashish, and I wanted to know what that meant for us.

He said, "No worries, I can quit because there is no pure opium here in the States."

I told him that he had to stay in the house and not go anywhere until he started to pick up his weight. He had thirty days until he had to report for duty. He agreed and then started to tell me that he had to report to Cannon Air Force Base in Clovis, New Mexico. He told me that if I did not want to go, he would understand and would buy me and the kids a home on his GI (Government Issue) Bill in York.

I took a deep breath and said, "Where in the heck is that?"

He said, "Far, and I want you and the kids to go with me."

I told him I wanted to go with him. He stayed in the house for almost two weeks, and he was gaining some weight, just enough that he no longer looked like a scarecrow.

Everyone was inquisitive about his weight, and we told them that he'd lost weight due to hepatitis. I did not let anyone come into my house except Renee, Doug, and Mom. I did not want anyone to see him in that state. To my surprise, he did not get any withdrawal symptoms. For all I knew, he still had something he was taking. *Shit, a drug dealer with hepatitis and an opium/hashish habit, Lord what have I walked myself into? Don't let it be!*

He soon ventured out of the house, and I was glad that he was looking much better. He told me he was going to go around the corner to the local bar for a pack of cigarettes. He was not gone very long. When he returned, he told me he ran into Mary's husband, Clabber, who had a mouthful of information about me and Bruce.

I did not speak, I just looked at him, and he said, "That was the past, Sandra. I am looking only at the future right now for us and our family. I can tell you this: I have done things but there will never be any children or any women coming to confront you as long as we are married. I want to know if you are still my wife and will you and my children be going to Clovis, New Mexico with me?"

I asked him if he wanted me to go, and he said, "If you are still my wife."

I said, "Are you forgiving me?" and he said, "You are already forgiven."

I had tears in my eyes, and I felt some kind of way. He was more grown-up than I thought for his age. "How will we get there?"

He said, "Let's figure it out before it is time for me to leave."

That was the last time I ever heard anything about that situation. He kept his word and never brought it up.

# Chapter Twenty: The Move to Clovis, New Mexico

It was all decided that we were to join Aaron in Clovis, New Mexico. We decided that the kids and I would travel by bus. I asked Mary if Tracey could go with us, and she said that it was okay with her if Tracey wanted to go with us, and Tracey told us both that she wanted to go.

It was going to be a long ride, twenty-five hours. At least we would change buses only one time, in Oklahoma. Aaron helped us to pack all of my things that I wanted him to have shipped to New Mexico before he flew out right after Labor Day. Military housing would give me the date that our things would be picked up.

He called me when he arrived at his new base and told me he was given ten days to find housing for us. We needed a house before we left. About a week later, he called and said he found a house about three miles from the base, and he gave me the address to share with my family and friends. Our address was 716 Hondo Street, Clovis New Mexico (the house still stands; you can google it). I was starting to feel homesick already, and we had not even boarded a bus.

I gave away all of my furniture to siblings and friends. We traveled with suitcases containing only our clothing. The movers picked our things up right after Labor Day: dishes, blankets, televisions, etc. This would be the last year for Kimmy Jo's Jerry Lewis Penny Carnival Telethon, and I sure hoped that she would not remember it when the following year arrived.

We left York at the end of September, and I hoped Aaron had worked out the school situation for the kids. The kids became so restless on the bus ride, especially Keenan Wynn and Karmentrina. I had packed food, snacks, and coloring books for the trip, but that did not last long.

At every stop we got off of the bus so we could move around a little bit, stretch our legs, and go to the bathroom. On long stops, we ate at the terminals from the vending machines. We had a long layover in Oklahoma, where Aaron's brother Michael was now stationed. I had never met him before but was looking forward to it.

We finally arrived at the bus terminal in Oklahoma City. I phoned Michael but did not get an answer. It was most likely a bad number or the wrong number. We were there for about an hour, and then it was time to board the next bus.

The kids and I were literally exhausted from the bus ride. We finally arrived two and a half days later. As soon as I saw the sign *Welcome to Clovis, New Mexico*, I was homesick. I pointed out the sign to the kids, and Tracey said, "We are here, guys."

I reiterated, "Yep, we are surely here."

It looked like we were in the desert when we arrived. Just open plains and tumbleweeds all over the place. Clovis, New Mexico was only nine miles west of the Texas border.

Aaron was at the bus terminal waiting for us when we arrived. One of his military friends, Gene Sistrunk, an older man who mentored Aaron in Thailand, picked us up and took us to 716 Hondo Street. It was right around the corner from a mobile home park where Gene lived. The weather was so hot and dry. The house was a one-level L-shaped house with a garage that had a two-car width concrete driveway, a fence in the front with an old storage shed in the back yard with no grass, just dry light brown sandy looking dirt. The back yard fence was about four feet high and all wood, painted white. You could not see through it. The front fence was four feet high with metal gate fencing. There was a walkway to the front door about fifteen feet long. The fence enclosed the driveway also. The house had three medium-sized bedrooms, a kitchen, living room, and one bathroom. There were sizable windows in the front and back of the house and in all of the bedrooms.

The only furniture we had was what Aaron had sent from Thailand. A large papasan chair and all of his clothing and boxes and boxes of jazz and rhythm and blues albums and a record player. More boxes from Pittsburgh showed up from his sister Kaye, who had all of his books sent to him. An assortment of all kinds of titles. I would come to hate those books.

Aaron would go into the bathroom late in the evening and stay in there forever. I knew there was no way it took anyone that long to use the bathroom unless he was constipated every evening after the kids went to bed. One evening I knocked on the door and he said he would be right out. Twenty minutes later he was still in there. I went to the door and used a wire hanger to pop the lock and found him sitting on the commode with his feet propped up on a stool, reading a book and smoking a cigarette. I wanted to go into the living room and pick up all of those books stacked against the wall and burn them. I would much later find out that his mom and siblings all had that reading in the bathroom habit.

He found a kitchen table on base from the thrift store for fifty dollars. A refrigerator came with the house, but there was no washer or dryer. There were clothes lines already put up in the vast backyard, four of them. That was right up my alley. I used to go to the laundromat when we were living in the projects to wash clothes and then bring them back to the house to hang them out to dry. Now, I would need a washing board because I knew we would not be able to afford a washing machine just yet. I was not looking forward to that. I remember watching Dot use her washing board when I was a little girl. I had the skill, but I was not looking forward to using it.

Everything that we had packed for the military to send here from York to include dishes, pots, pans, my knickknacks, pictures, important papers, blankets, quilts, and all of our clothing arrived. Thank goodness for the quilts because we were all going to be sleeping on the floor for a while. I would have to find a job as soon as possible if we were going to survive financially.

Aaron would be getting a housing allowance because he would be living off the Air Force Base with his family. That would help. But I wanted to take some college classes while we were stationed there. If we were able to afford it. I would have to keep my fingers crossed on that. We had neighbors to the right of us, and Aaron would introduce me to them later. The husband was in the military also.

I assigned everyone their bedrooms and gave everyone quilts and blankets. It was not too cold; the weather was mild. I was hoping that my children's Social Security check would come on time, for I had changed the address in plenty of time. The first thing on the agenda was to enroll the kids in school.

Aaron suggested that we all walk up to the corner store, it was called Allsups 7-11 (Allsups) because they sold ready-to-eat food. We did that and also purchased cereal and milk for the next day and then returned to the house and ate. We looked through the boxes and found our pajamas and clothing for tomorrow. Got everyone settled, brushed their teeth and then made the beds on the floor. Aaron and I slept on the fluffy papasan chair cushion. The next morning when everyone was up, it was time to eat and then head out to register the kids for school.

Aaron asked his friend Gene if we could borrow his car to take the kids to school, and he allowed us to. I was thinking how nice of him. We first went to the junior high school Sacred Heart because it would be closest. Tracey was in the seventh grade. We filled out her paperwork in the office, then we were taken to meet her teacher, Sister Bernard, whom we left her with. Sister Bernard told us that she would be sure to get Tracey on the right bus after school to go home. Then it was off to Our Lady of Guadeloupe, the elementary school, for the rest of the children. Kimmy Jo would be entering fourth grade, Kevin second grade, Karmentrina first grade, and Keenan Wynn would be going into all-day kindergarten.

It took quite a lot of time completing all of the school paperwork for all of them. Thank goodness I had all of their school records and baby shot records with me. We did not have to worry about transportation, for the Catholic school had a bus system. The bus stop was right in front of our house. Now we just hoped that all of the kids came home on the bus. I had asked the principal to please make sure all of my children were together when boarding the bus home. They all made it home from school on their buses. All worked out okay.

Tracey did not feel comfortable at school. This would be the first time she attended a Catholic school, and she was the only Black child in her class, whereas Kevin, Kimmy Jo, and Karmentrina had been the only Blacks in their class before.

I felt she would adapt. I thought things were going well in the schools until one day I came home from work and Tracey met me at the front door and told me Karmentrina had an accident on herself in school because the sister would not let her go to the bathroom.

Karmentrina was in my room sitting on the papasan cushion and looking so sad with teary eyes. I asked her what happened, and she told me she raised her hand to ask to go to the bathroom and her teacher, Sister Anne Monica, told her to go and sit down. She said she raised her hand again because she really had to go to the bathroom, and she said she started to cry and that Sister Anne Monica told her to stop her crying and to go and sit down, *monkey see, monkey do, I am not having it in my class.* Babygirl told me she had to poop so badly she used her pencil box and then threw it in the trash. On the way home on the bus, she said she felt so bad because students were whispering, "What is that smell?" My baby was so sad and embarrassed riding that school bus home. She said she ran into the house and told Tracey, and Tracey bathed her and helped her to change her clothing.

I was furious and could hardly sleep that night. I felt my baby's pain, and that sister was going to know at the start of school the next day how I was feeling right now. That bitch obviously did not know whose child she was messing with, but she would know tomorrow morning.

When Aaron arrived home from work, I told him about the incident. He went into Karmentrina's room and sat and talked with her for a while. Later that night, I told him that I was going up to that damn school and give Sister Anne Monica a piece of my mind and that every sister in that fucking school was going to know not to mess with our kids and that none of my kids were monkeys.

Aaron looked at me with a very serious look, not that it bothered me because I knew what he was thinking. He really at that time did not know me. He told me not to go up to that school and get the kids kicked out because that was the only school they could go to in our district. If they went out of the district, we would have to provide transportation, and we had no means of transportation.

The next morning, I took a taxi to the school. I went to the principal, Sister Barbara Anne's, office and asked to speak with her. I was offered a seat, but I stood. I was mentally trying to calm myself down before the principal arrived in the office. Sister Barbara Anne finally showed up and escorted me to her small office in the back of the front office. I told her my concerns, and she had Karmentrina sent to the office. After she listened to Karmentrina she summoned Sister Anne Monica. It took about ten minutes because another teacher had to cover her class. When she arrived, I was introduced, and I had the opportunity to let her know that if Karmentrina asked to go to the bathroom, she needed to go. I told her that I did not appreciate her saying to my child, "monkey see, monkey do" because my child felt she was calling her a monkey and I felt the same way.

I let Sister Anne Monica and the principal know that my child had an accident on herself and had to ride the school bus home with all of the students making comments about the smell. To make a long story short, when I left that school, from that day on, neither my babygirl nor any of my kids ever had a problem at Our Lady of Guadalupe. After school, it was quiet at home, and Karmentrina was so happy that I had gone to her school. She told all the kids about how Sister Anne Monica was scared of Mom, and how "Mom made her apologize to me."

That evening when Aaron came home from work, he had a pet lizard for the kids. The lizard's name was Soho. Aaron told them that they would have to catch grasshoppers to feed it. Kevin wanted to be in charge of the lizard, and Kimmy Jo and Tracey wanted nothing to do with it. The problem was Kevin was afraid to catch the grasshoppers to feed the lizard, so Karmentrina and Keenan decided that they would catch the grasshoppers if they could be in charge of the cage sometimes. Kevin agreed.

Keenan's kindergarten teacher, Sister Herrea, gave him a certificate of distinction for his participation in the Bilingual Program, and the only thing he could say in Spanish was *good morning, good afternoon, good evening,* and *how are you.* Kimmy Jo was quiet in school, and her teacher Sister Claire noted on her progress report that we needed to help her with her penmanship. As for Kevin, Sister Marie Dolorine said he was doing quite well. If Kevin had enough to eat for breakfast and lunch, I knew he would be okay.

Keenan came home from school one day and told me he saw Karmentrina doing cartwheels in the hallway and the principal let her get away with it. I scolded Karmentrina and told her to stop showing off in school before she got her butt whipped. I guess my conference with the two sisters paid off; no one was going to mess with Sandra Lee's children.

We found out a month or so later that Tracey was not doing well in class. I was notified by mail to come for a parent teacher conference and to bring Tracey with me. When Aaron and I arrived at the school along with Tracey, we were taken to Sister Bernard's room, which was Tracey's home room. The sister was showing us some of Tracey's work, and all the papers had failing marks.

I asked why we had not been notified before now, and Sister Bernard said, "Mrs. Stockton, you signed all of the notes that were sent home with Tracey for your signature." I was boiling inside because I knew at that moment that Tracey must have forged my signature. I asked Sister Bernard to show me and Aaron the papers with my signature. I did not freak out at the meeting, but Tracey knew she was going to have to deal with me later. We walked home, and no one was doing any talking.

We arrived home, and I guess the kids could see that our faces were not looking happy. I told Tracey that she was deserving of an ass whipping, forging my name and lying, what was she thinking? I told her to go into her room and I would be in there soon. I took my time going in there because I wanted to be in control of the strap. I told all of the other kids to go into the kitchen with Dad and do their homework. Kevin said that he did not have any homework and I told him to find some if he did not want to get the same thing Tracey was about to get.

When I entered the girls' room, Tracey asked me if Uncle Aaron could give her a whipping and not me. I told her no way and walked over to her. She lay down on the floor and started crying and telling me, "I am going to hold my breath until I die."

I started hitting her little legs with the strap, and she started holding her breath and turning red and, in a few seconds, she started screaming like I was killing her. She elected to stay in her room until dinner. The next day she hardly spoke to me, and I knew she was angry, but one day she would thank me for keeping her in line.

Because education is of most importance in this day and age for negro people. From that point on, things went well with Tracey and her schoolwork; she brought assignments home and got help from me and Aaron. One morning before she left for school, she gave me a letter she wanted me to mail to her nanny. I decided to steam that letter open to see what she had written.

Wow, it was a bombshell. She started off telling Mom that she hated me, my husband, and all of my kids. She said that she felt like a little slave, and all I let her do was go to school and babysit the kids. I was upset at first and then I shrugged it off because she was a little girl. I remembered back when I convinced Mabel to go with me to the police station in York when we were teens because Mom took some of our pay checks to help with utilities. As teens we get a pass sometimes. This was one of those times.

I never sent the letter and have it to this day. Tracey did very well for the remainder of the school year and passed to the eighth grade with very good grades.

Every day while the kids were in school, I would walk to the corner store or the gas station across the highway and talk with the owners. I was building bridges for us to have safe passage to what we were going to need during our stay in New Mexico. One morning the manager at the Allsups gas station asked me if I wanted a job, and I told him I did indeed. He asked me if I had ever been a cashier, and I told him no but that I was a quick study. He took me up on it and hired me.

I learned the job quickly and became the store supervisor. The store had a problem with local young Mexican men and women coming in in groups and stealing. The store was losing thousands of dollars a week. I convinced him to hire Aaron and one of his friends part-time. He did.

I managed the schedule. I was on the day shift, Aaron evening shift from three p.m. to eleven p.m. but he did not get off duty until three, so I stayed until he arrived. His friend Wolff, who was also in the military, had the night shift. The store owner and his wife worked the store on Saturdays and Sundays with their son. We cut their losses down to less than six hundred dollars a month. They were so happy.

I kept asking him for a raise for all of us, and he kept saying the store could not afford it. I knew that was a lie, because I did the books. The white man just thought I was dumb and would accept whatever he said.

So I decided how we were going to get that raise. I am not going to put that information in this book because I do not know how long the statute of limitations is in Clovis, New Mexico. We like our freedom. If you ever meet me, you are at liberty to ask me. We only shopped at the Piggly Wiggly grocery store for meat because Allsups took care of the rest.

Although I was working and the kids were settled in school as well as Aaron was at his job, I was so very homesick and damn sick of washing clothes on a washing board, feeling like I was a slave. I used to play "Midnight Train to Georgia" by Gladys Knight and the Pips almost every night while I was rolling up Karmentrina's plats to curl on the ends. I used to save bread bag twisty ties and wrap pieces of brown paper bags around them to roll up her plats and the girls' hair if I needed to. I could not afford any hair curlers. Karmentrina wanted her hair to be curly like the little Mexican girls. An impossibility with her coarse hair, but the curled ends on her plats worked out just as well. She thought she was so cute, and she was. I played it so much the kids were running around the house singing "Midnight Train to Georgia."

Every chance I got I called my mom to complain about something. I remember calling her to complain that one evening when I arrived home from the University of Clovis, trying to enroll in a course, Aaron had done the laundry and ironed all of the kid's school uniforms. He had food on the stove when I arrived home and told me to just rest if I wanted to because he could handle things. I told Mom he was trying to make it look like I could not keep up the housework.

Mom started raising her voice at me like a crazy woman. She said, "You should be glad that you have a husband who is willing to do the laundry, cook, and tell you to take it easy. Are you crazy, Sandra? Grow up and be a wife, and stop calling me collect because I cannot afford it."

I was at the corner phone booth crying for a minute. When I walked home from the store, Aaron asked if I was all right, and I said yes, some sand blew in my eyes when a car drove by. That night I was feeling like Mom was a traitor. That incident started me on a path to grow. Sure, Aaron wanted to do the laundry now, for we now had a washing machine, but he was not volunteering when I was scrubbing out his dirty drawers on that damn washing board. After I got over my conversation I had with my mom, I fell asleep, and slept well. She was right. I needed to grow up a little bit.

The next day, Saturday, Aaron had duty on the base. When he came home, he took me next door to meet our neighbors. I had been speaking to them over the fence while hanging up the laundry but not much of a conversation. Cathy was Mexican, and her husband was Caucasian, and they had three little kids about the ages of our kids. Karmentrina, only in the first grade, fell in love with their son Timmy, and Kevin fell in love with their little girl.

Karmentrina was always in love with some little boy. At McKinley-Cookes Child Development Center back in York, Pennsylvania, she'd fallen in love with a little boy named Troy. I knew she was the one I would have to watch like a hawk. There would be no teen parents in this family if I had anything to do with it.

Cathy called her husband Peckerwood. Cathy and I became very good friends. One day when our kids were in school, she came next door and asked me to go shopping for magazines with her. I told her I did not have any money to buy magazines, but I would go with her to keep her company. It was sometime in October, and the weather was changing. I grabbed a jacket and went with Cathy. I jumped into her car and we took off. She was driving like forever, and I did not see any stores. I finally asked her where she had to go to buy magazines. We had passed Sears and Montgomery Wards in town. The only two department stores they had and they were small.

She told me we were going to Beverly Hills, and I said, "What? That is in California! You are driving to California?"

She said no, it was the Beverly Hills of Clovis, New Mexico. It was where all the rich Mexican/white people lived, and they threw away the best magazines at the end of the month. I never thought I would find myself rooting through rich white and Mexican folks' trash for magazines. But they were the best ones that I always looked at in stores but could not afford. She told me not to worry about getting caught; they did not care if we looked through their trash for magazines.

As we made our way through the back alley, a young woman yelled out to Cathy, "How are you doing, Cathy? How are the kids?"

I said, "She called you by name. Do not tell her my name, please!"

We talked all the way back home laughing and joking. When we arrived, we said our goodbyes. After I took my magazines in the house, I told Aaron and the kids. They were laughing at me. That is when I got hooked on Publishers Clearing House Contest and would enter for many years to come. I used to love to look at the automobile magazine pictures, so classy. One day I saw a Volvo and it was beautiful. I promised myself that one day I would buy a candy apple red convertible Volvo. We did trash can rooting once a month and a couple times a month during the holidays. I could not believe what rich people threw away.

We finally saved enough money to buy some furniture for the kids. We went downtown and started looking in local mom and pop stores. We came across bunk beds that we wanted for the boys and single beds for the girls. The store manager asked us what we were looking for and we told him about the beds.

I asked him if we could put them on layaway and he asked, "Do you have a job?"

I said, "Yes, and my husband is in the Air Force."

He said, "Then I will set up a store credit account for you and deliver the beds next week to your house." He was an older Mexican man, and he told us that he owned the store. He also told us that he knew how hard it was to get started in building credit. He directed us to go across the street and open a Sears and Montgomery Ward's store credit card and that they would give it to us because we had military identification cards. After we completed the paperwork, we thanked him for his kindness and proceeded over to the two stores and it was a piece of cake opening the store credit accounts. Our limits were five hundred dollars on each one. We were very happy about this. We did not worry about a bed for us; the papasan cushion worked just fine. We were so broke from buying Catholic school uniforms for the kids and our washing machine.

The holidays were quickly approaching, and we had to think about money for Christmas for the kids. I started picking up extra hours on the weekend to help out. We cooked our Thanksgiving dinner together. It was our first Thanksgiving holiday together. I had Aaron peel the onions for my potato salad and stuffing. His eyes were tearing and red, and he just kept on peeling. Made me remember when I got the job of peeling onions for Mom.

It was strange not seeing my family during the holidays, but it worked out; we were happy. A few days after the Thanksgiving holiday, Aaron came home from work and had a brilliant idea. He told me that Peckerwood invited us to go with him and Cathy to pick potatoes for two weeks to make extra money for Christmas. Peckerwood told him that he and Cathy did it every year, and the money was good.

I agreed, and Aaron put in for two weeks leave. I worked it out with my boss to cover me in the mornings until I arrived. He agreed. Aaron kept his shift and sometimes worked part of my shift because the potato fields wiped me out. Tracey was in the seventh grade and her job was to make sure everyone got up on time, ate breakfast and not miss the school bus. I would always set the clock so she would not oversleep.

A big truck came by for us early in the morning when it was still dark and the only thing in the sky was stars. We had to climb into the back. Cathy spoke to them in Spanish. We did not know what she said, but they all struck up a conversation. I was hoping they were not laughing about us because we were a sight to see with our heavy clothing and scarves over half of our faces. We were the only Blacks on the truck. They obviously knew each other.

Peckerwood never said anything. Later Cathy told me he could not speak Spanish. It was so cold in the back of the truck I was sitting very close to Aaron and thinking, *What have I let him talk me into?* The sun was not even up yet at five o'clock in the morning. We drove for about forty-five minutes and the truck came to a stop. We unloaded.

As far as I could see, there were potato fields. They gave directions in Spanish, then Cathy explained to us what we had to do. We were bundled up with scarves over our noses and mouths to keep the dust out. Everyone lined up on either side of the truck. I made sure to not be separated from Aaron. We had to walk along side of the trucks and keep pace with the driver. We all had to dig up with our hands enough potatoes to fill our sacks and then throw them onto the truck. I could hardly lift my sack when it was full. Aaron threw my sack up on the truck. He had double duty because he had to throw his on the truck as well. It seemed like every two hours or so I had to pee. Cathy and I would run to go pee in the field. I am sure potatoes got peed on and not just by me.

Aaron was so quick; he kept pace and did my share as well as his. He must have been a slave in another life. After that first day, I could barely walk and did not want to go back the next day. Black dirt was all over our faces; the scarves hardly did anything to protect our faces, and dirt was in our noses, ears, hair, and fingernails. We even had on hats that did nothing to protect our heads from the cold weather. We were so happy to jump off of the back of that truck on arrival to our house. The driver yelled to all of us, me, Aaron, Cathy and Peckerwood, "See you early tomorrow morning."

Aaron took a shower and went up to Allsups to start his shift. I sent the kids to the store to get something to eat after Aaron was on duty. The kids retuned from the store to eat their food. They had fries and hot links, and I knew the hot links were for Tracey; she just loved them. The hotdogs were for the rest of the kids. They were happy and so was I. I stayed in bed for about four hours until it was time for me to relieve Aaron so he could get some rest. We split his evening shift. I told the kids they could stay up for a while, until nine o'clock and not to make a lot of noise so Aaron could sleep. We had a television with local stations, nothing much to watch but they were adjusting quite well to Clovis. When I finished the shift at eleven p.m., I returned home, and Aaron did not even feel me getting on the papasan cushion with him.

Before we knew it, the alarm clock started ringing loudly. It seemed like four o'clock in the morning came so darn fast. We were up before the crack of dawn. I finally got the hang of it and made it through the rest of the two weeks, which I thought would never end. Cathy praised me for doing so well as it was my first time and she said that I would do even better next year. I told her the only way I would ever pick a potato again would be from a grocery store. She laughed.

The best thing about picking potatoes was when we were paid, and for some reason, they paid me more than Aaron. I told him to stop crying about it because the money was going to the same place. We made good money during the two weeks. We had enough money for me to register for an English class at the university and to buy two second-hand dressers for the kids' clothing and the toys that they wanted for Christmas. We would hold on to the rest and continue to save for a used car. I saw one with a sign on it at the gas station across the highway from Allsups. I soon told Aaron about the car, and we decided we would go together to inquire about it.

It was now January 1975, and I was so very homesick, as were the kids for their nanny. We would write often to everyone at home, and they would write back to us. Mabel wrote to me the most and asked if she could come to visit in the summer by bus for a week, and I told her it would be fine.

My class went just fine. It was a Saturday class, so I did not have to miss work. I knew that Aaron was to be stationed in Clovis until the end of September 1975, but not me and the kids. I was going to do whatever I had to do to convince him that I wanted to go back home when the school year was over. That night after dinner, I brought it up to him, and he said he would think about. I agreed.

In the meantime when I went to work the next day, I walked across the highway to ask about the old station wagon with the for-sale sign on it. I decided not to wait for Aaron to go with me to inquire about the car. The gas station owner wanted seven hundred and fifty dollars for it. I asked him if he would consider me paying it off in two months and he said, "Are you married?"

I told him I was and that my husband was in the military stationed at Cannon AFB. I showed him my military dependent identification card. He told me to bring my husband by tomorrow to talk about it, and I did. The following day Aaron hitchhiked from the base to the gas station on his lunch break. Everyone hitchhiked back and forth to the base and downtown in those days. I had three hundred dollars in cash with me. The owner told us he would take the money as a down payment and we could take the station wagon immediately, but he would keep the title until we paid it off. We paid it off in six weeks and had our car, a nineteen sixty-five Chevy station wagon.

As soon as we got the station wagon, Aaron signed the boys up for a karate defense class. I found out that my husband was a Bruce Lee fanatic. I would be the driver for them until Aaron got his driver's license and then only if I felt they would be safe in the car with him. On the weekends he would practice karate with the boys, and we would also have tag wresting events, the boys against the girls. That was too crazy. Aaron always made sure that the girls won or it was a tie.

We now had a car, which meant no more hitchhiking back and forth to the base and downtown. The problem was that Aaron did not know how to drive, and he needed to learn. I worked around my schedule to teach him how to drive as much as possible. I picked up a driver's handbook from the motor vehicle administration.

One Saturday we were out driving, and Aaron was feeling himself. He decided he would drive with one hand and his other hand propped on the door of the open window. I said to him that the turn to our house was coming up, and he had to make a right turn. Just then a car in front of him came down the street to make a left in front of us, and he panicked and turned a hard right and almost hit a telephone pole. I told him to turn the car off and he did. I got myself out of the station wagon and started to walk home.

He got out of the station wagon and started calling, "Babe, you can drive, I will walk."

I said, "Take the car home Aaron." My life flashed in front of me and there were some things that I had not accomplished yet. That night we shared a bottle of cheap sweet wine and decided that Aaron would drive to work every morning with me in the car. It was a straight highway and would be safer for him to get more driving experience and to get his confidence level up.

That went well, until one day he was driving and he looked up into his rearview mirror and saw Karmentrina in the back seat. He said, "Karmentrina, what are you doing in the car?"

I said, "Stop playing. I am not in the mood."

Aaron told Karmentrina to sit on the seat and I then looked back and saw her. I told him to pull off of the road and stop the car. I yelled at Karmentrina to get out of the car right then and there and for her to walk home. It was now spring, and the weather was warmer and we were only about a block from the house, but to her it probably seemed like a long way. She started crying and sat there shaken. I told her to get out before I snatched her out of the car. She got out of the car crying and sucking her thumb. I got out as well to make sure she was far off the road. I told her to start walking, and she did. I told her she better not get hit by a car or I would kill her when I got home.

Aaron said, "Sandra, we cannot do this."

I said, "We are not doing this. I am. Get walking, Karmentrina!"

I got back in the car and was a little worried, but I was teaching her a hard lesson. Inside I was feeling pretty low, a part of William was in my head, and I needed to figure out how to get rid of it. His attitude and his upbringing in my life for ten years made a negative impression on my behavior, and I needed to change somehow.

She was safe when I returned home. She was in her room sitting on her bed with all of the kids. They were looking sad for Karmentrina. They knew that Karmentrina was in for a spanking. I gave her a break. I thought she'd learned quite enough for that day. I told her to go to the bathroom and wipe her face. I followed her into the bathroom and hugged her and told her that she can never just do things without asking because only moms and dads are allowed to do that.

She said, "Okay, Mommy, I love you."

I squeezed her a little tight and told her I loved her too.

One early Saturday evening, I walked up to Allsups for a Slurpee. Aaron told me not to go because the weatherman on the television set said a tumbleweed storm was coming that evening. I did not know what that meant, and I told him I would hurry. The sky was a little gray, no big deal.

On the way back with my cherry Slurpee, the sky turned very dark, and the wind was blowing so hard, out of nowhere, and giant weeds were flying everywhere. I could hardly walk without being pulled across the road. My cherry Slurpee blew out of my hand. I made it to a pole next to our yard and held on for dear life. Aaron and the kids were yelling out of the window to hold on. "Mommy, please don't let go."

I had never experienced any such ordeal. I had never seen weeds so big. When the wind stopped, Aaron walked over to the pole for me. I asked him why he did not come to get me and he said there was no need for both of us to be blown away somewhere. I now knew what a tumbleweed storm was and would most certainly respect the warning if I have to again.

That may have been my punishment for making Karmentrina get out of the car the other morning against Aaron's judgment.

Aaron was getting comfortable with his driving and said he was ready to go and take the driver's test. So we went to take the test, and he passed. He had to drive in some open fields with no lights or stop signs. It was nothing like the driver's test I'd taken back home in York.

He started taking the car on the weekends to go play cards with his friends Jackson and Wolff. It was okay for a while, then I had a problem with it. I was home with the kids on the weekend studying, and the only friend I had was Cathy.

She told me not to take his shit. She said, "Let Peckerwood try that shit on me. I would slit his throat."

I told her I did not want to slit Aaron's throat. The car issue continued until I got fed up with it. I told him that I was going to leave and take the kids back home if he kept it up.

He said, "I would not try that if I were you, Sandra."

I asked him if that was a threat and he said no, but if you want to go, leave, just let me know which half of our kids are you taking? I told him that was not very funny, and he said he did not mean it to be. He started having his boy pick him up and leaving the car with me. I think he was testing me. Well, I was not going to go until I finished my class in May anyway.

I thought I had a hiding place in the house to stash money for the trip home, and one day I went to add money to my stash, and it was gone.

At bedtime he took out my envelope and said, "Is this what you were looking for earlier? What was your plan?"

I asked for my money, and he gave it to me and said in the next breath, "I dare you to take my kids, Sandra. Remember we are married now, and I have rights. If I come home and find that station wagon and my kids gone, I am going to call the highway patrol and tell them that you stole the kids. I will tell them you are a danger to the kids because of your mental condition and you know that when the police pull you over you would snap out about what I told them, and they would believe you were mentally unstable."

I had another plan. I told Aaron that we could ask the kids if they wanted to go with me or stay with him, and he agreed. The next evening at dinner we had a family meeting, and I told the kids that I wanted to move back to York and they could go with me or stay with Dad; it would be their decision.

Immediately Karmentrina, the traitor, said that she was going to stay with her dad because he would be lonely living in New Mexico by himself, and Kevin signed on with her. Kimmy Jo, Tracey, and Keenan said they were going to go with me.

Keenan tried to bribe Karmentrina, telling her that she would not see nanny. It did not work. I decided that I was not leaving without my kids, all of them. So I settled down and decided to stay put. Aaron stopped the card playing weekends and stayed home with us. We started to get along better and stopped fussing about the station wagon.

The following weekend, he drove me to Tijuana, Mexico for a short trip. Our friends PJ and her husband watched Karmentrina and Keenan and took them to Carlsbad Caverns while we were away. Wolff and his girlfriend watched Tracey,

Kimmy Jo, and Kevin for us. It seemed like we were driving for days. We arrived and parked on the American side of the border and walked through customs. Aaron said that would be safer for us and our car. We only needed a driver's license to get through the customs border crossing gate.

It was my first time out of the United States. I had never seen so many children just following behind us begging for pennies. We did not stay long; it bothered me somewhat. We purchased a few things for the kids and decided to drive back home, a fifteen-hour drive. We were so tired from the drive there. We decided to stop and get a motel room and found one on the side of the road on US-60. It was a room with a bed. I was worried that bedbugs might be in the bed covers. The blanket looked like it was about ready for the trash. My nose was in the air, and Aaron was feeling that I did not want to stay in that room. But given his driving experience, he needed to sleep.

He used the bathroom and then lay on the bed and was out in a few minutes, snoring so loudly that I knew I would not get to sleep. But I tried. I sat in a chair and propped my feet up on the bottom of the bed and soon fell asleep. I slept for about four hours, and Aaron was still snoring. I pulled the blanket off of him to wake him up.

He turned over and said, "You ready to go?"

I responded, "Yep, let's get out of here."

# Chapter Twenty-One: Summer 1975

School was now over, and everybody was promoted to the next grade and I passed my English college class. I was wondering how we would make it through the summer with the kids. There were no playgrounds in the immediate area, and we had no money for amusement parks.

Since we were not using the old shed in the back yard, Aaron decided to turn it into a playhouse. He was working on it for days. He hooked it up with a fresh coat of white paint, a carpeted floor with a table, and little chairs sitting around. I was in awe when I saw it, thinking back to when he could not figure out how to put together the kids' Christmas toys.

I told him it was very nice, and he replied, "Sandra, I do have some skills." We agreed that we would take the kids to the movies and the youth center on the base more often. Karate classes were expensive, so we could not afford too much more. However, there was a local park where we picnicked and hung out with some of Aaron's military friends and families. It was so hot in New Mexico and very dry.

One Saturday afternoon in June, Aaron and I were playing cards and there was a knock at the front door. Aaron answered the door, and there was a young white man in military uniform who told Aaron that our kids were throwing stones at the passing cars when they drove by. The only ones in the yard were Kevin, Keenan, and Karmentrina. Tracey and Kimmy Jo were in their room. Aaron asked the soldier if there was any damage to his car and he said there was not.

I was thinking to myself, *This is going to be a long summer.* I got up from the kitchen table and walked over to the back door that led to the back yard, and they knew what I wanted. They obviously saw the car stop in front of our house. Before I could get one word out of my mouth, Karmentrina and Keenan were already crying, and Kevin was blaming it on Keenan.

Karmentrina, being the little diplomat, said, "Mom, I know we are going to get a beating, but can Dad beat us?

I told her, "No way; I know he really does not give you guys the whipping that you deserve." I told her to just stop sucking her thumb because she was not getting out of it. After that incident, the kids knew that throwing stones at passing cars was not a good idea.

That night, Aaron and I had one of our talks about family issues. He told me that maybe it would be a good time for me and the kids to relocate back home to York before the school year started. I asked him when and he said by the end of July. I was thinking *Why not now?* but I remembered that Mabel was coming for a visit in July for a week. So it was settled that night, and boy was I glad! I would not have to play "Midnight Train to Georgia" much longer. The days were going slowly, but Mabel would arrive soon. She was taking that long-ass bus ride from York, Pennsylvania. At least she was not traveling with restless kids.

Mabel arrived the second week in July just after her birthday on July eighth. We were very happy to see each other, and she really wanted to see Kimmy Jo, her favorite niece, for she had no girls. We had a blast. We took her on base so she could see what it was like. She got a kick out of us going through the gate and seeing the soldiers in uniform checking identification cards.

She was at the house during the daytime with the kids because I had to work. She did not mind that. I told her beforehand that I could not afford to take off from work because we were saving for the trip back home. The week was coming to an end, and Mabel wanted to know if she could take Kimmy Jo back with her on the bus, and I told her I would let her know after I talked it over with Aaron. That evening when we were alone, I brought it up to Aaron. At first, he said no, because she might steal her again. I reminded him that we were just teens then and Mabel now lived in York and not in the countryside of Bel Air, Maryland. Aaron agreed that Mabel could take Kimmy Jo back to York with her on the bus.

The rest of us would not be leaving until the second week of August, just three weeks before school was to start there. The other kids were a little jealous that only Kimmy Jo had the opportunity to go back with Aunt Mabel. However, I reminded them that we all would be going back very soon. They got over it pretty quickly. Whew! Where did the time go?

It was now August the first, and we were leaving in thirteen days. Aaron had already reserved a medium U-Haul truck, and all of our things were boxed up and ready to go. We would pick up the truck the day before the move. Some of Aaron's buddies promised to help us load it.

# Chapter Twenty-Two: Moving Day

Early Saturday morning, every one of us were up at the crack of dawn. I'd driven Aaron to pick up the U-Haul truck the day before. His friends were to be at the house by 0800 hours, and they were right on time. It seemed like forever filling the truck and making everything fit. Moving things around and repacking to make everything fit was a task.

Finally, the truck was fully packed, and the few things that would not fit would have to be sent home later. Aaron planned on getting a one-room apartment for the rest of his tour and has already put a security deposit down on it. The station wagon was full of the kid's small toys, coloring books, snacks, and water for the road. Early Sunday morning, we pulled out. Aaron drove the truck, and I drove the station wagon. It was to be a long twenty-five-hour drive. I was kind of nervous about him driving the truck, for he had not had his driver's license very long.

About a few minutes on the road, I saw Aaron in back of me in the truck start to swerve side to side, and I got scared. He seemed to slow up and take control of the truck. I pulled off of the road as soon as I found an area for both of us to safely stop. I told him that we would have to go the speed limit only and for him to stay in back of me, and he did.

Kevin asked if he could get into the truck with his dad, and against my better judgment, I allowed him to. That worked out better, for we were less crowded in the station wagon.

We stopped often, for I had never driven on such a long road trip, and I knew that I was more experienced a driver than Aaron. After the first night, we decided not to drive past eight o'clock in the evening to be safe and rested.

We were caught in a rain storm the first night and were driving about thirty miles an hour with our flashing lights on. At some point, I pulled over and Aaron followed because my visibility was so bad that I could hardly see at all. A truck driver in a big tractor trailer pulled over in front of us. He got out of his truck and came over to my window to see if I needed help. I told him we were reluctant to continue driving because of the rain and that was my husband following me in the U-Haul.

He told me we could not stay in that area for it was not safe sitting on the side of the road, for he could hardly see us. If we stayed there, we would definitely get hit, for that was a truck route. He told us to follow him to the next truck stop, where we would be safe. My dad William once told me that truck stops were a safe place to stop on the road when traveling. Once we arrived, we thanked the truck driver for helping us to get there safely. We took the kids to the bathroom and then we went back to sleep in the vehicles, Aaron in the truck and the rest of us in the station wagon. Kevin in the back, Keenan and Karmentrina in the middle seat, and Tracey and I in the front seat. It was hot, muggy, and uncomfortable. Kimmy Jo was lucky; she'd gone home on an air-conditioned bus with Aunt Mabel.

We woke up before daybreak and got the kids out of the station wagon and took them inside to wash their faces and brush their teeth. I brought a quart of milk, and we ate cereal outside by the truck, for I was prepared with cereal, small bowls and spoons.

As soon as we started to drive, Keenan wanted to know if we were almost at Nanny's house, and I told him it would be two more nights to sleep outside and then we would be there.

Day two, good weather and Aaron's driving was good for a new driver. That little swerve when leaving Clovis must have spooked him pretty good. We stopped at a truck stop for a break and to eat lunch and then got right back on the road until just before dark. We were all tired and restless. The truck stop was a nice place with a big store and clean restrooms. We ate dinner inside of the truck stop restaurant: burgers and fries with soda.

Karmentrina could not eat all of her food and said to me, "I'm full, Mom." No sooner were the words out of her mouth than Kevin said, "I'll have it Karmen," and I said, "No, you will not."

Kevin had just eaten two burgers and some of Keenan's fries, and there was no way he could still be hungry. Boy must have worms or something. After we finished, we visited the truck stop store and purchased a few things for all of us, mostly candy and chips. Then we went back outside to our vehicles to decide how we were going to sleep because the night before sleeping in the station wagon was too crowded. Aaron probably had the best sleep in the truck cab alone. It was getting late, and we were ready to get some sleep.

Aaron decided that the girls would sleep in the station wagon and he and the boys would sleep outside on the ground between the trailer and the station wagon. We made a sleeping pallet with our blankets that were in the back of the U-Haul truck.

The girls went to sleep quickly, as did Aaron and Keenan outside. Kevin was playing with his little toy soldiers that he brought along on the trip. I figured I better get some sleep and I told Kevin not to go anywhere, but just then he said he had to pee.

"Lord Jesus, Kevin! I am not walking over to that bathroom." I said, "Come here, boy and pee in back of this truck."

He did and then wanted to know how he was going to wash his hands. I took a bottle of water out of the cooler and poured it over his hands and told him to shake them dry. I was thinking that boy better not ask me for any soap. I kept a watch on him for a while, and he finally fell asleep. I dozed off at some point.

The next thing I knew Aaron was waking me up and asking if I was ready to go. It was about five in the morning. We woke up the kids and made everyone go to the bathroom; we would stop in a few hours to eat breakfast.

We were all ready to go when Kevin said to Aaron, "Dad, my two army men are missing." So we all got out on the ground looking for the toy army men. Crawling on our knees looking under the station wagon and the truck and all around the area, there were no army men to be found.

After about twenty minutes, I was tired of looking. Tracey said, "Dad, can you just buy Kevin some more army men?"

Kevin was still crying, and Karmentrina and Keenan were hugging him and saying, "Don't cry, Kevin. Dad is going to get you some more army men when we get to Nanny's house."

Aaron went to calm him down and told him that he would buy him more army men when we got home. That worked out, but Kevin was not going to let him forget about the army men he promised him. We stopped about nine o'clock to eat breakfast and go to the bathrooms. We were about seven hours from York, Pennsylvania, and boy was I glad. We told the kids that we were driving straight through with one stop only for the bathroom. Of course, three hours later we made that stop because I had to pee.

# Chapter Twenty-Three: Home Coming at Mom's House

I finally, saw the sign for Harrisburg, York, Lancaster. I was excited and woke up the kids to tell them we would be at Nanny's house in an hour or so. We finally pulled up on West College Avenue and parked alongside of Mom's house.

Mabel, Kimmy Jo, and the whole clan were there to greet us. Keenan looked out of the window and saw his cousin Sean. He was yelling, "There's Sean, Mom!" and trying to get out of the station wagon by climbing over the seat.

I told him to just wait a minute until Karmentrina and Tracey got out and then he could climb over the seat. We all crammed into Mom's house, and the party was on. Mom had food on the kitchen table like it was Thanksgiving or something. I really had missed Mom's food on the holidays. I knew I was home now, for real. Sisters, brother, nieces, and nephews were everywhere. We all had missed them so much, for we were always at each other's houses when we lived in York. The kids were asking to spend the night with their cousins. Aaron and I were more than happy to let them.

Tracey went home with her mom Mary, Kimmy stayed with Aunt Mabel, and the rest of the kids stayed next door at Mom's house with Aunt Bonita. Finally, after midnight, everyone kind of cleared out. Aaron fell asleep in a living room chair. Mom covered him with a blanket. I am sure that chair felt a lot better than that hard ground at the truck stop. I got comfortable on the sofa and slept quite well.

The next day, Bucky and Wayne helped us to unload the U-Haul. I do not know how we crammed all of our stuff into Mom's attic, but we did. Aaron would return the truck the next morning. Aaron was on a ten-day leave and would hop back to New Mexico from Andrews Air Force Base. As much as I wanted to return home, I did not want to be without him here, but I knew he would be back by the end of September.

I had enough to do with getting the kids situated for school and looking for a place for us to live. The kids were up early and came over to Mom's house with Bonita. Mom cooked breakfast—pancakes and scrapple, which I had not had in a long time. We all sat down and ate until we were bloated. Kevin as usual ate a whole lot and asked for seconds, and his nanny obliged him.

Mom and I started discussing my living arrangements. Bonita interrupted and said that the kids and I could move in with her and her kids for a while. I asked her to check with Barrion to make sure it would be okay with him. She later cleared it with him, and it was done. It was good, for me and my kids would not have to cram into Mom's house. After all, Bucky, Wayne, Bubbles, and Bernard lived with Mom and Mr. Bill. It would be good, for we are only lived next door now.

It was just six more days until Aaron had to leave to return to his duty station, and he wanted to catch up with Doug before he left. Mom had Aunt Vera's (rest in peace) phone number. I called her to get Doug's number for Aaron. I could hardly get off of the phone. Aunt Vera was so excited that I was back. I told her that I would stop by to see her soon.

Aunt Vera had been my idol since I was just a little girl. Aaron called Doug, and he came over to Mom's house to visit and pick him up. Before they left, I told Aaron not to get lost. Doug and Yvette had purchased a house in the East End side of York. Aaron was back around dinner time and was excited about Doug and Yvette's house. He wanted me to go over to see it, and I did the next day. It was nice. They gave us their real estate agent's contact information for later when Aaron would come back home.

We settled in at Bonita's house before Aaron had to leave and decided where everyone was going to sleep. It was a big house with plenty of space. Our kids were around the same ages, so that worked out well. Bonita loved to cook, so I did not have to worry about that.

One thing I would miss when Aaron left was him ironing our clothes. He always did all of the ironing. He told me he received a lot of experience with ironing because he worked summers while in high school at a cleaner's. That was a good trade-off; after washing all of our laundry on a washing board and hanging out all of the clothes on the clothe lines, I deserved to get out of ironing.

I would get over it quickly. I had no choice. Aaron's leave was winding down, and he would have to return to Clovis. I was starting to miss him already, and I did not think that I would. That year in New Mexico, we both grew up together, rearing our children and making joint decisions. Little did I know that my conversation with Joanne would be constantly on my mind. It was as clear as day her asking me if I loved Aaron two years ago in the projects sitting in her kitchen. If she were to ask me that now, the answer would be different.

The night before Aaron was to leave, he took the kids to McDonald's in our station wagon and talked to them about leaving, and they seemed okay with it. They promised Aaron that they would be good while he was gone. The next morning Mr. Bill and Bucky drove Aaron to Andrews Air Force Base. I did not ride along because I thought saying goodbye would be a little too emotional for me. I am one who does not like to show my emotions, if I can help it.

Mr. Bill and Bucky returned later and told me that they dropped Aaron off at the base terminal and that he said he would call me later on. That evening Aaron phoned me at Mom's house. He told me that no sooner had he arrived at Andrews Air Force Base than he'd hopped a plane to Cannon

Air Force Base (AFB), New Mexico. He told me he was very lucky because planes seldom go to Cannon AFB.

He now had to clean out the house for it to pass inspection for our deposit to be returned to us. He already had his one-bedroom apartment and could move into it right away. About two days later I received a call letting me know that the house passed inspection and that he'd received our two hundred dollar deposit back from the landlord.

In the next breath, he told he had already spent the money on an old car, a 1964 Oldsmobile 88. I could not very well argue with him, for I had the station wagon, and he needed transportation because his apartment was not off of the main highway any longer, and hitching would have been more troublesome for him. He said he would be okay with me keeping the housing allowance for he had decided to continue working at Allsups part time evenings. He ended the conversation with the only thing he was going to miss was me and the kids being there with him in Clovis. I told him to chill, he only had one month to be there and then he would be stationed close to home back at Andrews Air Force Base.

# Chapter Twenty-Four: My Old Stomping Ground

School started in two days, and I had to get my children transferred back into the York County school system. I did not have to worry about Tracey, for she went back to live with Mary. Kimmy Jo would be in the fifth grade, Kevin Scott in the third grade, Karmentrina in the second grade, and Keenan Wynn would be in the first grade. Finally, everyone would be in the same school—Saint Patrick's Elementary School at 219 South Beaver Street.

The registration was easy, for I had their report cards from the school in Clovis. For the first week, I walked them all the way to school, then I walked them across the College Avenue Bridge because I knew Kimmy Jo could manage from there. This would be Keenan's first year at Saint Patrick's; everyone else had attended prior to moving to Clovis, New Mexico. It would not take long until they had the routine down.

I would soon hook up with Renee and Wanda, my home girls. It was like I had never left. They heard that I was at Mom's house and stopped by. We sat on the front porch and talked for what seemed like hours, catching up on all of the latest gossip. Who was now dead, who was sleeping with who, and who went to jail for whatever.

You know I had to ask about Bruce, and I was told that he had left York. Damn, just a thought. But it was a good thing, because he was my weakness for sure. I needed to act like I was a wife, and that was what I was going to do. I asked Bonita to help me to put on a small party, and she did. We had it at Mom's house with her permission so the kids would be next door.

We invited my old crew, my sister Portia, and her friend Cathy from Baltimore. Mom Bernice came along to hang out with Mom Dot in the kitchen. Bucky Branch, Sam, Tiny, Smickle, and too many more to name. We partied damn near all night.

Portia, Cathy, and Mom Bernice left after the party. I was worried about them driving back so late to Baltimore, but Portia said, "I got it." She was to call me to let me know when they arrived back home, and she did.

Pretty soon, everyone cleared out. I was so tired. When I woke up the next morning, I felt like I'd outgrown the old ways, like that atmosphere was no longer for me. I guess I kind of grew up, like Mom told me to on that telephone call when I was back in Clovis.

I knew Aaron would be home in less than a month, and I was ready for us to find a house for our family. My plan was to stay in York, and he would commute back and forth.

I took it upon myself to call the real estate agent Doug and Yvette had referred us to. I looked at several houses but was only interested in the one about two blocks from Doug and Yvette on the next street over in the same numbered block.

So when Aaron came home the first week in October for thirty days, I let him know that I did indeed want to stay in York. He showed up in his 1964 Oldsmobile, and he had the car stuffed with his clothes and a wire cage with live mice in it, telling me he won them at a casino night contest at Clovis AFB non-commissioned officers club (NCO).

I said, "What the hell are we going to do with them?"

He responded that they were his pets, and he planned to keep them. There were about eight of them in a wired cage with a plastic water tank and a tube for them to run through. He pointed to the one he called Ben. I was not feeling that and wondered where we would keep them. He decided he would put them in the attic. All I had to do was feed and water them, and as soon as he figured out his living arrangements in the Andrews AFB area, he would get them. He was no longer permitted to stay at the AFB because he was married and receiving a housing allowance.

So I agreed to keep the mice until he came back for them. All of the kids were excited about the mice except Kimmy Jo. Aaron taught them how to feed the babies to the big mice. They were not afraid to pick them up. I was supposed to keep watch to see when babies were born in the cage so the big mice could eat them. That was how we were to keep the mice population down.

After the mice conversation, I took him to look at the outside of the house that I was interested in. We walked around and peeked through the windows. It was a small corner lot with a fenced back yard and a concrete driveway at the rear of the house. He thought it was a good option for thirty-six thousand dollars, so we called the agent so Aaron could see inside of the house, and he liked it. The next day we met the agent at his office and filled out the contract paperwork. Aaron had a copy of his certificate of eligibility for a veteran-backed (VA) loan.

We were approved in forty-five days with no money down. We were so happy because we could be in our new home before the holidays. Aaron returned for the settlement meeting where we had to sign all paperwork and pick up our keys to the house. It would be the first time Aaron had ever purchased a house, but the second time for me, so I kind of knew what to expect. It was special this time—I was now married, and the struggle would not just be mine but ours together.

The following weekend, the end of October, Aaron came home, and we rented a large U-Haul that Mr. Bill drove for us. My brothers and several of our friends helped us to move our stuff from Mom's attic and basement and from Bonita's house to our house. There were three bedrooms, attic, kitchen, dining room, living room, one small bathroom with a mini tub and shower, a wooden back porch, and a basement. The basement floor was half concreted. This house was much bigger than the house back in Clovis. The girls would share, the boys would share, and we would get the master bedroom. We had bedroom furniture for the children, a washing machine, kitchen table and chairs, and our large papasan chair.

After we were finished moving all of our belongings into the house, we sat down for a while. We decided to unpack all of the boxes the next day. Bucky and Aaron returned the U-Haul truck, and when they came back, the party was on. They set up a table to play spades and had purchased beer and wine on their way back to the house.

Pokey and Mabel stopped by but left after we finished emptying the truck. Mary pulled a bottle out of her purse and shared some of it.

Bucky tried to take a swig out of the bottle and she said, "Don't do it Bucky, because I am going to slap the shit out of you if you do." All eyes were on Bucky, and he decided he had better not try Big Red (Mary's nick name).

We played cards until the wee hours of the night, and finally all decided to leave. Aaron drove whoever needed a ride home. Mary made sure to grab her bottle of liquor that we did not finish. Dottie Mae decided to spend the night; she was half-ass drunk and slept on the papasan chair. Aaron and I as usual slept on the floor with quilts. The kids and Bonita went home with Mom and Mr. Bill after the truck was unloaded.

We soon went to Sears to purchase a bedroom set for us and a living room set, but our credit limit was too low to get what we wanted. The clerk asked us if we wanted to request an increase of our credit line, and of course we said yes. He took our military identification cards, and voilà, our credit increased to nine hundred and fifty dollars. Wow, the military IDs worked magic once again. We were in business.

Aaron went over to Bonita's house to get the mice out of her attic before he left. He put them in our basement. The weekend went quickly, and it was time for him to return to Andrews.

He took his time leaving, for he no longer had to depend on anyone to take him back to Maryland or to the Greyhound bus terminal. The following weekend when Aaron returned and went down to our basement to check on the mice, only Ben was still living. He had a fit and he said to me, "Babe, I thought you were going to watch them."

I responded, "Lord Jesus, I am so sorry. I forgot all about them mice. I had so much to do and you calling every damn night, how do you expect me to remember to feed Ben and his family? How in the hell was I supposed to know the big mice would eat the big ones? You said they only eat the babies. You need to let greedy-ass Ben starve to death. Greedy-ass rat eating his own kind."

Aaron decided to take Ben back with him since he was staying with his sister Helena in Virginia. He told me later he had to terminate Ben because Helena said she was not having no Ben in her apartment. She told him that she had a choice if she wanted mice in her house, not like when they were kids in the projects back in Roanoke, Virginia where they had no choice of having rodents. I did not feel sorry for Ben and his greedy ass. Hopefully Aaron would never get any mice for pets again.

# Chapter Twenty-Five: Constant Change

The kids and I were very comfortable in our new home at 245 East Prospect Street. The only problem was not having Aaron there each and every day. I guess I had gotten used to being around him. School was going well, and I wanted to look for a job, but missing Aaron made me forget that mission because I wanted to go with him.

The holidays were approaching, and I was restless. I started going out and shopping for Christmas toys for the kids. I put several things on layaway for them, to include but not limited to a bumper pool table.

Aaron had not been home for a few weeks but was going to be home the week of Thanksgiving for several days. I had planned to let him know what my plan for me was going to be moving forward. Thanksgiving was at Mom's house like always, and we were looking forward to being with the entire family, for we'd missed the big dinner last year. It was always so much fun being there, playing music, dancing, and talking trash when other family and friends stopped by to get a plate.

The family managed to get through the evening without any sister arguments—somebody was always mad at somebody for something. I had not seen anyone for a year, so I had no current beefs with any one of them. Christmas was right around the corner, and I had planned to have Christmas with our family: me, Aaron, and our kids, just us in our new home.

Our first Christmas went well. Toys were everywhere. Aaron brought dolls for the girls and trucks and cars for the boys and some toy army soldiers for Kevin, which he'd promised to get him when we moved back home. I was glad that he remembered and kept his word to Kevin. Aunt Vera and Uncle Herman (rest in peace) stopped over a few days after Christmas. They played bumper pool in the basement for the longest time. I loved watching them and thinking one day that would be me and Aaron happily married for years and years to come. Well, maybe! Hard to say with me.

They were such good role models for me. They were married with children, and they had a house with a yard, and I never saw them be mad at each other. Not like William, who damn near beat Dot to death in front of me and my siblings when we were small children.

That night after the kids went to bed, I told Aaron that I wanted to live with him, and he said, "No problem; I am sure Helena would not mind."

When he left that Sunday after Thanksgiving Day, I approached my mom and told her what I wanted to do. We sat down at her kitchen table, and I told her that I wanted to leave York and go with Aaron but I would need her and Bonita to keep my kids until Aaron and I found housing in Maryland. I told her she could move into the house on Prospect Street rent free; that way she would not have to pay rent any longer.

She looked over at me after sipping her black coffee and said, "I don't know about that, Sandra! What if you get mad at Aaron and decide to come back home and want your house back?"

I promised her that would never happen because I did not plan on coming back, and if it did not work out for me, she would not have to move. I would make other arrangements. Mom agreed, and now all I had to do was clear it with Bonita and I knew she would be cool if the money was right.

That Sunday night, I told the kids what I was going to do. The plan was for the boys to be with Mom and the girls to be with

Bonita. I left after the spring school break in April to go to Maryland with Aaron.

Aaron and I put all of our things into storage, and Mom moved from West College Avenue to East Prospect Street. I left York once again to live with Aaron at his sister's apartment in Alexandria, Virginia.

Space was tight, for Helena and her husband lived in an apartment just big enough for them and their two children, Amye and Larry Junior. We had our own bedroom. There were about three more months of school left in the school year, and I was hoping we would have housing before the next school year started. We were already on the base priority housing list because we had four children. I went home on the weekends during the rest of the school year like Aaron used to do when we lived in the projects.

Karmentrina did not like Aunt Bonita's rules and asked me if she could stay with her nanny, and I allowed her to move from Bonita's house. It was okay with Mom. When school was out, I stayed in York with Mom, and the kids were now all with me at her house. So it was not so bad.

Aaron was notified at the end of June that our name came up on the list and our move-in date was scheduled for August Friday the fiftieth. Aaron said the date for pickup was Monday, July twenty-eighth. We were so happy and told the kids together when Aaron came up for the weekend. I knew the kids would take this in stride, for we had moved quite a bit during their young lives.

The following weeks, the kids and I drove around in the station wagon to grocery stores to collect boxes to pack up our clothing and their toys. Dottie Mae and Bonita came over to the house and helped me pack up almost everything. When Aaron came up on the few weekends that were left, we finished the packing. Our belongings were boxed up and ready to go for the military to pick up. All-important paperwork would travel with me in the station wagon with the kids. I remember when Mom was running from William, she grabbed all of her important papers and pictures. Aaron would be picking up the house keys on the move-in date. The kids and I would get there on Saturday the sixteenth. We were to meet Aaron at the McDonald's across the road from the main gate.

# Chapter Twenty-Six: 1179-B Hall Court AFB

The car was acting up on the way to meet Aaron, and Keenan kept on asking, "Are we there yet?" I was so tired of him asking me that. I was worried that the car would not make it there; it was smoking and acting like it could not go fast at times. I could not wait to get there myself.

We'd packed plenty of blankets, for we had not planned on going back to York that night. We finally met Aaron about ten o'clock in the morning at the McDonald's. I told him about the car, and he checked the oil while we were stopped. The oil was just too low, turned out to be no big deal. The kids were so excited. Karmentrina asked if she could ride with Dad, and I told her it was fine.

Keenan quickly added, "I want to go with Dad too, Mom."

I said, "Okay, hurry up and get into the back seat, both of you."

Kevin, Kimmy Jo, and I followed them in the station wagon on to the base. The base was not new to me, but to the kids it was a whole new world. Seeing the airmen posted at the gates with guns and dogs was a strange thing to them. They were asking so many questions. I told them that they were there to protect us after we moved onto the base.

We followed Aaron around Perimeter Road on the base for a while. That road circles the entire base. I knew he was just showing the kids around, for I had been there several times before.

We finally arrived at our quarters: a duplex on the corner of the Main Street, Menoher Drive, and Hall Court, two blocks from the main hospital and the dental clinic. Our house number was 1179-B, and the neighbors on the right side of the duplex was 1179-A. They were a white family who had recently moved in, just like us. The wife came out and introduced herself and her children to us. The neighbor in the next duplex next to us on the left was Black. Her name was Clemmie, and her husband's name was Charles, and they had six boys. We would become very good friends. Our kids became friends as well, quickly.

There was a large single car garage with a manual door to open and close. A kitchen, large living room/dining room combined, laundry, powder room on the first floor as well as a small pantry, three bedrooms, and a full bath on the second floor as well as a master bedroom with a full bath. There were new appliances, but we would have to purchase our own washer and dryer. I was sure the kids would like having a pantry again, for that is where they used to have their decision-making meetings in the projects. Kimmy Jo would bribe them to be on her side with chocolate milk and candy. They would double cross her and be on my side and Dad's side most of the times.

It was a sizable house, and the base housing area was for new enlisted personnel only. Officer base housing was in a different area because enlisted and officer personnel were never mixed in housing areas or the clubs. Straight-up segregation if you ask me, but it was the way it was. I was surprised when I saw officers in the commissary and the base exchange (BX) together. I was wondering why the officers did not have their own shopping stores.

We looked around the house for phone jacks, and there were none. Aaron drove to the housing office to find out how we could get telephone service. They gave him the number to the local telephone company, and he called while he was at the housing office. They told him he would have to pay to have the telephone cable installed, for telephones had never been in that area. It would cost us one hundred and twenty-five dollars plus a cost for each jack that we wanted. The housing officer told Aaron that Andrews would not pay for it.

When Aaron told me that, I was truly pissed off. What kind of shit? It wasn't like enlisted people made a lot of money. We decided that phone service could wait for a few pay periods to pass. I had other things to think about. About two pay periods later, we had five phone jacks in the house, one for the kitchen, our bedroom, and one in all of the kid's bedrooms. We put a yellow phone in the kitchen and in Kimmy Jo's room, a pink phone in Karmentrina's room, a blue phone in the boy's room, and a black phone in our room. The kids thought they were living large.

Our belongings were to arrive two weeks before Labor Day. And I still needed to register the kids at Saint Phillips Catholic School about five miles from the base. Aaron already had the paperwork, and we were to complete it and return it to the school on any weekday. I knew that once we found out about school uniforms that would set us back a little bit. Catholic boys' uniforms were much cheaper—brown pants or navy blue and a white shirt and a bow tie with black or brown shoes.

We were prepared for the first day of school. We drove them the first day because we did not know the bus assignment for them. I went inside of the school to speak with someone to be sure my kids were going to be directed to the right bus back to the base after school was over. I had hoped that this Catholic school would not get on my damn nerves too bad. They had already started getting under my skin when we went to register them for school; they gave us a pack of white envelopes for our weekly tithes. That was a first! When the kids attended Catholic school in New Mexico and in York, Pennsylvania, all we had to pay was their school tuition, buy uniforms, and go to the required meetings and all events that included them. No one ever gave me a pack of white envelopes. Those two schools probably knew better than that.

The kids were so proud that they got on the right bus from school and knew where their stop was. I could always depend on big sister Kimmy Jo. I was at the school bus stop waiting for them. It was fairly easy for them because we lived directly across from the shoppette, and they saw me standing there.

While the kids attended school, I got the house in some kind of order. We did not have curtains for the windows, so we covered them with sheets temporary. Every day when Aaron came home from work, he painted. I chose colors that were more like me—no, I did not have him paint the kitchen black, red, and silver, like I had in the projects a long time ago. That drove Mom crazy. I chose a canary yellow paint for the kitchen, white for the powder room, beige for living room and hallway up and down stairs, sky blue for the boys' room, peach for Karmentrina's room to go along with her white bunk beds, light green for Kimmy Jo's room to go along with her brown trundle bed, and white for our room and the bathrooms upstairs.

In about two weeks, the entire house was painted. I never knew Aaron could paint so well. Even though he had dripped pain on many things, the walls looked good, and we got up most of the paint drippings.

We did not have a storage area or a play area for the kids to hang out in. Since we had a long concrete driveway that both of our automobiles could fit onto without having to be parked on the street, Aaron decided to paint the garage and fix it up for storage and a hangout place for the kids and their friends when they got them. I was sure that would not take very long because the next-door neighbor Timmy with his blond hair and blue eyes was hanging over our fence in the back yard talking to Kimmy Jo every chance he got. I knew I had to keep my eye on him. I was glad they did not go to the same school.

We placed dark bluish gray indoor/outdoor carpet on the garage floor. It looked nice, and the kids loved it. We knew we would need a heater when the winter arrived.

My whole family came down for a picnic and to see the house. Mr. Bill, Dottie Mae, Bucky, and Mom came early on a Saturday morning. Bucky had Tameca with him as well. Mom always had her. Mary, Mabel, Bonita, and Pokey came later with all of their kids. We left their names at the main gate so they would be able to get on the base, and Aaron met them there as they arrived.

Mom just loved it. She kept talking about the experience coming through the main gate, just like the kids did the first time. Everyone stayed 'til late evening and then left. Mr. Bill, Dottie Mae, Mom, Bucky, and Tameca spent the night. Tameca was sleepy and would be asleep soon in Karmentrina's room with her.

We all just talked about the good old days. That Saturday evening before dark and before they all left, Bucky asked the kids to go to the shoppette to get soda for the liquor and some chips. Kevin volunteered to go to the store because Bucky said whoever went could get a dollar.

Kevin returned after about twenty minutes, and it was then dark outside. Bucky asked Kevin where were the soda and chips.

Kevin replied in his whining voice, "Shoot, Uncle Bucky, it's dark outside" and Bucky responded to him, "It was not dark when you left."

Everybody burst out laughing. I chimed in and told Bucky to leave my son alone. Kevin at that time did not like being outside when it was dark. He grew out of that as soon as he started being interested in girls.

Mom saw my makeshift window curtains with sheets and told me she would make some curtains for us. She took measurements and told me to give her a week or so and she would make some cute curtains, and she did. They left to go back to York early that evening.

We took the whole family up a week or so later to visit and pick up the curtains. They were so cute. She had only made enough for the kids' bedrooms and the kitchen window, which was a big front window. That would be good, for one would have to walk past that window to enter the front door. The entire kitchen could be viewed through that window.

We would later get Venetian blinds for the living room and our bedroom. Time was flying by, and the kids were having no problems in school, and by this time we knew everyone's little friends in the neighborhood. They adjusted well to the diversity of military life. It was new to me as well. The garage was a big hit. They played church a lot and used candy for communion. Kimmy Jo was such a church girl growing up.

A few weeks after we moved in, the next-door neighbor Timmy, the little white boy, wanted to know if Kimmy Jo could be his girlfriend, and I told him he would have to ask her. He wanted to know if he could take her to the movies and he said he would pay her way and buy her popcorn and candy. I told him that it was okay if Kimmy Jo wanted to go and if his mom and dad said it was okay. He came back to the front door a few minutes later and told me his mom and dad said it would be okay.

Kimmy Jo did go on that movie date. She said they had fun. I soon met Timmy's older brother, who was always on his skateboard and riding Karmentrina on his shoulders up and down the street. When I saw him with her on his shoulders, I wanted to yell, but that might have made them fall. When he got back in front of our house, I told him that he was not permitted to ride her on the skateboard with him. He tried to assure me that he was really good and would not drop her, but I insisted in a stiff verbal way without scaring him to death. Karmentrina was not happy about that, but she would be less happy if she had fallen while riding on his shoulders.

Kimmy Jo made friends first. She was the oldest and outgoing. Karmentrina followed suit with meeting her little girlfriend also on Hall Court, Sharonda and her sister. They would become lifelong friends. Kimmy Jo was always on the phone in her room talking to her girlfriends. She met a little girl named Stephanie Marshall, who was a neighbor on Hall Court. Her dad was stationed at Andrews also.

One day I came home with a new braided hairstyle and Stephanie was at the house with Kimmy Jo. They wanted to know how my hair got so long and I looked at them two little girls with a straight face and said, "The hairdresser stretched my hair with a special hot comb and then she braided it like this."

They both wanted to get their hair stretched like I did. It was so very funny; I could hear them in Kimmy Jo's room talking about how they were going to get me to take them to get their hair stretched. I finally told them after about an hour that it was hair braided into mine.

They were two funny little girls. Stephanie was taking family life classes in school, and she had heard several girls telling her that a girl could not get pregnant on the first time. Stephanie and Kimmy Jo approached me with the question. We all had a discussion in my bedroom, and I told them that a girl could get pregnant the first time. I told them they did not have to take their clothes off to get pregnant, that they could just slow dance with a guy and get pregnant if they danced too close. I went on to say that the boy's sperm could drip onto his underwear and seep out through his clothes and then pass through their clothes to their panties and they could become pregnant. They were in awe.

I would know soon, as they were approaching teenage years, that they would recognize that I made that shit up, but it worked for then, and that was all that I needed at that time. I told them if they ever felt like they needed to dance really close to come to me and I would take them both to the base clinic for birth control pills. The two little girls were too much. They would become lifelong friends. Keenan and Kevin were slower to make friends—I guess it was a boy thing. They hung around the next-door neighbor's house, for she had six sons.

The holidays were slowly approaching, and I knew where we were going for Thanksgiving dinner: to Mom's house, of course, in York. For Christmas we would stay home and have our first Christmas holiday in our new house like we did at East Prospect Street.

I found a part-time job for over the holidays at Memco Department Store across the road from Andrews in the appliance department. I worked all of the overtime I could get so Christmas would be good for the family. I put so many things on layaway for the kids and Aaron.

Kimmy Jo was the only one who knew there was no Santa Claus, but I knew she would not tell. They all received small televisions for their bedrooms and record players for their vinyl records as well as many toys, dolls, trucks, etc. Aaron found a tree for us, and we all decorated it with decorations we had from the previous years. I baked cookies and brought plenty of holiday candy. I did not put it all out at the same time because I knew it would not have lasted very long. We all had a sweet tooth. I found out early that Aaron was a cookie thief. I would put cookies out, and they would be gone in record time.

Aaron kept saying it was not him eating the cookies, and the kids denied that they were eating all of them up. I told the kids that I was going to do something to catch Dad. I told them not to eat any of the cookies, for they would get sick and I did not want them to get sick. While they were at school and Aaron was at work, I baked a batch of chocolate chip cookies, his favorite. I opened up the pack of cookie dough from the fridge and mixed ex-lax into half of the batter. Then I rolled it out and baked the cookies. They were smelling so good. I placed them on a tray and put them on the dining room table all nice and neat. I could not wait for his greedy ass to eat them cookies, keep blaming it on my damn kids.

The kids came home from school, and I showed which cookies not to eat before Aaron arrived from work. They went to do their homework until dinner. After dinner, we all went into the living room to watch television. We only had a long sofa and a big floor model TV. The dining room table and chairs were on the other side of the room.

We started to watch the Brady Bunch when Aaron decided he wanted a cup of coffee. He was in the kitchen for about ten minutes making his instant cup of coffee. I yelled to him and told him not to eat the cookies in the kitchen, for they were for the kids. His were all on the dining room table. He later came back and sat at the dining room table and lit up a cigarette. He had a cup of coffee and about five or six cookies on a plate and started to watch TV with us, having his coffee and his cookies. I asked the kids if they wanted some cookies and they said yes. I went into the kitchen and brought some cookies out to all of them, the ones without ex-lax in them. We watched TV for some time until it was time for the kids to go to bed. I told Aaron I was sleepy and was going to go to bed as well. I looked into the kitchen to see how many cookies were left and there were only three cookies left that had no ex-lax, so I indulged myself, smiling. I was feeling some kind of way and could not wait until the ex-lax that greedy ass ate in the cookies took effect. This was going to be good. That would teach him not to blame my kids for eating all of the cookies.

That night about two o'clock in the mooring I heard Aaron in the bathroom. He kept going back and forth. I finally asked him if he was okay, and he said he had an upset stomach. I asked him if he wanted me to get some Pepto Bismol for him, and he said yes. It was all I had not to laugh right in his face. When I came back upstairs, I approached him sitting on the commode with a straight face and gave him the Pepto Bismol. He kept saying that he never had diarrhea like that before in his life. I started to ask him what he had for lunch at work and he said, "I skipped lunch." I told him that if it did not get better, he should go to sick call in the morning and he agreed. I was on my side of the bed laughing to myself. Boy don't mess with my kids! When he came down to the kitchen in the morning, he asked me if the cookies could have been spoiled, and I told him that maybe they were because I did not know how long we had that cookie dough, but the kids and I did not get sick.

He went and got the plate from the dining room table with the rest of the cookies and threw them away, saying, "I don't want the kids to get sick."

I told him that was a good idea.

Christmas morning was like no other. We watched the kids open their gifts, and we opened ours. Aaron was like a big kid playing with Kimmy Jo and her dolls. He would pretend he was going on a plane ride with the dolls. Keenan would interrupt their play time by introducing his little army men, making them knock down Kimmy Jo's dolls. Keenan would make Kimmy Jo so angry at times. He always knew how to get under her skin.

Kevin and Karmentrina were in their own worlds with their gifts. You could not tell Kevin that his army men were not real. Karmentrina and her Easy-Bake Oven was something I wished I had not gotten her. Once she knew the light bulbs in the oven could cook real food, it was on. They were making such a ruckus in the house that Christmas morning. They were all so happy, and so was I. Christmas had gone well and my part-time job was ending, so I decided to investigate going to school in the fall.

# Chapter Twenty-Seven: Our First Vacation

Spring 1976 was upon us, and Aaron wanted to take us to Roanoke, Virginia to meet his mother and grandmother. We had the station wagon serviced and we joined AAA. We decided to make the trip to Roanoke in the summer when school was out because Aaron wanted to stay for several days. The school break would not be long enough.

So we made the trip in June. It was about four hours away. Aaron drove, and I read the directions on the map. We were welcomed into his grandmother's home. His mother was there also for a while. She lived in North Carolina but made the trip to meet me and the kids. His grandmother and mother planned a summer picnic so the whole Roanoke family could meet us and congratulate Aaron.

Many family members and friends showed up, and all were in the back yard. At one point, Helena asked me to go along with her to a local bar. She was trying to find an old friend of hers. I checked it out with Aaron, and he said it would be okay if I went along with her.

When Helena proceeded toward the yard gate, one of his aunts said to me, "Just where do you think you are going, young lady? You have children here."

I was thinking inside of my head, *No, that bitch did not call me out in front of all of these people. She does not know me well enough for that.* I thought I had to respond, and I did. I looked over at her, and all were watching. The talking got quiet, and you probably could have heard a pin drop in the grass. My 351 Stone Avenue Project attitude showed its face, and I said to her, "It is none of your business where I am going. My children's father is right over there."

Her face turned bright red for a Black woman. No one said anything. I followed Helena out of the yard and did not look back. I did not know how Aaron was taking it, but he yelled, "See you when you get back, babe."

I knew he was okay then. When Helena and I returned, their grandmother pulled me aside in the house and said that it was about time that someone put Inez in her place. She was married to one of Aaron's uncles. Apparently, she bullied everyone. I was not the only one.

Aaron's mom decided where the kids were going to sleep, for his grandmom only had a three-bedroom house. Kimmy Jo and Karmentrina spent the night at Aaron's Aunt Duck's house next door. She had three daughters: Kim, Tuts, and Keita. They loved it there.

The boys were to stay at Aunt Dot's house. They told us the next morning that it was like the Addams family house, spooky and dark. Moving forward, we kept the boys with us, and they slept on the floor.

That night when I went up to bed, I heard Aaron and his grandmom downstairs in the kitchen talking. She told him that she just loved me and the kids, and she thought he'd made a good choice. She also told him that Katherine, his mom, loved me too. That made me feel good.

Aaron finally came upstairs to bed after all of his aunts and uncles finished drinking and had gone home. I was glad because they were so loud talking about the good old days.

Aaron slid under the covers and tried to put his hands in a place where I knew what he wanted, and I told him, "Hell no. Your mom is next door and your grandmom is downstairs.

They can hear everything in this little house. As loud as your ass is, there is no way."

He said that he would have quiet sex, and I told him that I could not trust him. He was a begging ass that night, saying they knew what married people do. I told him that they did not know how loud his ass was during sex. There was no way I was going to take that chance.

# Chapter Twenty-Eight: We Are Going to Disney World

When we returned home from Roanoke, we decided that we would keep up with the vacations before school started for me and the kids that year. With a wing and a prayer, we were going on the trip of a lifetime. We only hoped that the station wagon would make the trip because that was all we had. It was going to be a long, hot drive without air conditioning in the station wagon.

I wanted us to go to Disney World in Florida. Aaron wanted to know how we were going to afford such a vacation, and I told him "I got this!" I started to figure out on paper how this plan was going to work out. Mom used to always work out everything on paper. The parks in Florida were very expensive. I went to AAA and picked up pamphlets about Disney and most of the parks. Epcot Center, Silver Spring Park/Busch Gardens, Six Gun Territory, Gatorland, Sea World, the Kennedy Space Center, and several more. We quickly planned a trip to Disney with AAA's help. They mapped out our route and starred places of interest for us to see on the way down to Florida. We budgeted out our money for all of the parks, gas, and the hotel. We made a reservation at a Days Inn on Irlo Bronson Highway, Orlando, Florida, about five miles from the Disney parks.

Our state and federal tax refund was quite a bit. I was always a coupon cutting person and a green stamp collecting person back in the day with Mom. It was not Greek to me. Aaron used to feel some kind of way about using coupons in the grocery store. But one time we purchased over three hundred dollars' worth of groceries and only used coupons and sixty-seven dollars in money. After that, Aaron would make sure to get the weekly Sunday paper for us to cut out coupons. It made him a believer. We were pros at cutting out grocery coupons from the newspapers.

We had seven hundred dollars' worth of food stamps because when I applied for food stamps several months before the trip, we were turned down. I challenged the Department of Social Services, and their decision was overturned. My experience working for clients in York, fighting their claims with the Department of Social Services back in the day paid off. I knew the welfare systems pretty well. I was not going to just take no for an answer the first time.

By the end of June, we were in Florida having the vacation of our lives. I took so many pictures of the kids and their new dad. When we arrived in the state of Florida, we saw so many orange groves and pine trees everywhere. It was breathtaking to see in real life, not on TV. The hotel room had a sofa bed in the sitting room and two full sized beds in the bedroom as well as a kitchenette.

Every day we were at a different park, sometimes two or three places in one day. On the fourth day we went to Disney World. The cost was six dollars for adults and four dollars and fifty cents for children five to nine years of age. Parents did not have to pay for children four years of age and younger.

We walked up to the gate and Aaron said to the guy in the booth; "I need two adult and three children's tickets."

The guy looked at Keenan and said, "How old are you, young man?" and Aaron answered quickly, "He is four."

Keenan looked at Aaron and said, "Dad, remember I had a birthday; I am five now."

Aaron said, "Boy, I know how old you are. You will be five next year."

Tears popped in Keenan's eyes, and he walked over to hold my hand. As soon as we entered the gate, I kneeled down and hugged my baby boy. I told him that Dad knew that he was five but he told a damn lie so he could have enough money for us to spend inside of the park. I told Keenan we would give him an extra dollar to spend. He was so happy with that. I also told him that if Dad lied about his age again, he would get an extra dollar each time.

We had a ball in Disney World. We must have gotten on all of the rides twice, and the Disney parade was an experience that I knew none of us would ever forget. The first ride we got on was one where the Disney characters jumped out at us. I got into a car with the girls, and Aaron got into a car with the boys. Our car started moving first. We were screaming every time a character jumped out at us. It was some kind of scary ride. Our car came out first and then the boys with Aaron. I noticed that Kevin was not wearing his glasses, and I asked him about them.

He responded, "Mom, I was covering my face because I was scared of the things jumping out in front of me."

Aaron said that they must be in the car they had been riding in. We went to the end where the cars come out and checked every car that came out when the people would get out. Low and behold, we found Kevin's glasses, and they were not broken. I was so happy, for I had recently purchased them.

Kevin was always losing his glasses. That was the last day that he would have them on during the vacation. Kimmy Jo never lost her glasses. We continued to walk and eat.

Finally, we saw the roller coaster, and I was praying that no one wanted to get on that ride. I was always afraid of roller coasters, and I was not going to start liking them at Disney World. Back when I was about twelve years of age and living in Lancaster, Pennsylvania, a group of us friends walked to Rocky Springs for the day. It was within walking distance of where we lived. Everyone was hyped about getting on that roller coaster, and I played along. I did not want my friends to know that I was afraid. So we all paid our money to ride.

Back then, the rails were made of wood. That roller coaster started to climb up the first small hill, and I panicked. I opened up the gate on my side and climbed out of the car. I started walking down the side of the wooden tracks and thinking I was going to slip and fall to my death. I was too afraid to cry, and I just kept climbing down the tracks until I got to the bottom platform.

The old white man kicked me off the platform and told me not to ever come back to his roller coaster ever again. Little did he know I was not planning on it. I finally told Aaron that I was afraid and he told the kids. Keenan and Karmentrina volunteered to ride with me and hold my hand. Kevin chimed in to tell me that it was just little hills, but Kimmy Jo clarified it for me, saying that some of the hills were steep.

That was it for me. Aaron rode with Karmentrina, and Keenan and Kimmy Jo and Kevin rode together. They had a ball and rode it several other times while I enjoyed myself eating candy.

We stayed until the park closed. We were on our way to the exit gate when Kevin started crying. I looked at him and asked him what was wrong. By now he was crying even more as we got closer to the gate, and snot was coming down his face with his tears.

He looked up at me and said, "Mom, I did not spend all of my money." He still had a five-dollar bill crumpled up in his hand. I took the end of his shirt and cleaned off his face. I was not putting all of that snot and tears on my shirt. I told him that I would take him out the next day to a store so he could spend his money, and he seemed to be happy about that.

We made it outside of the gate, and I asked Aaron where we'd parked, and he said that he did not know. He went on to say, "I thought you wrote it down." All I could think about was the time he and his friend Paige could not find the car at the Springfield Mall in Virginia.

We got on the little trolly that took patrons to their cars. Everywhere it stopped, we could not see our brown station wagon. The conductor took us back to the gate and told us to just sit and wait for the lot to start to empty, then maybe we would spot our car. People were pouring out of the gate in droves, and finally the conductor took us out again, around the gigantic parking lots, and we spotted our brown station wagon in the Miss Minnie parking area. We were all exhausted, but we'd had a ball.

The next morning, the kids were restless. They had so much energy, but Aaron and I were tired. We decided we would stay near the hotel the last day. While Aaron and I were watching TV in the living room area after breakfast, we heard a loud noise coming from the bedroom where the kids were supposed to be watching TV.

Aaron yelled, "What the hell was that noise?" and we both went into the bedroom. Kimmy Jo was laying on her bed watching TV and eating candy. Kevin was saying, "It wasn't me, Dad."

We looked over at the closet where Keenan, Karmentrina, and Kevin were standing nearby. I asked all of them what had happened, and Kimmy Jo quickly told us that Karmentrina and Keenan were swinging in the closet on the rail like it was a monkey bar and it broke in half.

I took off my flip flop and went to flopping on their behinds. Kimmy Jo and Kevin got it too because they should have come and told us what Keenan and Karmentrina were doing in the closet. I was so darn mad at the kids, so I left the hotel and went down the road to shop for snacks for the trip home and made them stay in the hotel with Aaron.

We had quite a bit of food stamps left. When I returned, Aaron left out to go and get some tape to fix the pole in the closet. He somehow had it hanging up there pretty good. I could not tell it had been broken.

# Chapter Twenty-Nine: The Trip Back Home

We woke up early in the morning to pack up all of our stuff and to eat breakfast. We had purchased many Disney T-shirts from the different strip malls and collected stickers to put on the station wagon from every amusement park we went to. The kids wanted to put them on the station wagon before we left, so I left that to them and Aaron. We knew it was going to be a long, hot drive back home.

Along the way, we stopped at Daytona Beach and collected sea shells from the ocean for about an hour or so then continued on our way. We stopped in Saint Augustine, Florida and visited several places of interest, including the oldest modern school in the United States of America. We were given a certificate for visiting from the United States Department of the Interior.

We drove and drove and drove and finally stopped to eat food and snacks several times. It seemed like no one had to pee at the same time.

We finally made it to South of the Border and ate at a very prejudiced small restaurant. We could feel the presence of them not wanting us there. The kids had no clue at their ages. We pretended that we did not notice it. It was daytime hours, so we felt fairly safe. As soon as we were done eating, we left the area, and we did not leave a tip.

We saw very few Blacks at Disney World but never felt like we did not belong there. It took about seventeen hours for us to return back to Andrews Air Force Base because we stopped so many times. We now knew that we could go anywhere we wanted to go if we just planned for it. Until we make it, we will fake it in this life. No one ever has to know how much one makes, if you are using food stamps or not or where you are from.

Finally, about one in the morning we were pulling up to the gate. The next few days the kids bragged about going to Florida and showing off the stickers on the car. We were proud too that we were able to show them a small part of the world.

# Chapter Twenty-Thirty: Education is a Priority

School year September 1976/77—By now the kids all had many friends. School would be one aspect of life that I would always take seriously, for I was the only one of my parents' seven children who had graduated high school at that time.

William dropped out of school at an early age; he completed the sixth grade. He could read and write. Mom dropped out of school in the tenth grade in Columbia, Pennsylvania. She told me she was one of three Black children in her classroom and that the teacher would always call on her to pass out papers to the students.

She said that on one particular day she was passing out papers. One female classmate pushed her paper to the floor and told Mom to pick it up, and she did. The white student pushed it on the floor again and Mom refused to pick it up. Mom told me that she walked to her desk and picked up her coat and left the school to never go back again.

She always instilled in us to finish school; however, not everyone paid attention to what part education would play in their lives. I was determined that all of mine would graduate from high school, even if it was the death of me. We were not doing dropouts! I would drill into them that they would need college or a trade to be able to support themselves in this world.

The kids were back to school, and I was registered for classes at the local Prince George's Community College (PGCC) in Largo, Maryland. We were going to need another car because I would be needing to drive back and forth to college on a daily basis. Aaron had gotten rid of his Oldsmobile because the gas was too costly. He would take it upon himself to start to look for a car, and he finally found one. A sergeant in his unit was going overseas and was selling his 1964 blue Ford Mustang. That worked out perfectly.

I registered for general studies and decided to take only classes pertaining to nursing so that they would transfer easily. The program accepted my credits from the University of Clovis, so I had a jump start on my associate college degree. I signed up as a full-time student and would be in class during the same time the kids would be in school. Since we had a vehicle, there were no transportation issues.

It was strange going back to school full-time, but it felt good. It was almost like being a senior back in Edmondson High School. It took a little getting used to, but everything fell into place for me. That first semester for me was fairly easy. I only took three classes because Keenan was starting to have behavior issues in school, and I needed to have time to deal with them. He was now in the third grade and struggling.

I decided to take a summer class so my semesters could be a lighter load when the fall came around. Taking fifteen credits gave me no time for anything else but studying day and night, and Keenan needed me now. The children kept telling me that the Catholic school was prejudiced, but I did not want to believe it. They were the only Black children in the school. I should have listened to them.

That fall, I decided to take anatomy and physiology, and it was so very hard for me. I was struggling. The first examination I received a D+. I was devastated. I knew I would not survive with grades like that. The instructor called me at home one evening to ask me if I wanted him to refer me to a classmate who was doing well, and I told him that I would.

He set up a meeting after class the next week, and I met a white student in our class who was in the two-year nursing degree course there at PGCC. She agreed to tutor me. I started studying with her at her home near Rosecroft Raceway near Andrews.

The first time I studied with her she told me a secret. She said, "Sandra, I am probably not smarter than you are; however, I have taught myself to memorize words that clue me to the answers on the exams."

From that point on, I followed her lead, making flash cards to study for exams. Karmentrina at eight years old became my flash card study partner. She used to piss me off when I would miss an answer. She would say, "That is enough, Mom. You knew that answer a few minutes ago, so when I show it to you again, you better know the answer, Mom, or you will have to write it down until you can remember it."

To this day Karmentrina is able to remember anything you tell her just one time, numbers or words. I earned a B+ in that class. It was smooth sailing after that. I had a year and a half to go to complete the two-year associate's degree in general studies. Miss Walker was right: God makes a way for you.

School year September 1977/78 was upon us, and I worried about how Keenan would do in the fourth grade. Things did not get any better; he had no attention span for school.

Aaron and I decided to remove him from Catholic school, and we did. We registered him at Woodley Knolls Elementary School. I did not feel comfortable putting him there alone without any of his siblings, but against my better judgment, I did. Karmentrina was so upset. She wanted to go to public school with him as well. We would not allow that at first, but would soon change our mind.

Keenan started to display even more behavior issues, coming home with pencils of all colors in his book bag. We started to check his book bag when his teacher called and told us that Keenan had taken a pack of pencils off of her desk. We thought we could get ahead of that problem. Aaron and I purchased black number two pencils for him and told him that those pencils were the only ones he was permitted to have in his book bag and in school. Things were going okay for about two weeks, when I received a call from his teacher that he had taken jewelry from home and was giving it to little girls. At that point I decided to pop visit his classroom and not tell him when I would come. He knew it was going to happen, but he did not know when. Things seemed to smooth out, somewhat.

The following school year, Kimmy would complete the eighth grade and go on to public school at James Madison Junior High for the ninth grade. At that time, it would be decided for all of them to go to the public school system: Kevin at James Madison as well in the seventh grade and Karmentrina at Woodley Knoll Elementary School with Keenan in the sixth grade.

Aaron had planned on taking the kids out of Catholic school when they reached the sixth grade because the Catholic school had no sports in their program. One good thing about it: no more stacks of white envelopes for tithes.

Kimmy Jo would become very popular in school. She took up music, which she was good at. There she met several new friends. Two in particular were Rhonda Ford and Darrell Terry. They would become lifelong friends. I believe Darrell was her first boyfriend. Kimmy Jo was so hurt when they broke up, but she bounced back with little difficulty. That's my girl! My family would become connected with Rhonda's family for many years.

Keenan was acting out again at school. One day the teacher had a round table session with her students. Per the teacher, each student was to read a sentence that she assigned to them and answer the question that they read. Apparently, the little girl before Keenan would miss her question, so the teacher told Keenan to read the question and answer it. Well! He was not having that. He told the teacher that it was not his question, and he was not going to read and answer it.

He ended up in the office, and I had to pick him up. He had already memorized the answer to his question. They did not suspend him that day, but tomorrow would be a different day for Keenan to continue being Keenan Wynn.

The next day, parents were allowed to visit the classrooms, so Aaron and I were going to visit his classroom as well as Karmentrina's. Keenan was not in his classroom when we arrived there. Per his teacher, he was sent to the office because of an incident in class prior to our arrival. When parents were walking into the classroom to visit, another student said to Keenan, "There goes your mom, Keenan."

Keenan supposedly responded, "That ugly lady ain't my damn mom. My mom is pretty." That earned him three days in school suspension.

The pediatric clinic at Malcolm Grow Medical Center referred us to a psychiatrist for Keenan to have testing done. We were already in weekly family therapy with a Catholic Charities counselor in Washington, DC. Her name was Doctor Barbera Suiter.

He would go to therapy for a while. She did her initial sessions with him alone and then pulled Aaron and me in later and wanted to talk with Kevin. We wondered why, but made the appointment for her to see Kevin.

She told us that Keenan thought that his father had been murdered when was a baby. Kevin had gotten in his head with all of his thoughts about seeing his dad get shot. Kevin was only two years old at the time of his father's death. They always shared a room together, so Kevin had years to tell Keenan stories that did not belong to Keenan's life. She also told us that Keenan did not want to share me with Aaron. She suggested that we never close our door when we were in our room unless it was bedtime. Prior to that direction from her, we would close our door if we were watching TV or just chilling during the day. He and Karmentrina would knock on our door every five minutes for something. Aaron and I should have taken the hint.

We also started a family game night once a week with Monopoly. Aaron was always the banker, and he was always the one winning. I would always play power moves to get the kids to be on my side because I knew they would.

# Chapter Thirty-One: Vacation Time Again – Canada

That summer, July 1977, before the school year started, I decided that we needed another vacation, and Aaron agreed. Like last year, our income tax and state tax refunds were pretty good, and we stashed some of it in our Andrews Federal Credit Union Savings Account. We chose to visit Niagara Falls and Toronto, Canada. We had the old station wagon serviced once more and prayed that it would survive the trip.

This would be the third country that I had visited. It would be another driving trip, and we would use AAA once again to map out the route for us. We left early on a Sunday morning and drove straight through for seven and a half hours to Niagara Falls. We drove through the Holland Tunnel, and the kids were amazed while we drove through. I had never been through the tunnel either.

My kids and I were finding out that there was a bigger world than York, Pennsylvania. We checked into our hotel, the Holiday Inn in Geneseo, New York, the first night and did some sightseeing at Niagara Falls the next morning, which was close by. The next day we drove to Toronto, Canada, where we checked into the Ramada Inn Hotel. Going across the border to Canada and through customs was just as easy as crossing the border into Mexico a few years before.

While we were there in Toronto, we visited the downtown area and took a boat trip to the Fantasy Island Park and toured the Tower of Canada. After the first four days, we hung out at the hotel, and Aaron took time to teach me how to swim. I felt so much fear in that water. I could not stop thinking about William and the fishing boots.

During the last days, Karmentrina, Keenan, and Kevin developed some kind of code that only they could understand. They would look at each other and then burst out laughing. I kept threatening them to stop, and Kimmy Jo said to me, "Mom, they are just trying to irritate me."

I told Kimmy Jo not to worry about them and to just ignore them. That was easy for Kimmy Jo because she knew how to shut people out. Aaron was getting his trunks on to go swimming, and I told him that only Kimmy Jo was allowed to go with him. I went into their bedroom and asked who wanted to go swimming with Dad, and they all responded that they wanted to go.

I said, "Well, that is just too bad" because only Kimmy Jo would be going. I looked at Kimmy Jo and Aaron, and we all started laughing. I bet those three did not think that was so funny.

The secret conversations stopped for the rest of that trip. Vacation came to a close, and it was time to drive back home. More stickers for the station wagon. We returned home just in time for the boys to start their flag football camp on the base.

We decided that it would be a good time to buy a dog because we had promised the kids a dog for some time now. I grew up with dogs, so I did not mind at all. The family went to Landover Mall in Largo, Maryland to look for a dog. We settled on a black Great Dane puppy named Lovers Sapphire. She cost us a lot, over two hundred dollars.

Everyone was happy about getting the dog except Kimmy Jo. She was like her Aunt Mary: She did not like dogs, cats, or anything else. I knew if she ever had her own kids, they would never have a pet.

Kevin loved the dog more than any of us, he was always hugging and kissing the slobbering dog. That dog would be with us for more than thirteen years.

Aaron started to complain about the cost of the dog food, for Sapphire was growing so big and tall. I would tell him that I could not work anymore than I was, and he needed to figure out what we were to do. He suggested that we get rid of the dog and buy a smaller one. I looked at him like he had lost his mind.

He caught my look and said to me, "I was just playing."

Aaron decided that he needed to make extra money, so he decided on cleaning houses for move-out inspections. He said it would be a piece a cake.

The first house he agreed to clean was a disaster. He agreed to help an officer clean his house for a move-out inspection clearance. It was such a waste of time and effort. That house would never pass inspection no matter how much work we put into it. I believe it was because it was an officer's quarters, he was never going to be happy.

Aaron did not get the money he was promised because the inspection failed, and the officer had to pay someone else to clean the house, so he said. The officer told us the house failed; we never saw any paperwork. We knew he was just getting over on us. The kids and I spent hours trying to help Aaron to pass that damn inspection. He never did. I was so angry with him agreeing to do it without checking with me beforehand.

He did get a dog out of the deal. A Great Dane named Lochmanor Slade, which we all hated. That damn dog ate a hole through our kitchen door when Aaron locked him in the garage away from Sapphire; he was always humping her. We now would have to replace the entire door.

Sapphire would be pregnant soon, and at that discovery time it would be time for Slade to have another home. I told Aaron that Slade had to go. He agreed! He found a farmer in Upper Marlboro who wanted the dog, and we were glad to see him gone. The Lord knows!

Sapphire would soon deliver nine pups, but one of them did not make it. She started delivering them when I was home alone, and I was panicking. The first two came out after much panting, then another. I called Aaron to come home from work; his job was across the street about a block away. When he arrived, I left to go meet the kids at their bus stop, for it was due.

I arrived at the bus stop and saw them get off. I ran toward them, telling them that Sapphire was having her puppies. They all ran and left me. There were four puppies by the time we got home and another one on the way. It was not breathing on delivery, so Aaron did CPR on it, but the pup did not make it. Aaron wrapped up the little pup and took it into the garage. We would later have a funeral for the pup and bury him in the back yard.

Four more pups soon followed, and they all lived. The puppies were growing so fast, and dogs were everywhere. The cost of the puppy shots and the puppy food was putting a dent in our budget. It was time for them to go soon. At two months old Aaron started to give them away or sell them when he could. To include Doug, Mom, and several other military friends.

We kept one puppy, a male, and named him Bocious. Bocious the Ferocious was Aaron's father's nickname. The kids just loved him. Bocious started to show signs of not being healthy. He started to have seizures all the time. I took him to our veterinarian, and they referred me to a specialist in Alexandria, Virginia. I was given medication for his seizures and nausea and vomiting.

That worked somewhat, but as Bocious grew older, but still a puppy, he started to do the strangest things. Out of nowhere food started missing from the kitchen table, and I thought the kids were just eating up everything. They kept denying it. One morning I woke up and saw that a loaf of bread that I had purchased the evening before was gone.

Now I was pissed. I checked in the trash cans to see if the empty wrapper for the loaf of bread was there, and it was not. I phoned Aaron at work and asked about the loaf of bread, and he told me it was on the kitchen table when he left for work. The kids were not up yet. I was thinking, *Lord do not let any ghost be in this house* and was hoping no bad spirits had followed us to Hall Court.

Soon all of the kids were down for breakfast. I was making a cup of tea when Bocious started to vomit. I hate seeing vomit and was wishing that Aaron was home. Bocious was gagging something terrible, and I reached in his mouth to see what was in his mouth and saw the plastic wrapper from the loaf of bread. I pulled it all the way out and got some of his medication into him. We now knew where the food was disappearing to.

Sapphire knew something was wrong and went over and started to lick his face. I made an appointment with the veterinarian in Alexandria for that evening. Aaron and I took him there, and the doctor told us that Bocious was not going to get better and no telling what else we might have had to deal with.

I asked, "What are you suggesting?"

He was straightforward and told us we should consider putting him down because he was in constant pain and suffering. We decided to leave Bocious there to be put to sleep forever.

When we returned home, the kids wanted to know where Bocious was, and we told them. Karmentrina and Keenan broke down crying, and Kevin was without words. Kimmy even looked somewhat sad. Looking back on that time, I wish we had done it differently so that the kids could have said their goodbyes.

To catch up on our savings, Aaron decided to take another job at a day care center as a janitor not far from Andrews. It was going to be a night shift job, which went well until Aaron started looking drained from all of his little jobs.

He decided that the kids and I would help and that it would be good for the kids to know that they get allowance for helping the family. I told him to just hold up on that because they had house chores that they got allowance for. "Are you advocating that you will raise their allowances?" I asked.

He looked at me funny, and I looked at him the same way. He decided that if he wanted the kids to help, they would need an increase in their allowance. He readily agreed to an increase of one dollar more a week. The janitorial job was going well until he had to strip, wax, and buff floors.

Sometimes the kids and I would go, and they would do their jobs that Aaron gave them to do. It took a lot of time to complete the floors, and I had to help him into the late hours of the morning. I would put up the little beds for the kids all to get some sleep, for they had school in the morning. After about three months of that, I told Aaron that the kids and I were done. He quit a few weeks later.

It was getting warmer, and the kids and I were glad that the school janitor job was over. But one day when Aaron came home from work, he had a white pet mouse in a cage and all of the equipment for a habitat.

Everyone was happy about it except Kimmy Jo and me. I was so pissed, and Aaron knew it. It was all I could do to refrain from cussing his ass out in front of the kids. He told me he would keep it in the garage and that he would take care of it. Of course, his name was Ben. I told him that the house mice would start to come around because they would be able to smell Ben. What do you know; a little black house mouse came around and Aaron put it in the cage. A few hours later the house mouse was lying in the cage lifeless.

I said to Aaron, "I told you that it would draw house mice."

If that was not enough, one evening after dinner, all of the kids were watching TV. I just happened to see a mouse run across the floor under the TV when I was going up the stairs to my bedroom. None of them saw it. They were all into the cartoons.

So I said to them, "Hey did you all see the mouse that just ran under the TV? Oh, my goodness! You did not see that mouse?"

They all started hollering and jumping up on the sofa. It was a sight to see. No one was interested in any cartoons then.

When Aaron came home from work, I told him about the mouse in the living room. He took off his uniform and put on a pair of jeans. He went into the living room with a hammer and asked me which way did the mouse run and I told him from under the sofa across the floor to under the TV. He pulled the sofa out away from the wall and there was a damn family of mice living inside the bottom lining of the sofa.

The kids and I were screaming and getting out of the way. We were standing in the doorway. Aaron took his hammer and started smashing them one by one. One mouse tried to get away, but Aaron chased it down putting a hole into the wall trying to get to it. Soon they were all dead. Aaron then went to the kitchen to boil some water and then he poured the boiling hot water over all of them to make sure they were all dead.

I told him that was overkill, and Karmentrina said, "Yeah, Dad!"

Aaron would repair the hole in the wall soon after, and no one would have ever known a hole was in that wall behind the sofa.

That night, Kevin decided that he would get one of the dead mice out of the trash can to scare Keenan with it. I heard Keenan yelling at the top of his lungs "Mom! Mom! Kevin has a mouse in here scaring me."

I was so mad at him; I did not punish Kevin that night. I just gave him a mom death stare and said, "So you thought that was funny? Okay!" The next night while he was asleep, I put a dead mouse on this pillow. He woke up early in the morning and encountered that dead mouse, and he started screaming like he saw a ghost. I took my time going to the boys' room because I wanted to teach Kevin a lesson.

I opened the bedroom door and went over and picked up the dead mouse by its tail and walked toward Kevin, who was hysterically scared. I made him promise to never scare his little brother again for any reason. He was crying with snot running down his little face and saying, "Mom, I'm sorry."

I said, "No, tell your brother that you are sorry," and he did.

The next morning when Aaron was ready to leave for work, I told him to take that damn white mouse, Ben and his cage out of the house, and he did. I did not care what the hell he did with it, as long as it was no longer residing at 1179 B Hall Court.

When Aaron left, the kids and I decided to put his name in the doghouse. This was something we had instituted not too long before, and we put Kevin in there with him. (It was a board on the wall with a dog house and little wooden dogs hanging on it, and all of us had one with our name on it. No one ever wanted their name in the doghouse because it meant losing something: allowance, TV time, no friends visiting, etc.)

All of the kids had their share of the doghouse, especially when they would argue about the telephones. I started to think that having TVs and telephones in their rooms was a mistake; after all, we'd managed with just one phone when we lived in New Mexico, two phones in the projects, and now five phones, and it was a mess. Somebody was always arguing about somebody on the phone too long. Lord Jesus, they just about drove me nuts with the telephones, and I had to get on them about leaving their TVs on all night long.

Kevin was the main one. One night about eleven-thirty, I went into Kevin and Keenan's room and the TV was not turned off.

They were sound asleep. I went over to Kevin's bed and woke him up to have him turn the TV off. I was irritated because I always had to tell Kevin that. He sat up and kept looking at me. I helped him down off of his bed and walked him over to the TV that was sitting on the TV stand and told him to turn it off.

He looked up at me and said, "Mom, there used to be a television in here, but I don't know where it went to."

I replied, "You are looking at the TV, Kevin. Turn it off."

He said he could not find the knob that used to be on the TV. A part of me wanted to laugh out loud, but I did not. By now Aaron was at the door and telling me to leave Kevin alone because he was still sleeping. I ignored Aaron because I had been getting on Kevin daily about that TV. He was supposed to turn it off at nine o'clock. He had a clock in his room, as did his sisters, and he was going to learn.

Kevin won that battle. However, I put him in the doghouse for a week, and he lost his bedroom TV privileges. I took the TV out of the boys' room and allowed Keenan to watch TV in my room before his bedtime. After a week of TV withdrawal, the problem was corrected. TVs had to be turned off before bedtime and no TV watching during thunderstorms.

Speaking of that, one afternoon it was storming outside, and I told all of the kids to turn off the lights and unplug their TVs so they did not get electrocuted. Grandmom Mabel used to tell me and my sisters that the lightning could come in through the window and hit the TV and electrocute us.

Well, I did not know if that was true or not, but I always unplugged everything and turned off the lights, just like Mom used to do. That particular afternoon, I was in the kitchen when I heard a loud noise, like a bomb dropped on our house. I ran upstairs yelling, "What happened?"

Kimmy and the boys were in the hallway by now and visibly shaken. I opened Karmentrina's bedroom door, and she was on her bed crying. Her TV was smoking like crazy. She did not unplug her TV like she was told. Well, it was going to be a sunny day in hell when she would get another TV for her bedroom. She deserved to be in the doghouse for damn near blowing up the house.

Kevin ran downstairs to put Karmentrina's name in the doghouse. He was sure glad to get his name out of there. Spoiled ass kids.

# Chapter Thirty-Two: Tracey Is Having Problems

September 1977, early October, Mom called me and asked if I would come for Tracey and bring her back with me to live in Maryland because she was not going to school and was acting out. I asked her what Mary had said, and she told me not to worry about it because Tracey was at her house.

I went to York to talk with Tracey and asked her if she wanted to come with me, and she agreed to come. I told her she would have to go to school, and she was okay with that. I registered her at James Madison Junior High for the ninth grade; she was back a grade for not going to school in Pennsylvania.

She had a difficult time at the school, students teasing her and calling her out of her name, like, "high yellow bitch." One day she'd had all she could take. Two girls who were sisters and much bigger than she was cornered her in the girl's bathroom. Tracey told me that her only way out was to fight dirty. So she beat the crap out of them with heels of her pumps. Gossip on Hall Court was "you do not want to mess with Tracey Smallwood, Kimmy Jo's cousin at 1179B Hall Court." After that, none of the girls at school bothered her. The principal did not suspend her because she was defending herself.

About a year later, Mary called me to ask if Tracey's sister Tara could come to stay with me for a while because she was having difficulty in school. Tara was the same age as Karmentrina. As much as I wanted to say no because our house was already crowded, I did not. I could never say no to anyone, especially my siblings. I knew we were struggling financially, but I remember Mom telling us that there was always room for one more. I was having a hard time believing that, but at that point, I had to, so be it. Tara and Karmentrina attended

Woodley Knoll Elementary in the fifth grade. Tara would stay about half of the year because her dad, Clabber, demanded that I return her to Mary, and I did.

Tracey was more grown up than the last time I had seen her. She made friends quickly with the older girls on Hall Court. She formed a singing group with a girl named Sandy, and their group of three girls started entering the talent shows on base and singing at the club on Bolling AFB.

She was fitting into the military lifestyle just fine. She soon met a young airman by the name of Kevin. Aaron and I knew he was too old for her, and Aaron asked him to stay away from her, but that did not work out. The next year when she was in the tenth grade, she started sneaking out to see him whenever she could.

Tracey shared a room with Kimmy Jo. Keenan had told me that Tracey was throwing stones up at their bedroom window at night so Kevin would go downstairs and open the back door for her to get into the house when she was sneaking out to meet her boyfriend. So I started to check Tracey and Kimmy Jo's room every night, and one night she had fluffed her pillows up in her bed to make it look like she was in her bed. I figured out she was not there and woke up Kimmy Jo to ask if she knew where Tracey was, and she said, "No, Mom, she always sneaks out."

This particular night I set a trap for her. She threw the stones up at the boys' window, and Kevin woke up. I told him to go downstairs and let her in, but I was with him. I wish you could have seen the look on her face when she saw me.

The following year in the eleventh grade, Tracey's relationship with Kevin would grow. She became pregnant and wanted me to sign for her to get married, but neither I nor Mary would do it. She dropped out of school at seventeen and moved to Baltimore with her boyfriend in January 1979. She had a baby girl in August, Caprisha. As soon as she reached eighteen years of age, which was about a month away from the birth of her baby girl, she and Keven would marry in Baltimore. They would visit often, for we were only about forty-five minutes from them.

# Chapter Thirty-Three: Educational Success

May 1978, I completed the required math classes and my required twelve credits for English. On the twenty-seventh day of May 1978, I earned my Associate of Arts two-year degree from PGCC. It was time to apply to a four-year school for a nursing program. My mom was so very happy, even more than I was. However, it would not be now. We were even more financially strapped, and I needed a job to help Aaron make ends meet.

I applied for an on-the-job training program to become a nursing assistant. I completed the program and started to work part time at George Washington University Hospital in Washington, DC. I paid attention and learned all that I could there and then signed on part-time on-call for other hospitals in the area. I also accepted a part-time position at Southern Maryland Hospital Center as a unit secretary and worked only evening and night shift, where I found time to study.

The money helped us quite a bit, but if I had worked full-time, it would have been better. I hardly saw the kids during the two years while I was going to PGCC. I was not feeling that. So Aaron suggested that I think about entering the Air Force Reserves. I was sure he had already decided that I was going to do it.

He took me to a recruiting station, and we picked up some brochures. After looking through them, I decided that it would not work for me because I was not athletic. He started talking to me about the money I could make to help us out doing one weekend a month and two weeks in the summer; that was all I would have to do. He convinced me to do it, and we then returned to the recruiting station to set up my appointment for testing. I told the recruiter that I wanted to be in the medical field. He told me I had to be a high school graduate and that if I scored high enough, forty-four or better on the Armed Forces Vocational Aptitude Battery Test (ASVAB), I would be able to enter that field. My date was scheduled for early August. I went back and passed the entry exam. I was to leave in December, but I told the recruiter that I did not want to go until after the holidays.

In January, the recruiter called me and asked if I was ready to go, and I asked for an extension for May 1979. Aaron asked me why I'd asked for the extension, and I told him that I was afraid to go and that I had to get my nerve up. Kimmy Jo was in the eighth grade now and on the girls' track team and gymnastics team at school. She told me she would help me to practice my running on the track around the corner from our house. Aaron helped me to practice doing pushups, and that damn near convinced me to change my mind. He also spent time teaching me what to expect in basic training. He told me that no matter what the training instructors (TI) did there in San Antonio, Texas, they could not put their hands on me.

I worked hard on the track with Kimmy Jo. I would try to give up, and she would yell, "Mom, don't be a quitter!" After how many times I'd said that to her, now I knew how it felt. I was not too worried about the kids being with Aaron alone while I was away for a little while. Kimmy Jo and Kevin were older now and could help out a lot.

The kids hung out with their friends at the youth center dances. Kimmy Jo's friend Deb Warner was with her a lot. Debra used to always call during the kids' singing practice time, and it used to piss me and Aaron off because it was always her. I would yell at Kimmy Jo to remind her about the times they had singing practice and Karmentrina responded. Even though no one asked her for her two cents, she responded, "That's all the time, Mom." That was why she always got her little mouth slapped always having something to say when no one asked her for her opinion.

Debra and Kimmy Jo would become good friends, going to the ever-popular Tops in Blues Annual Shows and movies on base as well as to the baseball games held on base. Aaron and I would also attend the Tops in Blues Annual Shows with the other kids. Now I knew they were not into baseball, and they were only going to look at the cute boys. I always caught Debra looking at Kevin. I could tell she had a crush on him. It fizzed out later.

Kimmy Jo and Debra were both artists in their own right, Kimmy Jo a vocalist and Debra a dancer. She was in a dance group with Johnita Wilson, Melissa, and Vanessa. Kimmy Jo would become friends with Johnita as well. They would all entertain the military masses at talent shows and fashion shows.

I would sometimes enter talent shows with my kids. I once sang Diana Ross's "Love Hangover" with Kimmy Jo at a base talent show. We both had on gowns, and her young friends thought I was her sister. She just loved it. One particular time, I entered them in a talent show off base for money. The first prize was one hundred dollars, money that my kids would love to have. I went to the tryouts and found out that there were no age categories. That meant that adults would be judged against children. I listened to some of the contestants and decided that they were not going to win that talent show. I entered the kids by their last name, Kearse, and mine by Stockton. I took first place and they took second place. We left with one hundred and fifty dollars. Money that we claimed. We split the money five ways, thanks to Roosevelt Smith (rest in peace), a young keyboard player who played our music. We had known him for some time because the kids practiced at Howard University with him about every two weeks or so.

They won the Metropolitan District of Columbia Metro Talent search hosted by Debbie Allen and many more talent competitions. Since they knew how to sing, I thought they should know how to dance. So I put them in a tap dance class with the Bren Car Dancers in Washington, DC. Kevin was an awesome pop-a-lot break dancer and made sure to enter all of the competitions on the base. They were all good at their craft.

# Chapter Thirty-Four: Basic Training

I joined the United States Air Force reserves in May of 1979 at the age of twenty-nine and went to basic training in Texas at Lackland Air Force Base for eight weeks. I was assigned to Squadron 3706 Fight W150 Lackland Air Force Base, Texas. I thought that I would never make it out of basic training. I was used to me yelling at my children when I needed to, but grown people yelling at me 24/7 was just too much. It felt like prison, and I had never ever been in a prison and hoped I never would be.

During that first week of the eight-week training camp, we were given the name of our training instructor (TI) and too many rules to remember. His name was Staff Sargent Tiller (SGT Tiller), a young white airman. He did not move me at all. One rule in particular was that we could not wear a watch ever. TI made that something we needed to be aware of at the top of the list of demands. It was clear that we were on the military timeline, and no matter what, that was where we would be until basic training was over.

We were given a handbook, and it was the only thing we could read when at ease. One day after I was assigned the squad leader position, while standing in line for chow, I allowed my squadron to read their handbooks after putting them at parade rest. A black female TI came by and saw us and called our squadron to attention, demanding to know who had given us permission to be at parade rest to read our handbooks.

I asked permission to speak, and she granted it. I went on to inform her that our handbooks given to us in week one said that we were allowed to read the handbook when at parade rest, which was the command I gave my squadron.

She put us at parade rest and said, "Carry on, Airman Stockton." I knew then I had some power and I was never afraid to speak up.

There were no times we had to keep track of. We were told when to make any and all moves. It was like they were trying to brainwash us—well, I was not having it. I kept my watch in my bra always, and whenever I was alone, I checked the time. I was older than all of the recruits in my unit. That was cool because I was made a squad leader during the first week. Therefore, I still had kids I could yell at if I wanted to. However, I found that most of them needed a mother. Some had never been away from home and or right out of high school. Some cried all the time at night. I would set by their bed and comfort them.

My twelve-person squad was always on point. I assigned each recruit in my squad a duty. Whoever was good at one of our requirements had the job of making sure everyone could pass that measure. From making bed linens so tight a coin could bounce off of it to making sure one's clothing drawer was in order, all items measured off in the correct military manner. I assigned four recruits to weekly laundry for the entire squad, all clothing was identifiable with the last four number of one's social security number. Two recruits were assigned to boot duty and uniform spot checks.

My group knew what teamwork meant, and that it was the only way we would all make it out of the basic training camp as enlisted airmen. We all had to be up at five in the morning for physical training (PT). This one particular morning, we had a different TI, another young white male. He put us at attention and then asked if anyone had the time.

One silly little girl pulled out her watch and said, "I do, sir!" She remembered after that day not to have a watch on her person. He made her drop and do fifty pushups, but she never completed them. The TI asked if anyone wanted to help her complete the pushups, and a few girls volunteered because there was no way I was going to help her out. She was not one of my squad members and not my responsibility.

Basic training was tiresome. I was so glad I'd practiced running on the track with Kimmy Jo and pushups and sit-ups with Aaron. We had to walk for miles almost every day. About four weeks in, we were allowed to make a ten-minute collect phone call home. The only thing that kept me going during that time was reading letters from my kids and Aaron. I received so many letters. They would tell me how much they missed me. I would write back to them in a group letter because I did not have time to write to them individually. One letter in particular was from Kevin where he asked me to write and tell Dad to let him stay out until twelve midnight because he had a girlfriend in Virginia that he met on the base. I found the time to write to him to let him know I would talk with him about it when I returned home. It never came up when I went home.

I could not wait to speak to Aaron and the kids. Aaron put them on the phone first for about a minute or so each. Karmentrina told me she had a new girlfriend that she met on the school bus, Julie Holley from the Philippines, and she was so excited. Kimmy Jo told me that she and Kevin were helping dad out a lot and that all of them were being good. Keenan told me he was being good almost every day.

Then it was Aaron's turn. I cursed him so bad, yelling at him and telling him that he'd lied about basic training and that it was like a prison camp. I would not allow him to get a word in until I was out of breath. He then spoke and asked me if anyone had hit me and I said no but they yell in my face so close that their damn spit touches my face.

Before I knew it, my ten minutes were up, and the phone went dead. I could not wait to get another phone call home. There were four more weeks to go, and we were given passes for on base to shop at the base exchange and the shoppette.

I always called Aaron collect when I was on a pass and was able to speak with the kids more often. Things were going well because the routine became manageable psychologically. I knew how to play spades, so I took adventures on my passes to play cards with some male airmen recruits in the recreation center that I met from our basic training class.

There were two more weeks to go, and I was feeling myself. We were given a pass one evening to leave the base until eight. One of the recruits in my squad that I friended, Gloria from Texas, had an aunt in San Antonio who came on the base to pick four of us recruits up about ten in the morning. We had our civilian clothes that we'd purchased when we shopped at the BX with us to change into when we arrived at her house.

We had a ball, eating good food, not like at the chow hall, drinking wine, beer, and hard liquor, which I skipped. I only drank the wine and soda. There were a lot of people there, mostly family. We were dancing to "Ring My Bell" by Anita Ward. The clock was winding down, and by six o'clock, Gloria's aunt told us we could have no more drinks and to put our military uniforms back on. She got us back to the base by seven forty-five, and we made roll call at eight o'clock pm. We had a ball.

A week left to go and we had to complete the obstacle course and pass all of the challenges before we could get our completion certificates. I was so worried. I had heard about the six-foot wall we had to climb over, and the monkey bars that were over water. I could not swim, and all I thought about was not making it over the bars and falling into the water and drowning. I had mastered the sit-ups, push-ups and running, so I was not worried about them. I had the hardest time getting over that damn wall; my teammates came back to help me over it. They made a ladder with their bodies and got me over. I missed the rope to get down on the other side and dropped and hurt my knees. I limped all the way through the rest of the obstacle course. Then the monkey bars were right in front of my face. The day I would most likely drop into the water and drown, and my kids would never see me again. Aaron be damned; he'd talked me into this bullshit.

Everyone was making it across, and no one fell. Then it was my turn. I got up there, and it took me forever to move. I was in shock. Then the TI came up behind me and told me to go, for he would not let me fall. I started across and made it about halfway and had no strength to go any further. I knew I was going to let go of the bars, and I prayed that God would not let me drown. I dropped and went under the water. I was splashing and thinking I was drowning, and the TI said, "Airman Stockton, stop slashing and stand up."

The water only came up to my waist. Everyone was laughing and clapping for me. I did not think it was funny at all. I knew I was going to be set back, and there was no way I wanted to repeat that obstacle course. The TI came over to me later and told me that they would not fail anyone who could not pass the obstacle course, only written work. Boy was I ever happy about that.

A few days after the obstacle course was over, the TI summoned me and another recruit who was Puerto Rican to his office. She was a squad leader as well. He took us to lunch and said it was for training—liar.

He wanted to know whom we knew that was in the military services. All of her brothers were in the US Army, and my husband was in the US Air Force. He then said that he knew someone guided us for we never broke down and were always quoting from the handbook.

I went on to tell him that I knew he could not touch any of us recruits and that I did not give a damn about him yelling because my dad, William, was a holy terror when I was a child and I was never afraid of him or anyone else yelling.

The easiest thing about that basic training was going home. I missed my family. I was so happy to see all of them except Aaron at that time. I forgave him later that night. I was assigned to on-the-job training as a medic at Andrews Air Force Base and then one weekend a month training and two weeks annual training a year at Andrews Air Force Base. It was convenient.

The following weekend, Mom had a cookout for my homecoming from basic training at her house in York. The whole family and a host of friends were at her house when we arrived. Mom was in shock when she saw how small I was, and she asked me if I were sick. I told her no, I had to lose weight to meet my weight requirement for the Air Force.

She said, "Child, if you have to be that skinny to be in the military, get out before you get sick."

I told her I had to do four years and that I felt healthy.

August 1979, we all drove up to Mom's house one Saturday afternoon prior to the new school year starting. When we pulled up to park, we heard loud music coming from Mom's house. "Busting Loose" by Chuck Brown was playing, and when I peered through the window, I saw Candy in the living room dancing.

I was surprised to see her. She was now married, and her Air Force husband, Wendell Brown, was with her. She was equally surprised to see me. She was down from Connecticut visiting one of her aunts. We caught up on family news. She now had a son. They stayed at Mom's house until the late evening. We exchanged current contact information and would stay in touch.

Mom had always accepted Candy. Candy called her Mom Dot. Mom always taught us that a child is not responsible for the decisions of their parents, and I wholeheartedly agree. Candy and I were so much alike, and I was glad that she came into my life. We drove back to Maryland that night because we'd forgotten to feed Sapphire.

After the kids were all in bed and the house was quiet, Aaron and I were sitting in the living room watching TV when he dropped a bombshell.

A commercial came on, and he turned off the set. He looked at me and told me that he had orders to go overseas in October. That would be only two months away. I asked him when did he get orders, and he had the nerve to say he had orders before I left for basic training camp. He said he did not tell me, for he thought I would have not gone to the training. I guess he knew me well, because I would not have gone. I was so upset because he knew I would be going to nursing school full-time at George Mason University in Fairfax, Virginia.

The next day, Karmentrina told me all about her new girlfriends, Julie Holley from the Philippines and Tonya from England. They were all going to the seventh grade in the public school system. They would enter James Madison Junior High School. I felt like it was such a blessing for my kids to be meeting and making friends with children from other countries, something that would not have happened if we had stayed in York.

They thought they were all that because big brother Kevin was there. Kevin used to be two grades behind Kimmy Jo, for he failed the first grade, but then he skipped a grade after going to summer school and would now be one year behind her. The school felt that he would feel out of place in the eighth grade for he was so much bigger and taller than the other children.

October came quickly, and I was feeling so unsure about everything, for I had not been away from Aaron for a long period of time since he was stationed in Thailand. Just when things were going so well for all of us. It was true that I was not far from Mom this time; however, it would be very difficult for me to be able to walk a few blocks to her house.

By now I was showing tears, and inside of me, I was hating him. Not only would the children be in school all day, but I would be going to college full-time. I told him that would feel like l was all alone again to handle all of the everyday tasks with the kids, the dog, my school, the issues that were more than likely to continue with Keenan in school, and running the household. Parent teacher meetings, weekly family therapy which we had started just last year with Catholic charities, football practice, practice at the youth center for talent shows with the kids, grocery shopping, and now I would have to iron our clothing. I was already feeling that I would fail trying to keep up with everything.

He moved closer to me on the sofa and placed his arm around me and said, "Babe, I had to take the short tour now so that you and the kids would not have to move from Andrews. This short tour guarantees me a home-based assignment coming back to the States. It will give us three to four more years here at Andrews. I know you do not want to move at this time, with your schooling and all."

Through my tears, I listened to him and did understand. We were already having little problems pop up with Keenan's behavior in school.

Aaron left in the middle of October without any issues. We all went out to dinner for his going away party and a birthday celebration for his birthday, which was coming up on November first. All of the kids told Aaron that they would be good and help me out during his absence.

# Chapter Thirty-Five: Guess Who Is Moving In?

A few days after Aaron left for his overseas tour, I received a call from Bonita. She wanted to know if she and her kids could come to Maryland to live with me because she was in a serious domestic violence situation with Barrion.

It was just before Halloween. I did not have to think twice about that and responded, "Yes, you may come here."

At the time when I told her she could, I did not realize that I would need permission from the base commander. My next-door neighbor Clemmie told me how to get the permission for her to stay with me temporarily. It was relatively easy.

Two weeks later, she was at 1179 B Hall Court with all of her belongings that could fit into Mr. Bill's car along with Sean in the sixth grade, Barronita in the second grade, and Cora Mae not in school yet. Sean and Keenan were in the same grade; however, I had moved Keenan to North Forestville Elementary school for the sixth grade on recommendation from his school counselors. It was a public school for children with behavior issues. The worst mistake I ever made in my life.

Those kids were crazy. I used to go and observe through a window, and my kid would be sitting in his chair just keeping to himself and others were out of their seats, swearing at the teachers and throwing things. It was horrible. I would move him to James Madison Junior High for the seventh grade the following year. Karmentrina would be there so I would not have to worry about him.

Halloween came, and all of the kids were working on their costumes. I would allow them to go alone since we were on the base. Keenan and Sean went together. They were only supposed to go trick-or-treating in our neighborhood not more than three streets over. Karmentrina and Barronita came back early, and their little bags were full. Cora Mae was too young to go with them, and they were so happy counting how much candy they had collected. Kimmy Jo and Kevin were not too far behind them. By ten o'clock, Keenan and Sean had not returned. I decided to go out to look for them, and I could not find them.

At that point, Bonita and I were beside ourselves with worry. I called the military police, and they came over and got descriptions of them. They left and told us they would return. About twelve midnight, here came Keenan and Sean. I was so darn mad. I snatched both of their bags of candy and told them to get upstairs because they were getting their little butts whipped. I called the police to let them know the boys had returned and that they were just fine.

They never got that butt whipping, but I went through their bags and confiscated quite a few goodies for me and Bonita. Moving forward, we had to keep our eyes on those two little boys. Keenan was always up to something; I knew he would easily persuade Sean into doing bad stuff.

Like when I found out they were skipping their Sunday School classes and sneaking down to the basement to steal doughnuts. I only caught them because Sean had some sticking out of his coat pocket when they came home from Sunday School. Keenan had eaten all of his evidence. He was the slick one.

The kids had no bonding issues, for Bonita and I had lived together with our kids once before in York. We agreed on a plan as to who was responsible for what. It worked out fairly well. The only issue my kids had was the tooth paste that she brought. They liked Aim, and she purchased a no-name brand that was much cheaper. They did not like the taste of it. Once I explained it to her, she switched and started to buy Aim.

I wrote and told Aaron that she was living with us, so I was not alone. The holidays came and went. We spent the

Thanksgiving and Christmas holidays at home. Bonita and I had enough money to get gifts for the kids.

Bonita started to get out and meet people on the base and build her own friends. She met a young man named Sterling, and I did not like him. I do not think she really cared for him; anyway, it did not last long. She would later meet a young man by the name of Michael Swan. He was okay, a quiet kind of guy.

Summer 1980 rolled around, and we were all okay. Big Wheels were out during that time, but our kids did not have one, so Sean and Keenan decided they would steal one from some kids who had one near us on the base. Well, the two little brats got caught. The security police brought them home.

Sean was crying and saying, "Aunt Sandi, I told the police what happened because I did not want to go to Attica Prison."

I wanted to burst out laughing. I told them both to shut up and go into the house to their room. I told the officer there would be no more Big Wheel issues from those two. I wore their asses out with my bat and ball paddle. They both were put into the doghouse. Since Bonita and her kids moved in, their names were added with a marker on the opposite side of some of the other little doggies.

I paid them back for coming back late on trick-or-treat night too. When I shut the door, I heard Keenan telling Sean that he was such a tattletale, and Sean responded, "I did not want to go to Attica prison, Keenan."

Keenan told him that they could not go to Attica because they were only little kids. There were no more Big Wheel issues or any other issues from those two for a minute.

By now, all of the children had many friends. They all were members of the youth center and the recreation center where they participated in many talent shows with their singing group, the Kearse Four. Although I never did meet Kevin's girlfriend in Virginia, he did introduce me to his new friend

Steve Durham, who lived on the other side of the base in the officers' housing quarters. We would allow Kevin to ride his bike the distance about two miles to visit him. He would not have to leave the base.

Kevin showed me the box car with wheels that they made together. They were so proud of it. He loved going crabbing with Steve and his father in Calvert County, as well as camping at Solomons Island, Maryland, a place for military families to vacation.

Bonita soon felt connected to Michael, and she and her kids moved into his father's house with him in Capital Heights, MD. She would come to marry him later. I did not really want to see her go, but I was happy for her because Aaron would be returning home soon. It would just be our family once again.

September 1980 came. The school year started with no issues, and the kids were doing okay. Kimmy Jo met and made friends with a girl named Angela who lived across the street from the base. She convinced Kimmy Jo to ask us if she could go to a Catholic girls' high school. We asked Kimmy Jo if she was sure because she'd just transferred to Madison the year before, and she begged to go there, a public school.

She told us she was sure she wanted to go. So I registered her at Saint Cecilia's All Girls High School in Washington, DC. for the tenth grade. We were so getting used to not paying school tuition. Oh well! Kimmy Jo felt that she had to stand up for her friend Angela, always telling me issues about that child. Her parents were very strict. They would never let her spend the night at our house but would allow Kimmy Jo to spend the night at their house. Really weird!

The child was being bullied at school and at home. One evening Angela ran away and came to our house. I felt I needed to phone her mother and let her know that her daughter was at our house, and I gave her mother our address. She and her military husband came to get Angela, and she refused to go. The military man was her stepfather, and she had an older sister and two younger half-brothers at home. I would not make Angela leave at that time. I told her parents that I would bring her home the next day, and I did. I let her parents know about all of the issues that Angela had shared with me and Kimmy Jo, and I told them that I would not hesitate to use the information she shared with me with his commander on Andrews AFB, if need be.

Later, Angela told Kimmy Jo that things were better at home. Kimmy Jo stayed there for a year then transferred back to public school at Frederick Douglass High School in Upper Marlboro, Maryland. Kimmy Jo told us that she wanted to leave because some girls at school were starting to look at her funny in the gym when they had to take showers. I was thinking, but did not say it, that girls after one year just started looking at her funny. Great, no more tuition.

# Chapter Thirty-Six: The Korea Tour Is Over

We were so happy to see Aaron, and me more than anyone else. He surprised us and showed up at the front door in early November on a Sunday morning. He told me he flew into Travis AFB California from Korea and then hopped (free military plane) to Scott AFB in Saint Louis and then a hop from there to Andrews AFB.

He only had a duffle bag with him and said his things would come later. He had so many things packed in there for the kids, they thought it was Christmas. He brought a jade statute for me. It was beautiful. He asked me what was going on, and I told him everything: my struggles with Keenan and my struggle making it through school. Just before he came back home, the station wagon broke down about an hour's drive from home. I pulled over at a gas station across from the school, and the station owner told me I had a dead battery. I explained to him that I did not have any money and I needed to get home. I offered him my military ID card for insurance that I would return with the money for the battery in two days when I had classes again. I was praying that he would trust me, and he did.

I still had three years of college to complete my nursing degree. I would go during the summers to crunch the time. That would allow me to finish a half a year earlier. It was a good experience going to college full-time. There were only two Blacks in my class, myself and a female student from South Africa. She and I bonded quickly, and we studied together most of the time. I also friended a young white female student named Terry, whom I adored. I often studied with her at her house, and I met her family, and soon her family knew all about my family. We would stay connected years after graduation and then Terry would marry, and we would lose touch with each other.

Aaron and I discussed getting a second car because I did not want to leave him on the base without transportation while I was at school. Soon after that conversation, we started going to the lemon lot (used cars) on base to look for a car. We finally found a used two-door yellow Chevy Vega. That car lasted us throughout college, and it never broke down. Our mechanic told us to keep up with the oil changes and transmission fluid as needed.

We had been living on base for almost six years, and I was ready to move off of the base. It seemed like our house was getting too small for all of us. Aaron and I were always stepping over our kids and their many friends. Julie and Tanya were around so much that I started to believe that they belonged to us.

One afternoon I was eavesdropping on one of their many conversations. They were all in junior high by then. They called themselves the "Base Crew," special K (Karmentrina), Juicy J (Julie), and Luscious L (LaTonya). They were making up what they called cool sayings; "never that" and "none of that." They would all get together to go and ride their bikes on the base probably places where they were not supposed to be, so grown.

I used to put a glass against the wall in my bathroom wall to spy on Kevin and Keenan. I did the same to Karmentrina; I would listen through the boys' room which was next to her room. I had Kevin believing that I knew everything. He would try to make Keenan a believer, but the girls would not fall for it. Karmentrina was arguing with Kevin one day and telling him that "Mom cannot read minds or tell the future; she is tricking you and Keenan." Only Karmentrina would try to mess up my kid control.

I started getting the Sunday paper weekly just to look at houses and cut out grocery coupons for food shopping. Karmentrina would always volunteer to go with me. Kimmy Jo always refused, saying it was so boring. I remember one time when I took Karmentrina with me to an appointment and I got lost. We had only been in Maryland for a few months. I was so frustrated. I would stop and ask people to help me, and it seemed like we were going in circles for hours. I had lost it. I was swearing like William used to a long time ago. Karmentrina was afraid, and she started crying. I stopped at a store, and there was a man who wrote down directions for us. I purchased some snacks for both of us. I felt so horrible, frightening her. I knew what she was feeling, for I had experienced that kind of outburst too many times to count while I was growing up with Dot and William. That was something that I knew I would have to work on: anger outbursts. We were so happy that I finally found the way home. Karmentrina and I did that for about one and half years, just looking at houses and dreaming.

# Chapter Thirty-Seven: I Want to Move Away from Andrews AFB

I was now in my senior year and would be graduating in the spring of 1982. Karmentrina and I continued house hunting on the weekends and found a house in Upper Marlboro, Maryland listed as a HUD house with a realtor's name on the sign. I did not know what United States Housing and Urban Development (HUD) meant at that time. I phoned the agent and asked about the house. He made an appointment to meet with me at the property.

I went to the appointment alone to see the house. It was a total dump, but I started to think like Mom, about all of the hidden possibilities. Aaron was out of town at a military conference in Mississippi at that time for a week. The agent told me that I could bid on the house. I told him that I did not have any money, and he told me that I did not need any money if I could get a promissory letter from a parent for three hundred and fifty dollars. I could only think of my mom.

I drove to York to get the letter from Mom. She was reluctant to sign the promissory note, for she thought she might go to jail if she did not come up with the money. She looked at me so seriously and said, "I only have a few dollars and it is for my lottery tickets."

I assured her that Aaron and I would come up with the money and for her not to worry about it. I told Aaron all about the house when he returned home and drove him to see it. He was on board but wanted to know how we were going to pull it off. I told him we both had to get part-time jobs, and we did. We both got jobs at the base Commissary on the night shift stocking shelves, and Aaron got an extra job buffing floors in the Air Force Systems Command building, which was two blocks from our house.

# Chapter Thirty-Eight: 5018 Brimfield Drive

We were tired all the time, but we made the money to cover the promissory note that Mom wrote and for all of the extra stuff that we knew we had to get for the house. We settled twenty days before I graduated in May of 1982. I would be taking my Maryland State Board examination in September. I applied for a graduate nurse position at the Washington, DC. Veterans Hospital Center (WDVAHC) and was hired on an orthopedic ward.

I did a twelve-week orientation with a nurse named Ms. Posey, and then I was assigned my first solo charge nurse position on a night shift with a licensed practical nurse and two nursing assistants. It was a disaster for me. Before the shift changed, I received a report from the evening off-going nurse. When her shift left, I made rounds, and half of the patients' intravenous fluid (IV) bags were dry or damned near dry. It seemed like every call light was ringing for pain medication or the bed pan.

I wanted to quit right on the spot, but I knew I could not abandon my shift. I could not wait for the change of shift. I made sure that all of my work was done and no one had dry IV bags. Foleys were emptied, and all patients were comfortable.

After I gave morning report, I drove home. I called my preceptor, Ms. Posey, at home. I knew she was off that day. I told her what had happened, and she responded to me, "What did you learn, Sandra?"

I was quiet and did not respond, and she started speaking. She told me that I had to always arrive to work at least thirty minutes before my shift to give myself time to make rounds before taking report. That way I could tell the off-going nurse what needed to be done before her shift ended. That was the best tip ever. I was never caught off guard again.

We were homeowners once again at 5018 Brimfield Drive, Upper Marlboro, Maryland. There was no hurry for us to move off of the base. So we took about thirty days to get the house livable. Aaron took leave for ten days. The first week of the ten days, he painted the entire first floor: the kitchen, living room, dining room, and three bedrooms. He painted the recreation room in the basement where he and I slept temporarily, and he painted a bedroom in the basement for Karmentrina.

All of the children had their own room. There was a fireplace in the recreation room, and we put a big screen TV down there with a couch and chairs. We brought all of the kids' bedroom furniture to the new house first as well as the kitchen set and all of our dishes so we could start to stay there. We moved the rest of our furniture and household goods from the base housing area during the rest of the month.

Aaron and I got the base house ready for inspection, and we passed the first time. I would bet money that the house we cleaned back on Andrews did indeed pass inspection, but the officer did not want to pay Aaron.

No sooner were we settled than Tracey called me to ask if she and her baby Caprisha could move back home with us because the marriage was not working out. I would never say no to her and my great niece. I was now glad that I did not sign for her to marry her husband. She also told me that his mother and sister were threatening to take her to court to have her declared an unfit mother and take her baby. I assured her that it would be over my dead body.

I stepped in with the funds for her attorney, and she walked away with her divorce and her baby. If I did not know anything, I knew that my mom taught me and my siblings to fight for our children.

I guess moving off the base gave Kevin a new lease on life. He thought he could just go and come whenever he pleased. I told Aaron that we had to come up with a plan to put Kevin in check. Aaron made a plan with a military security police officer who was a friend of his.

Aaron came home from work one evening and told Kevin that he had to take him on base to the police station because they wanted to speak with him. I played along with it and said to Aaron, "Police station for what? We don't even live on base anymore."

He replied, "I do not know what, but they came to my job today to tell me they needed to see my son, Kevin Kearse."

When we three arrived there and went to the desk to ask for the officer who was Aaron's friend, he came out, and Aaron introduced him to Kevin. He escorted us to a room and closed the door behind the three of us. A few minutes later, the officer and two other military police officers entered the room and they told Kevin to stand up.

The one officer looked at Kevin eye to eye and said, "Yeah! He fits the description!"

The other officer approached, and they handcuffed Kevin. By now, Kevin was crying and saying to me and Aaron, "Mom, Dad, I did not do anything. I have not been on base since we moved."

I looked at Kevin with tears in my eyes and told him that I could not vouch for him, for he was always away from home without permission. Aaron's friend looked at us and told us to leave because they were locking Kevin up until they could be sure he was not the perpetrator who was breaking into cars on base. They gave us some Cokes and let us watch TV in their break room.

One of the officers came back in about an hour and told us that he thought Kevin had had enough. They were watching him on the cameras sniffling. They brought him out to us, and he was subdued. It was a quiet ride home.

I told Kevin that was one of the reasons he needed to let us know where he would be going when leaving the house. I also told him that we needed to be able to say that we knew where he was at all times. Things straightened out somewhat.

September was upon us, and I presented to Baltimore, Maryland to take my nursing board examination. It was long and tedious. I was not feeling good about it. The examinations were not computerized back then. One big room with many students spaced apart at small desks with number two pencils and a large package of multiple-choice questions.

It would not be long before I received the results of the exam. I was devastated for I had failed the maternity section and the psychology section. I told my preceptor the next day at work and she told me not to worry but to register for a review class for the two sections. I took her advice and paid over two hundred dollars to take a review course at the University of Maryland.

I completed the course and applied to take the exam for maternity and psychology the next exam date. It was necessary for me to pass the two sections because it would be the last year one could test for sections of the exam. In 1983 the rules would change. If a student failed any part of the exam, they would have to repeat the entire exam with all of the sections.

I was at work on the day shift at the WDVAMC when I was called to the front desk to answer a phone call. It was Tracey, and she said, "Mom, you have a letter from the Maryland State Board of Nursing Licensure. Do you want me to open it?"

All of the children knew I had previously failed parts of the exam. At first, I told her no, then I said, "Go ahead, Tracey, open it and read it to me."

She soon started to read, "Congratulations, Sandra L. Stockton." I stopped her right there. I knew I had passed the two sections. I would now be paid registered nurse pay instead of graduate nurse pay.

I was overwhelmed and could not wait to tell Aaron. By the time I arrived home, the kids had already told him. The first thing he asked me was how much my paycheck would go up. Only Aaron would ask that. My first full check surprised me.

Not too long after that, Aaron introduced me and the kids to his friend Pete Smith and his wife and three sons. I invited them to dinner. My mom was down that weekend with Mr. Bill and Bucky. Mom and I cooked enough food for all of us and there was a lot of leftover food.

I invited Pete's wife to take as much leftovers as she wanted to take. She told me that Pete did not allow the family to eat leftovers. Mom was in shock! She started to say something, and I kicked her under the table. When they left, Mom, Aaron, and I all laughed. Mom wanted to know where in the hell Aaron met such rich friends.

# Chapter Thirty-Nine: Separation Anxiety Again

Fall 1982. Kimmy Jo and Kevin were in senior high school and Karmentrina and Keenan were in junior high school. Things were going well. I quit my job at the WDVAHC. I was so tired of the heavy workload, lifting, and turning patients with little or no help, always short staffed, it was just too much for me, so I made a move.

During my night shifts I started searching the want ads and looking for a new position. The problem was that I had only a year's experience and only in orthopedics. I soon came across an ad for a hemodialysis nurse, new grads accepted. I did not know what it would be all about, but I did not hesitate to apply.

I applied and was hired. It was located in Camp Springs, only twenty minutes from where I lived. I wrote my resignation letter for my boss at the WDVAHC with a four-week notice. I wanted to do it on the right terms just in case the new job did not work out.

The new year, 1983, rolled in, and Aaron dropped the bomb: He had orders for four years at Scott AFB in Illinois. A special duty assignment at Headquarters Military Air Command (MAC). He also mentioned that Pete and his family had orders as well, so there would be someone there that we knew. Not that I cared about Pete's family going there! I was saddened about that news for me and the kids; we were so settled. I was so happy at our house and the kids were all teens with so many friends. I was the head nurse on the day shift at a hemodialysis center in Clinton, Maryland.

Aaron and I dropped the news on the kids after the holidays were over. They were all so mad at their dad. Aaron reminded us all that for seven years we did not have to move, and he could no longer be at Andrews AFB. Kimmy Jo was rolling her teary eyes and I could feel her anger and her sadness as well as the sad feelings from all of the kids.

Karmentrina had built new friends at school and in the neighborhood with Jennifer Jackson and Peggy White. They were getting along so well and always together. They had never had to leave their friends, but many of their friends' families had received orders and had to leave them in the past. I was sure Kevin would miss his friend Kenny Allen, they thought they were music geniuses. Keenan's friend was his cousin Sean, partner in crime. He would be okay. Julie's family had orders to go back to the Philippines soon, and Tanya's parents had orders to leave soon for Scott AFB as well, so it would not bother Karmentrina as much as it would bother Kimmy Jo, for none of her friends were going anywhere.

Kimmy Jo was adamant that she was staying in Maryland when she graduated in May, no matter what Aaron and I spoke. I went to her bedroom later that evening and told her that over my dead body would I leave my eighteen-year-old daughter in a state alone without me.

The summer came fairy quickly, and we all packed up and made the trip to Scott AFB. We did a DITY move (do it yourself) because we could get extra money if the military did not move us.

Tracey went back to York before we left. We rented a large U-Haul truck. Aaron was a much better driver than he had been back in Clovis, New Mexico. I drove our old Chevy station wagon, and Aaron drove the U-Haul. The kids and Sapphire were in the station wagon with me. We towed the 1964 Ford Mustang that Aaron bought from a soldier going overseas not long ago. I would be returning to an empty house and needed the Mustang to drive back to Maryland, to stay until I was able to get a job in Illinois and also to rent the house out.

The drive was an experience that I would not want to ever repeat. All the way there, Karmentrina and Kimmy Jo played the same songs—I was so sick of them, and so were the boys.

They played Renee and Angelo's "My First Love," Sergio Melendez' "Never Going to Let You Go," Pattie Austin's "How Do You Keep the Music Playing," Anita Baker's "Angel," and "I Want to Be Your Girl." I finally made them stop and started to play the radio off and on. The girls would take turns riding in the front passenger seat to read the AAA map for me. Karmentrina always fought to be in the front seat, and she always fell asleep.

It was going to be about a thirteen-hour drive. About three hours out, right outside of Pittsburgh, Pennsylvania on the turnpike, the truck broke down. I looked in my rearview mirror and saw Aaron pulling over in back of me. I pulled over in front of him. We had no mobile phones back then.

There was a rest stop on the other side of the turnpike. It was six lanes across. Aaron decided that he was going to cross the road. I was worried that he might slip and fall, but he insisted there was no other choice. He put the road cones by the vehicles, and I pulled farther off of the road and made all of the kids get out of the vehicles just in case someone did not see the truck and hit it or us. I left Sapphire in the car, for she might have ran into the road. Aaron was back in about thirty minutes to tell us a tow truck was on the way. About an hour or so later a tow truck from U-Haul came and towed the truck, and we followed them to a hotel where they told us to see if we could check in for the night. We were able to check in and dogs were allowed. They were like little cottages. The U-Haul tow driver said they would have our things reloaded to another U-Haul truck and have it back to us with in one day, and they did. We were still about ten hours' drive away from Scott AFB.

We started out after we ate breakfast and only stopped for bathroom breaks. We had packed food and drinks for the trip.

We arrived in downtown Belleville, Illinois about eight o'clock that evening. Aaron was now in front of us with the U-Haul and he was pulled over by the Belleville City police. I pulled over in back of them and one of the officers got out and started yelling at me to move. I tried to tell him that I was following the truck. He responded that he did not care who I was following and that I needed to move. Okay, new environment! I drove up ahead and parked at a meter to wait for Aaron.

Kimmy Jo started to cry and saying, "Mom, these white people could kill us, and Nanny would never know what happened to us." I told all of the kids to settle down, no one was going to kill us. Although I was somewhat nervous, I could not let the kids know that. About twenty minutes later, Aaron came down the street and I saw him and followed him. We were soon at Scott AFB. Aaron pulled off on the side of the road about two miles from the base and told us that the officers only gave him a warning. He said they were aggressive at first, but when he showed them his military ID card they softened up.

I said, "Thank God!"

There were no issues getting through the gate. Aaron called his sponsor from the gate, and he gave him directions to temporary enlisted housing. The next morning, Aaron was able to get the keys to our quarters at 2496 Firtree Lane on base. We had three days before the truck was due to be turned in. We emptied the truck within the three days and set up the house like we had been there for years. It was a one level three-bedroom duplex house. The girls shared and the boys shared. While I was in Illinois, I applied at the Veterans Hospital in Saint Louis (STVAHC), Missouri for their Hemodialysis unit. About a week later it was time for me to make the drive back to Maryland, praying that the Mustang would not fail me.

It was so spooky in our empty house on Brimfield Drive. I could not wait to get out of there. I had a sleeping bag, and it seemed like I could hear all kinds of noises in that empty house. I worked with a rental agency in Marlo Heights, Maryland and they found a renter. About two weeks after the house was rented out, I received a call from the nurse supervisor, Mrs. Sutton, from the Saint Louis VA Hospital with an offer, and I so readily accepted and told her I could report in two weeks, and that was fine with her. Bucky wanted to go out to Scott with me and stay for a while, and I checked with

Aaron who said it was fine with him. I told Bucky that he would have to sleep on a sofa bed in the living room because we did not have enough bedroom for him to have privacy and he was okay with that.

Even though Aaron had orders for four years at Scott, my plan was not to be there that long. I did not inform him about that but when the time was right I would. Bucky would stay for about a year. He applied and got a job at the enlisted club. He thought he was the man. He got Karmentrina to give him a Jheri curl, and with his blond hair and grey eyes, he pulled any girl he wanted at the club. I used to threaten to tell his girlfriend in York about him flirting out there. He knew I never would!

The kids acclimated to the base quickly it was just like being on Andrews AFB. They now were all old enough to frequent the recreation center where many teens hung out. They met and made many friends. They were still singing and dancing and entering contest because I insisted on it. But that did not last long. We went to the movie theatre in Belleville as a family, there was only one theatre and yes you guessed it, mainly whites were in attendance. After a while it did not bother us, but I still did not let my kids go alone or without friends. Summer flew by, and the holidays were upon us.

December of 1983, Helena phoned us, and I answered the phone. From her tone I knew something was wrong and I asked her what was wrong. She told me that her father died, and she needed Aaron to know of his death. She told me to tell him because she did not want to tell him on the phone herself.

Aaron was in the bedroom and did not know that his sister had called. I went into the bedroom to tell him that his father had passed early that morning. When I entered the room, I did not speak right away, and he looked up from the bed and said,

"What is it, Sandra?"

I told him that Helena called and said that his father had passed. He started crying, and I sat down beside him, and we just hugged. He soon said that we needed to tell the children for they had met him in Pittsburgh on one of our many trips there. It would be decided that Aaron would fly to Pittsburgh, Pennsylvania to attend his father's funeral. It would be a short stay. He was back home within three days. I felt some kind of way about supporting him. I was glad that I was the one to be able to comfort him during such a horrible time. I knew he would be okay. He never spoke much about his father's family besides the witchcraft that they believed in. I was sure Aaron did not believe in witchcraft.

Christmas was close and we were deciding what we would get the kids for Christmas. While Aaron and I were shopping at the base exchange (BX) one morning, a young woman was giving away puppies. They were all black. We asked for a boy, and she gave the puppy to us. We named him Bocious after a puppy we once had back at Andrews. We took the puppy home and called the kids into the living room to see it. They were so happy, but Karmentrina more than all of them. One Christmas gift down and a few more to go. Aaron was in the mood to find a part time job to help out, but I told him we would be fine on my salary and his military pay. He still came up with a crazy idea.

He and Bucky approached me with some crazy idea that they wanted to sell Christmas trees. They told me they would need five hundred dollars to buy the trees and that they were going to rent a corner lot for one hundred dollars during the Christmas season. I told Aaron to go to the bank and get the money from the savings account. Right after Thanksgiving they were up and running. They had their sign out, *Ace and Bucky's Christmas Trees, Real Cheap. Twenty-five dollars a tree.*

The other tree lots were selling their trees for thirty-five dollars and up. They were out there at their lot in the cold weather every day. Bucky was there in the daytime and Aaron joined him in the evening when he was off work. Every day when they came home in the late hours, I would ask, "How many trees did you guys sell?" Every night it would be the same answer.

"None!" About two weeks in they decided to lower their price to fifteen dollars a tree and still no buyers.

About five days before Christmas, they both came home and were very happy to tell me that they sold a tree for fifteen dollars. I asked them where the money was and Bucky responded, "Sis we were hungry, we bought something to eat." They felt like the trees would sell. The next couple of days would prove them wrong, no trees sold. So they reduced the price to ten dollars a tree and still no buyers. Christmas Eve they marked the trees down to free and left the lot with their two chairs and hibachi that they were using to keep warm.

The next day, Christmas morning, they went to see if the trees were still there, and they were all gone. After Christmas, Aaron had told one of his Caucasian military buddies at work about his Christmas tree dilemma. His friend told him that there was nothing wrong with his trees and that the problem was that he and Bucky were Black. He told him that Belleville, Illinois was red neck central.

When Aaron told me and Bucky about it, I was not surprised because of the incident we encountered on our way here driving through the town of Belleville. When the holiday was over and school started back up, Karmentrina came home one day and said Tonya was in her room. She said that her family had just arrived during the Christmas holiday, but that would be short-lived. By the summer, Tonya's father got orders back to England for a year.

Kimmy Jo found a part time job at a grocery store in Belleville. I was worried about her going there, and so I should have been after coming through the town of Belleville when we arrived. Kimmy Jo came home from work one evening and told me and her dad that a white woman in the grocery store called her a Black nigger. I was damn near in shock, mad as hell, Aaron not so much because he was exposed to such while growing up in the South.

I asked Kimmy Jo what had happened to make the white woman say those things to her, and she said, "Nothing, Mom." She went on to explain to us that the store was crowded, and hardly anyone was coming through her line and a white female manager walked over and said to folks in the store that "this line is open." Kimmy Jo said a few customers came to her line and one white woman from another crowded line, responded back to the manager, "I ain't letting no Black nigger touch my food."

I wanted to just scream and go up to that store and give them a piece of my mind. Kimmy Jo calmed me down by saying, "Mom, it did not scare me at all. She did not touch me and you taught all of us that words cannot define who we are and to ignore ignorant people, white or Black."

Moving forward, I was worried about Kimmy Jo driving into Belleville to work at that damn grocery store, but Aaron told me she would be fine and would become stronger when dealing with ignorant people in this world. It was surely not going to be the first time.

We instructed Kimmy Jo to lock her car doors as soon as she entered her car and to lock it when she left it to go into the store to work, so that no one could do anything to her car. For teenagers, my kids all had thick skin. I knew that we would have to teach our kids how to stay alive in Illinois.

Aaron had a meeting with all of the other kids while Kimmy Jo was at work after the incident that she went through. We used to have weekly family meetings to iron out issues. He told them all to remember to keep their mouth shut when being approached by any white people in authority if and when they were being accused of anything. They were to just let us know by phone or when they got home. They were all permitted to make a collect call to us if and when they needed to.

They had all been exposed to racial issues in the past at Catholic schools on the East Coast but not to this level. We reminded them that as long as there were racist-ass people in the world, they should expect these things to happen. Kimmy Jo stayed there for several months and then moved on to a job at a department store, where she had no further issues and we were happy about that. Although the kids had experience being the only Blacks in a crowd, it was nothing like this.

Kimmy Jo had her driver's license and would need transportation. Aaron found and bought a 1975 Oldsmobile burnt orange Omega with no power steering. It started to give Kimmy Jo a lot of problems, so Aaron would soon put it back on the lemon lot and sell it to someone else. He decided to let her drive his 1964 Mustang and that was not much better, but it was a car.

Aaron used to irritate me always on Kimmy Jo about the milage, telling her he knew she'd gone farther than where she said she would be going. It turned out to be true. Kimmy Jo met and started dating a young man from Saint Louis. Soon we would barely see her.

Kevin bugged me about getting his driver's license, and I took him to get his learners permit and the drivers' handbook. When he was ready, I took him to take his test. I pointed out when we got there that there was a stop sign right where he would start the course.

He looked at me and said, "I got this, Mom." Well, as soon as he drove down the street, he went right through the stop sign.

The officer had him park the car and get out. He gave Kevin his paperwork that said failed. All the way home Kevin complained that he failed because he was Black.

I said, "No! You failed because you did not stop for the stop sign at the corner. I told you it was there. I guess you will remember the next time."

About a month later, we went back, and Kevin passed the test. I knew Karmentrina would be asking me as soon as she was old enough to apply for her drivers' permit.

School was another thing. Keenan was in eight grade and in an all-white school. Keenan was a very dark complected young man. One day, the school called me to tell me to come and pick Keenan up from school because he was being suspended for slapping a white girl. I was off that day and arrived there as soon as I could. The white girl's parents were there, they were military. I knew that because the man was in a military uniform. I asked Keenan what happened in front of the girl's parents and the principal.

He said in front of them all, "Mom, she called me a Black nigger, so I slapped the heck out of her."

Inside of my head, I was thinking *You go son, defend yourself.* I said to them all that if they were going to suspend my son for three days, they better suspend her, or I would sue the school, and they did suspend her as well.

I praised my son. We went to McDonald's in celebration. No one at that school ever called my son out of his name again. In fact, everyone was nicer to him after that.

No sooner did I get through that hurdle than I got a letter from the high school about Kevin. I went to the meeting with his teacher. Apparently, Kevin was getting his lunch then going over to the a la carte table for extra food. Kevin did not realize that he had to pay for that food. They never had a la carte in the Maryland school system.

Once it was explained to Kevin, there were no more issues.

Later that year we received another letter from Kevin's school to attend a parent teacher meeting. I attended the meeting. Aaron never wanted to go with me, for he thought I might embarrass him. That Mascoutah High School was getting on my last nerve. I presented to the meeting with my invisible armor on. I went to the office, and the teacher and Kevin were called down to the office. Introductions were made. Then the female English teacher went on to say that Kevin was intimidating her, always looking down at her when she spoke to him. Again, all white school, all white teachers.

I responded, "Why don't we all stand up?" and everyone did. I said to the teacher and to the principal that my son was taller than all of us in the room, and bigger and Black. He had never disrespected any teachers throughout his school years and I did not think that he would start now, so please respect that he cannot change who he is, change his height or change his color.

Kevin had his sad face on, and I had my mom protective face on. If that was not enough for us to deal with, Karmentrina came home from school (she was in the tenth grade) one afternoon and told me and Aaron that she'd asked the principal, Mr. Dean what the school was going to do for Black History Month. And she told us that Dr. Dean stated in front of the entire class, "What did Black people ever do for America?"

Karmentrina told me her friends were upset; they were mostly military dependents. I knew Karmentrina was not going to let that get past her. She was so inquisitive beyond her age, stayed on the honor roll each and every year. Probably too smart for her own good at times!

I contacted the school board by phone and followed it up with a letter. I demanded that the school have Dr. Dean apologize to all of the students who were in that class. They did something even better. They made the principal apologize in the school cafeteria over the intercom. It was that or his job. Kevin and Karmentrina had no more issues at Mascoutah High School.

Kevin graduated without any issues. Soon after Kevin graduated, he left for the Job Corps in Paducah, Kentucky for cooking but soon changed to carpentry. They paved the way for Keenan. There were many things I would deal with as my children were growing up, but one of them was not tolerating anyone messing with my kids.

About a year of living on the Scott, Aaron came up with this idea for us to move to Mascoutah, Ill, across the street from the base, to a small mobile home with a garage so we could get our housing money added back to his check. It was more than the rent would be. It was so small, and we were cramped in there, but relatively clean. The kids could now have parties in the garage without anyone complaining of too much noise.

There was a beehive as big as five basketballs put together on a tree in the front yard. I told Aaron to call the owners to have it removed. In a few days, a company came and removed it. It was on a long country road. Thank goodness Bucky went back to York with his girlfriend when she visited for about a month; there would have been no room for him at the mobile home.

It was a mile from the kid's schools and now considered long distance from Belleville, which was across the street. So all telephone calls to the base were long distance. We saved change to walk across the street to make telephone calls unless it was an emergency.

Although it was a three-bedroom with two bathrooms, it was like a matchbox. Everyone hated it but Aaron. I had to support him, for he always supported me. Kimmy really did not want to stay with us. She moved away to the city of Saint Louis with her boyfriend, Keith, someone we had not met. She packed up her clothing and left. I could not stop her; after all, she was nineteen. If it didn't' work out, she would find her way back.

# Chapter Forty: Work and Education

Work was going well for me at the Veterans Hospital (VA). I built friendships with several of the nurses: Anita, Margorie, Penny, Mary Anne (she was the only Caucasian nurse on our unit) and others, and we would bond and stay close until I left the unit. After I was there for about six months, Mary Anne approached me and told me she completed her Master's Degree in Health Administration. She told me that I should consider it because I was so good with charge duties.

I told her that I could not afford it and she said, "Don't make excuses." She told me that she would be my mentor throughout the program. I ran it by Aaron, and he said he thought it was a good idea, but worried about the cost. So I checked it out and then applied. It was a two-year program, but I could do it in eighteen months if I worked hard at it. I looked at the curriculum and saw that statistics was a requirement. I remember how I'd barely passed that course when I was an undergrad. It was a challenge working full-time and taking classes full-time. I worked a lot of weekends so I could attend school during the day and evening hours.

I remember taking the first statistics class. The instructor had our results and passed them out. She walked to everyone's desk and placed them face down. Students were picking up their exam papers to review, but I would not pick up my exam paper. She put the class on a fifteen-minute break, and everyone left the room. I left my exam paper on my desk. When the break was over, I walked over to my desk and sat down. I picked up the exam paper and almost had a heart attack. I had received an A.

I knew then I would make it through the program. Nothing else worried me. When I reached the last two courses, I was out of money, so I asked Aaron if he would consider selling his Mustang to get the money for me. He looked at me like I'd just put a stake in his heart. He went outside on the porch to smoke a cigarette and later came back into the house to tell me he would sell the Mustang to get the money. I would soon graduate with my Masters of Arts Degree in Health Services Management.

It was now time for Karmentrina to get her driver's permit. She would not let me forget that. I took her out in that old Omega for practice. Aaron kept the oil and transmission fluid in it. I just needed it to last until Karmentrina passed her driver's test. I took her out to practice every chance I had.

One day we decided to stop at McDonald's while we were out. She pulled onto the lot so fast, and I told her to slow down and hug her curb on her side. She was pulling in right between two parked cards and hit one of them sightly.

I got out of the passenger side to look, and she said, "Stop looking, Mom, and go inside to get our food."

I told her we needed to wait to see whose car she had hit. She walked right past me and said, "Okay, it will be your insurance going up."

I followed her into the McDonald's, and while we were in there, the driver of that car went out and got in the car and pulled off. I drove that non power steering car home and told Aaron to get rid of it right away and I told him why. Karmentrina took her test in that car, and she passed.

# Chapter Forty-One: Kimmy Jo Growing Up

Halfway into our second year and Kimmy Jo had not been making contact with us very much. I told Karmentrina to ask her if she could spend the weekend with her, and Kimmy Jo agreed. She picked up Karmentrina along with her boyfriend Keith for the weekend.

When she brought Karmentrina home on Sunday, I waved at her from the porch. She waved back but exchanged no words. I could not wait to hear what Karmentrina had found out for me.

Karmentrina told me that her boyfriend was nice to her and that he and Kimmy Jo watched TV and talked a lot but when she was alone with her boyfriend's mother, she was told that her son beat Kimmy and one day ran her out of the house with no shoes on in the snow and went out and dragged her back into the house. She told Karmentrina that she was an invalid, and her son would beat her as well. She warned Karmentrina to tell me to come and get my daughter.

Kimmy Jo told Karmentrina later that the boyfriend's mother had passed. Now that meant no one would be knowing what was going on with my daughter. I had to figure out how to get her back. I would not leave that state until I did.

I came up with a plan to get her back. I called Kimmy and invited her and her boyfriend for dinner on a Sunday evening. They accepted. I told her siblings and Aaron to be nice and just have a friendly conversation because we had to figure out how to get Kimmy Jo back home with us. They showed up, and things were going well. We were eating and communicating. Aaron was not saying too much. Then all of a sudden Aaron stood up and told the young man that if he ever found out that he put his hands on his daughter again he would kill him.

Everyone got quiet. Kimmy Jo started to cry, and they got up and left. I looked at Aaron and said, "Thanks a lot, Dad."

Summer was coming to an end, and school would start soon. Karmentrina would be in the twelfth grade, and she wanted to go back to Maryland to graduate at Douglass Senior High with her friends Peggy and Jennifer. If I took her back, we would all go back and leave Aaron at Scott for the rest of his two-year term. We would have to see.

It was summer, and it seemed that four of my nieces wanted to come to Scott to visit us. So Aaron drove to York, PA in the old Chevy station wagon to pick up Barronita, Bonita's daughter, and Tameca, Bucky's daughter, for two weeks. He left Keenan in Maryland with his Aunt Bonita. They were both teens or close to it. I asked both of their moms if they knew what to do if they started their menses while at Scott. I was told they both knew.

Well, within two days of each other, they started. I empowered Karmentrina to teach them what to do. She was trying to teach them how to use tampons but it was no use when it came to Tameca; she gave up. I purchased pads for her and told her she could learn later from her mom when she went back home.

They had a ball going on base swimming and playing at the youth center. It was soon time for them to return, so Aaron made the trip again to return them and pick up Caprisha and Cora Mae (Barronita's sister). They were younger.

Kimmy Jo had returned home with us to stay. She called me at work one day to come and pick her up, and I did. Her boyfriend was at work when I went to get her. I helped her with her bags, and we left and never looked back. So she was there to help with her little cousins. That gave Karmentrina a break.

One afternoon they went swimming and when they returned, Kimmy Jo told me that Caprisha got into some water over her head and when she took her out of the water she was coughing, crying and yelling, "Kimmy Jo, I need CPR!"

Kimmy said there was an audience, and she told Caprisha to stop yelling because she was breathing. At that point, Kimmy Jo said it was time to take them home. I laughed so hard and hugged Caprisha and took her in my room to watch TV with me. She felt much better then.

Aaron and I took the little ones along with Keenan and Karmentrina to Six Flags one afternoon. Aaron and I were watching Cora Mae and Caprisha in the park. So we put them on a little train ride and showed them the gate to meet us at on the other side of the ride. We put them on and walked around to the other side. We were standing there talking and didn't' notice that the ride had stopped. It was soon another group of kids on the little train, and those two were nowhere to be seen.

I panicked, but Aaron told me to calm down. "They can't be far."

We walked for what seemed like hours, but it was more like twenty minutes. I looked in a bounce house and saw Caprisha's pink balls bouncing up and down. I pointed it out to Aaron, and we ran over there. I looked in there and yelled out both of their names. They saw me and thought they'd seen a ghost.

Cora Mae came out first, saying, "Aunt Sandi, it was Caprisha's idea."

I made them get their shoes and then I found a bench for us all to sit on. We were there for about a half hour when Aaron caved, and I started taking them to get on rides again. That scared me so much. My siblings would have hated me if something were to happen to their kids on my watch.

I was ready for the little ones to go back. Those two weeks could not go fast enough. I drove the girls back home and took Kimmy Jo and Karmentrina with me. When we arrived in Maryland and returned all of the kids, we picked up Keenan from Bonita and went to York for two weeks. When we returned to Illinois, I decided that we needed a dependable car, so I went car shopping alone and purchased a 1985 gold Chevy Horizon with no money down. It was only $7500.00. Aaron saw it and was jealous. He went to downtown Mascoutah to the Chevy dealer and purchased a gray one for himself. So damn jealous. Now we had two car notes. We still had the old station wagon, and it just always worked for us. It was so dependable.

# Chapter Forty-Two: Time for Me and the Kids to Leave

I finally told Aaron that I was going back to Maryland with the kids because Karmentrina wanted to graduate from Douglass high school like Kimmy Jo did. She had refused to graduate from Mascoutah public high school because she did not want a prejudiced school name on her graduation paperwork.

I agreed with her because I wanted a reason to leave that area. I called the rental agency in Maryland to let them know we were returning, and they told me that the renters had vacated the property about three months ago. I could not believe it; they'd never told us that. We should have guessed as much for we had not received any payment for a few months.

And that was not the total amount due. Kimmy Jo did not want to go back to Maryland, so Aaron and I convinced her to go to college at Webster University in Saint Louis. Aaron would be there for two more years, so she would have support from him. She applied and was accepted for the fall. We moved her into the dorm, purchased everything that she would need, and paid her meal plan and her monthly college tuition plan of eight hundred dollars a month. She was all set before I left the area permanently with Keenan and Karmentrina.

I could not really leave before getting a job back in Maryland. I worked it out with Kimmy's friend Rhonda's mom and dad for Karmentrina to live with them temporarily so she could start at Douglass High school on time in Upper Marlboro, Maryland. I paid a monthly fee for Karmentrina's room and board. I gave Karmentrina allowance to cover her lunch and her books. I drove Karmentrina in my new car to Maryland to register her for school and get her settled at Rhonda's parents' house. I would leave my car parked there and take a round trip rental car back to Illinois because we still had two cars out there. I would convince my brother Bucky to help me drive back. I rented the car for a week. Bucky was to drive it back and turn it in. He did not turn that car in for almost a month. I hounded Mom so much trying to get her to convince Bucky to return the car. I was so angry with him, for he knew better than to do that.

Aaron was so mad at my baby brother. I did not know how he was going to get past that. They were pretty good friends. Eventually everything was back to okay. I would get a transfer to the WDVAHC a couple of months later and given the position as assistant head nurse on my arrival. I felt good

about that. The master's degree was paying off, or so I thought.

I met up with so much resistance from the nurses on the ear, nose and throat (ENT) unit there in Washington DC. Several of them had applied for the assistant head nurse position and were denied. Once they found out that I had the credentials, I was treated better by most.

At the end of October, Aaron and I, along with Keenan and our two dogs, would drive to Maryland. The kids and I would remain. On our arrival we went directly to our house on Brimfield Drive. We had the keys. The house was non-livable. The fridge was packed with crawling roaches, as was the electric stove. The toilet bowls were as black as charcoal, as were the sinks. Old torn furniture and trash all over the place. I just wanted to cry. When I thought about all we had to do to make it livable when we purchased it, it just made me sick and Aaron probably sicker.

We knew we could not stay there. Aaron called Helena, and she told us to come and stay with her. Her mother and her son Christopher were living with her. We picked up Karmentrina to stay with us and picked up my Horizon as well. We parked the station wagon at the house on Brimfield Drive to make it look like someone was now living there. We were in the house in two weeks. We had set off foggers for roaches and bugs and put rat and mouse poison everywhere. We threw out all of the appliances and purchased new ones: fridge, stove, washer, dryer, and dishwasher. To think that damn rental agency was collecting money half the darn time and must have never sent anyone to see the property. Well, you know I just had to curse them the hell out.

We had to re-paint the entire house. That would be done when Aaron came home for the weekends. He came home each and every weekend from Scott to Andrews on a military plane with no cost to him. There was always space available because there was a two-star general stationed at Scott who had a nine-passenger plane. He would fly every weekend because his family was living on Andrews AFB. I really did not have time to miss Aaron.

Before Aaron left to go back to Scott, we decided it was time to get rid of the Chevy station wagon; it was about done. So we went to Sheehy Ford in Marlo Heights to try to trade it in for a new one.

Voilà, the power of the military ID cards. We were given five hundred dollars for the Chevy and credit instantly. That Chevy was done and probably worth nothing. I'm sure it was rolled into the price of the new station wagon. We drove away in our brand-new dark green Ford LTD station wagon. Now all of our automobiles were brand new.

# Chapter Forty-Three: Trying to Get Back on Track

Tonya and Julie magically showed up. When I walked into the house after arriving home from work, they were in the kitchen with Karmentrina. Although it was nice seeing them, I had plenty of questions, but I kept them to myself for the time being.

Karmentrina asked me if they both could spend the night, and I replied, "What about school?"

When we left from Maryland to re-locate to Illinois, they were all in the tenth grade. Both girls were older than Karmentrina, but when they arrived in the States and started school while living on Andrews AFB, they were put back a grade. Two years ago, when they both relocated back overseas, they were put up a grade and so graduated a year before Karmentrina did.

A few days went by and the girls were still staying at the house, so I asked Karmentrina why, and she told me that Julie's parents were still back in the Philippines, and Tonya's parents were in Philadelphia.

Aaron came home on weekends, and early one morning when he arrived in his uniform, it had an extra stripe. I noticed it right away and said, "Congrats, Technical Sargent (TSGT) Aaron Edward Stockton, you finally made it to E6."

I kissed him, and we hugged. He continued to the kitchen, and the girls were in their pajamas in the kitchen eating. He came down to our bedroom where I was folding laundry and asked why Julie and Tonya were still there because he saw them the previous weekend. I told him that they lived with us and they were sharing Kevin's old room while he was away in Job Corp.

I explained to him about their family situation, and he said it was okay with him if it was okay with me.

# Chapter Forty-Four: People Moving in People Moving Out

Fall of 1986 - It seemed that I was working all the time. I just never had enough money, and if that was not enough for me, Bonita called and asked to stay with us for a few weeks until she and Mike and her kids could move into their apartment.

I was thinking, *What could a few weeks hurt?* and I told her it was okay. She opted to drive her kids to their schools. Our house was full, and I could not wait for the three weeks to pass. It did, and I thought her issue was ironed out. Boy was I wrong! Bonita called because she was having problems with Sean and Mike's relationship. Sean was not going to accept taking orders from Mike, who was not his father or stepfather as of that time and never would be, as far as Sean was concerned.

I told Bonita to let Sean stay with me and go to school from my address. She gave me paperwork to allow Sean to stay with me. He would go to Douglass High School with Karmentrina and Keenan. I thought we had our house back in some kind of order when my nephew Bernard called to see if he could come to Maryland and stay with us until he found a job and got his own place.

I was working agency at Southern Maryland Hospital and had some contacts. I was able to help him to land a job in the kitchen. I would provide his transportation. Well, that worked out well: He left to go back to York after about three months. He was a nephew that Mom had raised. I knew he did not expect to come with me and not work.

My phone was ringing off the hook! What now? It was Aunt Marilyn, who needed a place to stay temporarily. Aunt Marilyn was a white woman who had married and divorced my mom's younger brother. She gave up her apartment in Baltimore because she did not want to sign a new lease. She was retiring soon from an auto insurance company and moving back to Pennsylvania.

Aunt Marilyn was a part-time court reporter and needed quiet space, so she shared Karmentrina's room. My siblings and I were all close to her before and after the divorce. I let Aaron know about all of the family who were at the house, and he could not believe it.

He was quiet for a few moments and said to me, "Sandra, you cannot save everyone, they have to go."

Now I was quiet because I knew he was right, and I told him that everyone would be gone before the holidays, and they were.

Bonita came over often to sit and hang out with Marilyn. One Saturday they wanted to borrow the station wagon to run some errands, and I let them. They had the nerve to get into a wreck. They promised to fix my station wagon, which never happened. A cost I had to absorb because I was so damn trusting, and I did not want Aaron to come home and see the car like that.

The three car notes were killing me. I got behind on the payments for the station wagon, and Ford was calling me every day. There was no caller ID at that time, so I gave Sean the job of answering the telephone calls. I gave him permission to handle those calls. I hid the station wagon at a friend's house until I caught up on the payments. I was trying to decide to either pay up the mortgage note or the car note. I was behind on both. I had a sister whom I asked to help me because I knew she had come into some money, but she refused. I was so hurt.

I did not have that many options, and I chose not to worry Aaron, for he was home all the time.

I finally went to a friend of mine who loaned me the money to get out of that financial situation. I repaid my friend back in sixty days, as I'd told my sister I would repay her. I was so happy when the bill collectors stopped calling me. I was working around the clock with my permanent job and agency nursing for extra shifts. I was under water.

You would think that Aaron would check with me before he would decide to take over payments on a three-bedroom mobile home from an airman who was leaving Scott. He told me happily on one of his weekend visits. I just looked at him and started to cry silently.

He said, "Babe, I thought we could find a place to put it and then rent it out to make some money."

Well, it sat in Linthicum, Maryland for the longest in storage while we struggled to pay the payments. We would eventually pay it off while it was in storage.

# Chapter Forty-Five: OH, NO! Not Korea Again

December of 1985 - Aaron called me from Scott one weekday evening and told me he had orders to Korea again. This time at Osan, Korea. I told him that I was under the impression that he had four years at Scott, which meant he had another year there. He told me he had no choice because he wanted to come back to Andrews, and the only way was to take another short tour which would guarantee his returning back to Andrews.

I did not believe him, for he was always going to the Far East. Why not England, Germany, Spain or any country other than Korea? I started to wonder if maybe there was something else in Korea that was calling him back there. I wanted to ask that question, but I chose not to because he told me a long time ago that he would never desert me and my children. I would have to trust and believe in him.

He went on to say that he had to report in ninety days. He would be home with us on leave for twenty-one days prior to leaving in January 1986. The separations seemed to have gotten the best of me. The kids were damn near grown and really finding their own identities. Kimmy Jo and Kevin would both be in their twenties when he returned from that tour. Aaron got off okay to his assignment. Before he left to go to Korea, he asked his friends Pete and Linda if he could count on them to look out for Kimmy Jo while she was in St. Louis attending Webster University. They agreed, and things went well while she was away from home. One thing we would not have to worry about, since neither of us would be in the area.

Karmentrina had four and a half months before graduation. She approached me with wanting to be an exchange student in

Spain, and I told her no way. Then she approached me with going on a senior trip with her classmates to Spain, and I denied her again, mostly out of fear. I knew it would have been a good experience, for she was fluent in Spanish. However, not only was money an issue, but her being there with chaperones who did not know my daughter and whom I did not know.

I offered her a trip to Korea with her dad for the summer. She was disappointed but decided that she wanted to go. Kevin returned home from the Job Corps in early May thinking he was a grown-ass man. He was strongly into the hip-hop music, and he would blast it so loud the house would seem to vibrate. He would open his bedroom window and he would be yelling along with the lyrics.

It got on my last nerve. I was now working as a hemodialysis nurse at Prince George's Doctors Community Hospital and had a bad day. So when I arrived home and pulled into the driveway and heard that hip-hop music blasting from his bedroom window, I went crazy for the moment.

I went into the house put my things down, went directly to Aarons' tool box, picked up a hammer, walked up the stairs to Kevin's room, smashed his equipment into pieces, and threw it all out of the window.

He just stood there looking at me with a deadly stare. I shook that hammer up in his face and said to him, "I wish you would. I brought you into this world, and I would have no problem taking you out of this world if it comes to me or you, so think about that for a moment."

I was worried about the influence Kevin would have on Keenan and Sean, so I decided that I would send Keenan on a trip to Korea with his sister as well. I took both of them to complete applications for their passports. I was told that it would be possible to obtain them in a week if we went to immigrations in downtown Washington, DC.

Keenan was not happy about going, but I gave him no choice. Julie decided to fly back to the Philippines to pursue a love that she had left behind, and they are married today. Tonya stayed on with us, for she was to be a bridesmaid in Bonita and Mike's wedding in August. She and Sean found summer jobs.

When Aaron came home in the middle of June, he had already made travel arrangement for all three of them to travel to Korea a week later. Separating Keenan and Sean was a good idea, and equally important for me to have Keenan away from Kevin for the time being. I was glad that some of the responsibility for raising the kids would now be on Aaron. Lord knows it had been so hard on me!

Aaron worked in outbound assignments and had a direct line to the States where he could call Andrews and they would connect him to our home. I spoke with the kids often.

About three weeks in, I received a long letter from Karmentrina telling me that Dad was living the life in Korea while we were struggling. She told me that Aaron even asked her and her brother for some of their rations.

The next time Aaron called me, I told him about Karmentrina's letter about how good he was doing over there. He apologized and told me that he did not realize that I was struggling so hard. In all fairness, I did not tell him, for I did not want him to worry while he was away. He decided to decrease the amount of his allotment he had coming to himself, and that helped quite a bit.

Karmentrina told me that she and Keenan both had summer jobs. Hers was at the recreation center assigning VHS tapes in and out to service members and their dependents. Keenan had a job in the gym and also DJing at the 9 Grand, a club in Osan. Keenan wrote to me in the middle of July and told me he wanted to come home to attend his Aunt Bonita and Mike's wedding, which was scheduled for August second. He told me that Bonita said he could be in her wedding. I told him I would ask Dad to make the arrangements for him to come home.

Karmentrina decided she would stay the entire summer and did not return with Keenan. She would later tell me that Keenan was mad at her for not coming home with him, for he was afraid to fly for the eighteen hours home alone.

Keenan arrived back in Washington, DC. the end of July. When I picked him up, I asked him how the plane ride was, and he said, "It was a piece of cake, Mom."

"Karmentrina told me you were afraid to fly alone."

He said, "Yeah, right!"

Kimmy Jo would also come home from college. She just showed up at the door with two suitcases for the summer. I said, "Wow, I was not expecting you."

She responded, "I know; I wanted to surprise you."

I told her, "You certainly did that!"

She was a go-getter! She found a job relatively fast at the Lunch Box in Washington, DC and started working and saving her money. She also helped Tonya to get a job there as well. She wanted me to co-sign on a car for her, and even though I was reluctant, I did. I may write about that later on in life. Smile!

# Chapter Forty-Six: Bonita and Mike Got Married

Reminiscing about my wedding to Aaron thirteen years ago. All of my children would attend, except Karmentrina, who remained in Korea. I had hoped that Bonita was going to be as happy as I was on my wedding day. She had been with Mike for five years, playing house. It was time to make it legal, so they did on August second of 1986.

Bonita was so happy in her white wedding gown and Mike in his white tuxedo. They were in wedding heaven. You would have thought it was Keenan's wedding the way he was hyped up about it. I guess he was serious when he told me he did not want to miss it.

Grown-ass Karmentrina told me, "I already attended one wedding of Aunt Bonita's. That one was enough."

It was a classic wedding of rainbow colors. The ushers were Keenan Wynn dressed in a white tuxedo with a burgundy bowtie and cummerbund and Sean in white tuxedo with a pink bowtie and matching cummerbund. Bucky gave Bonita away as he gave me away at my wedding. He wore a white tuxedo with a gold bowtie and matching cummerbund to match the groom's outfit.

Wayne Swan, the groom's brother, was the best man, and he wore a white tuxedo with a baby blue bowtie and matching cummerbund. The bridesmaids—Tameca, Lugenia, Barronita, and Tonya—wore dresses in full color matching the cummerbund of their escorts. Cora Mae was the flower girl, and she wore a light purple dress. Tonya (Tameka's mom) wore white; she was the maid of honor. Kimmy Jo wore bright yellow and sang "Endless Love" by Dianna Ross and Lionel Richie. Yes, Kimmy Jo brought everyone to tears.

Our whole immediate family from York was in attendance, including my guardian and her children, Portia, Wendy, and James Owens. My husband's family, mom, sister and one brother attended as well. Mom, Mr. Bill, and I were profiling. Yes! I had the nerve to wear white, and as broke as my ass was, I would give them an awesome gift.

All of the guests were dressed to impress. In spite of their happy union, Sean was not ready to live with his stepfather just yet. They would stay married and raise Barronita and Cora Mae. We saw each other frequently, for we only lived about twenty minutes from each other near Andrews AFB.

# Chapter Forty-Seven: Why Are the Police Calling Me?

Aaron called to let me know that I would need to pick Karmentrina up from the airport in Baltimore because she would be returning home the first week of September. He told me that Karmentrina chose to skip Bonita's wedding because she ran into an old flame from Scott AFB, and they were hanging out a lot until he left in the middle of August.

I picked her up without incidence and drove back to Upper Marlboro. The fall of 1986, Karmentrina would start acting out of her element. I was on the night shift one night and received a call from the Prince George's County Police Department (PGCPD). The officer on the other end said who he was and told me that Karmentrina and her friend had been arrested for a robbery gone bad plot.

He told me that he called me because he knew that they were in no way criminals. I was so angry! Karmentrina always tried to act like a thug, watching Scar Face too many times to count and any other crime movies she could get her little hands on. I would have banked money on the whole situation being Karmentrina's idea. She was so damn grown.

He told me that they would be put in jail at the PGCPD in Upper Marlboro, Maryland. They would see the judge in the morning and would most likely get bail. I was in a panic state, worrying about her. I did not give a damn about whoever her friend was at that moment. I called a friend of mine to help me figure out what to do. I had never come up against this type of issue.

My friend told me that he would come to my house to pick me up about eleven in the morning so we could go to the PGCPD to see if she was given bail. Then he went on to say that we would have to find someone who would be willing to bail her because women were a risk.

I asked why, and he responded, "They can change up things, like their name, their look, etc." He asked if I was willing to put up my house to get her out, with the risk that I would lose it if she ran. I told him that the only running she would do would be from me trying to beat her down like a stranger.

When I arrived home from work, Keenan and Sean were both home where they were supposed to be. Just who in the hell was Karmentrina with?

We went to Upper Marlboro and found out that she and her friend had gotten bail. We found someone who would bail her. I took it upon myself to bail her friend out as well. After putting up the bail money, we had to wait about forty minutes for them to be released. We went around the corner to the 7-11 corner store and purchased donuts and coffee; my friend opted for a Pepsi. We stayed parked there for about thirty minutes then drove back around to the jail house to wait for them.

They were both standing there looking like they had just lost their best friend. I now knew who her friend was—that child always followed whatever Karmentrina said. So sad!

We pulled up to them, and I shouted out of the window for them both to get into the car. I looked up into the rearview mirror and they were both looking up, and I said; "Don't say a fucking thing to me."

I told Karmentrina's friend that she could clean up at the house and then I would be taking her home. I warned her to tell her mom because I was going to check with her. I then raised my voice and said, "You better not jump bail and make me lose my house."

She was crying and apologizing. Karmentrina was not saying anything, but her quietness let me know that she did not know what to expect from me. I was never in jeopardy of losing my house because their bail was so low. My little secret! I just had to give up a very small amount of money to bail them both out.

On arrival to our house, I sent Karmentrina to her room and told all of the kids that I had just bailed her criminal ass and her girlfriend out of jail. I told Karmentrina that I would be calling her dad about the arrest. He would be the one going to court with her, not me. After all, she was Daddy's girl.

After I calmed down, I decided not to call Aaron. I finally got through that ordeal when Keenan was expelled permanently from Douglass Senior High School for fighting a white boy in gym class. I was told that Keenan picked up something to hit the boy with but did not hit him. Just threatened him. I was told that school policy stated that one could not threaten to hurt another person of bodily harm in any way, shape, or form.

I got a lawyer to help me fight the school, but found out that he would not be able to help because that incident was the third time that Keenan had been in trouble. I told the lawyer that I was never notified, and he showed me paperwork with supposedly, my signature. I could have just wrung Karmentrina's neck for signing my name. I am sure he begged her so I would not find out. If I had known, maybe the expulsion would have been avoided. I found out later that she was writing notes for Sean as well, but he listened and stayed out of trouble.

# Chapter Forty-Eight: Trouble Don't Last Always

I told Karmentrina that she and her friend now had a court date scheduled. She asked me how I knew, and I told her that I opened the letter that was addressed to her from the courts.

She looked over at me and said, "Mom, people go to jail for opening up mail that does not belong to them."

I took a sharp-sided look at her and said, "I know, people go to jail for robberies.

She responded, "Darn, Mom, I was only kidding."

I said, "I thought so!" I told her that I found out how she could have her record expunged once court was over and that her dad would be the one presenting to the courts with her to have that done.

Court ended up with probation for a year and three months' community service at the courthouse. She told me that she was so sorry, and I would not have to worry about her, for she had learned her lesson.

Karmentrina changed tremendously and was a big help to me at the house. I was happy about that because Kevin was being difficult right then, trying to figure out his manhood.

Aaron would follow Karmentrina home from Korea in March 1987. Four more months, give or take a day or so, and he would be at the door. Karmentrina got a job at the Lunch Box in Washington, DC, but a different location than where Kimmy Jo worked.

Moving forward, Karmentrina kept her word and stayed out of trouble, as far as I knew. She would work several different jobs to include Hecht's Department Stores but not limited to retail. She always had a job.

One day I was on duty at P. G. Doctors Hospital to make a delivery. She called me, and I walked over to the building where she was making a delivery. She was driving a big moving truck, and Tonya was her assistant.

I was like, "Who in the heck let you drive this big truck?"

Karmentrina said in her authoritative voice, "I got this, Mom, really!"

The kids were becoming their own persons right in front of my eyes, and they were who they were going to be. I came home from work one evening in September and took the scenic route to our house in order to come down the hill instead of going up the hill. On the drive down the hill, I noticed that Aaron's gray Horizon had been wrecked.

I was crazy with anger when I walked into the house, yelling, "What happened to Dad's car?"

Keenan was in the family room with Sean watching TV. He yelled, "Mom, me and Sean do not have a driver's license," and Karmentrina came into the room and said, "Mom, you know I only have permission to drive your gold Horizon, and you have been driving it."

Kimmy Jo must have heard the conversation. She walked past me toward the front door and said, "Not me; I got a car! See you later, Mom."

So now I knew that Kevin had taken the car without permission, and I would find out through childhood interrogation of Keenan and Sean that he had been taking the car on many occasions.

Aaron called soon after that car incident and asked me to come over to Korea with him during the Christmas break and fly back with him, for he was going to be reassigned back to the United States of America. He said we could go to the Philippines on the way back and stay a week with friends whom I met through him back at Andrews AFB. He also said that we could go from there to Hawaii before we returned home.

He would be stationed back in Maryland but not at Andrews AFB. He would be assigned special duty at the Bethesda Naval University of the Health Sciences, where all military physicians trained. I was excited but not that excited about being in the air for eighteen hours. Lord, don't let Keenan Wynn and Karmentrina know I was a little scared.

I agreed to go, but I would hope that Kevin Scott would not kill his little sister, Karmentrina, in my absence. They were always at each other's throats since he returned from Job Corps. Aaron told me he would get my ticket on his end in Korea because it would be cheaper. I liked cheaper.

The car issue was on my mind now more than ever. That car must be repaired before I left for Korea so that Aaron did not find out about Kevin taking it without my permission. I knew that I would not be able to go through our insurance company, for I would have to report the car stolen by him.

I drove the car to a mechanic, body and fender shop to find out the cost of the repairs. The cost was to be about seven hundred and fifty dollars, something that would stress me financially. I was already robbing Peter to pay Paul, but I knew I had to get it done, and I did. I cashed in saving bonds that I had saved for the kids when they were much younger. I was going to use them for a rainy day, and this was more than a rainy day. It was raining cats and dogs!

When the car was repaired, it looked brand new. No way Aaron would be able to tell that the car had been wrecked. I touched bases with Bonita to let her know that I was going to go away for about four weeks, and I needed her to check on the kids once a week. They were old enough to be left alone. Kimmy Jo was over twenty-one and home, but she was always doing things with her singing group and working. I gave Karmentrina the phone number to a friend that would assist her if anything went wrong in the house. Always some issues in the house. I made sure that all of the kids knew how to turn off the water to the entire house if anything started to leak, something that Doug taught me a long time ago when we lived on Prospect Street. I told Keenan and Sean that they had to be responsible and go to school like they were supposed to.

# Chapter Forty-Nine: Sandra's Trip to Korea - Winter of 1987

My travel day came up, and I was in the airport as nervous as ever thinking about that trip. This would be a four-week trip, two weeks in Korea, one week in the Philippines, and one week in Hawaii. I took a plane from Washington, DC to Missouri, where I changed planes.

When I boarded the Korean jumbo jet airliner, I was amazed. It was so big, nothing like the size of the plane I'd just transferred from. I found my seat and was glad I had an aisle seat. There were hundreds of seats and filled with mostly Asian passengers speaking in their native tongue.

Things quieted down just before the safety briefing. The briefing was done in so many languages. It was early morning and we were offered drinks: coffee, tea, and all sorts of juices. Lunch would follow not too long after. The menu was Greek to me, but it was good. There was no cost for food, drinks, or movies.

Soon the message came on in many languages that seat belts could be off. Many of these people must have made this trip before or other overseas trips like it. People were getting in and out of their seats from that point on. I got up often to go pee and to stretch my legs. There was no way I was going to get any clots in my legs.

It was daylight when we left the United States, and we never saw dark again. We were instructed to pull down our window shades when it was nine o'clock pm our time until six am the next morning our time. The US is eleven hours behind Korea. So after eighteen hours when we arrived it was still the same date at nightfall. I found out that we'd crossed the international date line. I did not know what that meant, but would find out later that the international date line serves as the "line of demarcation" between two calendar dates. It was established in the year of 1884, and it passes through the mid-Pacific Ocean and roughly follows a 180 degrees longitude north-south line on the earth.

So all we passengers ever saw was water, water, and more water. I was so amazed at seeing so much water and prayed often on that plane that I would make it to dry land. It would not even matter who could or could not swim, all that water farther than the naked eye could see. I don't think so!

We made a stop in Japan for some customers to deplane and others to board, then we had four more hours to fly into Seoul, Korea. I was so happy when we arrived in country. Getting through customs was another wakeup call as to how they do it in Korea. There were signs everywhere, and I could not read any of them. There was a customs officer who must have seen me looking quite lost, and he came over to me speaking in English; "You American?"

I shook my head affirmative, and he pointed me to the line I was supposed to go through. As I walked over to the line, it was written plain as day in English as to where I was supposed to go. There were so many lines and guards with guns. When I finally reached the customs officers' checkpoint, they asked me where I was going (in English), and I told them to Osan Air Force Base to visit my husband. The customs officer stamped my passport book and then I was directed to some long tables along with my luggage.

I would be told to open my suitcases, and I did. The officers at the table emptied out all of my things on the conveyor belts and rummaged through everything. They had the nerve to push me to the side and tell me to hurry up and put my things back in the suitcases and move on. I was thinking a lot of shit! but I did not say a word. Damn if I was going to be locked up in a foreign country. Everyone who was clearing customs were ushered to a different opening, where there seemed to be millions of people holding up signs.

I finally spotted a sign that had my name on it. I looked harder and saw Aaron. He had a big smile on his face, as did I. I was so happy to reach him after all that I had endured getting to him. I must say it was a learning experience. I had so many questions, and he was trying to answer me. We took my two suitcases outside to an awaiting bus that was going to Osan AFB. It was bitter cold outside.

Aaron told me that it was a bus that transported military members and their dependents to and from the airport for ten dollars round trip. On the way to the base, I told Aaron about Karmentrina's arrest. He was in disbelief! I told him to relax, that things were taken care of, but he would have to go to court with her because I was not going.

That being said, Aaron told me the plans that he had for us. We would go to his apartment for me to get settled and meet some of his friends. There was a foul odor when we got off of the bus, almost unbearable to me. Aaron said to me, "You will get used to it in a few days or so." He told me that the odor was from their septic conditions, and they did not have a good system as we had in the US.

Later that evening when his friends showed up and were all hanging around drinking, we would leave to go to Miss Lee McDonald food stand outside of his apartment to get something to eat. It was so cold outside, and I really did not want to go, but Aaron and his friends insisted that I go with them. I did want to see what the food stand was all about.

Well, it was not McDonald's, that was for sure. They all dug right in like they were eating the best burgers ever. I did not eat the food. I was not feeling the taste of the burger and fries. For all I knew it could have been dog burgers. I had heard that Koreans eat dog meat.

I was hungry so Aaron walked me to another place to get shrimp fried rice. When we walked into the restaurant, there were cats running all over the damn place. Aaron ordered shrimp fried rice for me. When our order was done it looked like an upside-down cake. I questioned the waitress about the order and that it did not look like shrimp fried rice. The owner came out and told me that it was indeed shrimp fried rice and what we get in the US was their version and not authentic Korean shrimp fried rice.

We sat down to eat, but I was not feeling it with them cats running around. So we left and took the food with us back to the apartment, where Aaron's friends were still hanging around. Once I tasted the food, there was no denying that it was delicious. That would be my spot for shrimp fired rice while in Korea.

After eating our food and all of the friends had left to go wherever they were going, we got ready for bed. Aaron had a futon bed which I went to lie down on, but he told me no, we were going to sleep on the floor because the futon bed was too small for both of us. I was thinking that he must have been out of his mind after riding eighteen hours sitting in a seat on a plane, I needed to stretch out. He went on to take the blankets to the living room and put them on the floor with pillows.

To my surprise, it was so comfortable and warm. I said, "Wow! Is heat coming from the floor?"

He responded, "Yes, the floors are heated."

That was where he usually slept, it was such a good sleep. That was our bed for the time left in Korea, and it was so cozy.

The next morning, Aaron had laid out plans for us to go shopping in the local markets. We first went out to get breakfast, and I spotted a Dunkin Donuts Store and asked to go there. I ordered a large hot chocolate and two cinnamon cake donuts. It was smelling so good in the shop. Aaron ordered black coffee.

I sipped my hot chocolate and took a bite of one of my donuts and damn near vomited. It did not taste like any donut I had ever eaten in the USA. I learned quickly that the bread and dough in Korea was nothing like in the States. I just could not eat it.

I would soon become hooked on the Korean pastries that we purchased in some of the bakeries near Aaron's apartment. Aaron decided that we would jump on a bus that went to the base to the dining hall. That was an ordeal. He said the bus was called the screamer. I soon found out what that meant. We walked to the main street about a block away and waited for the bus to take us to the base.

It arrived, and Korean nationals and military members with their families were waiting in a big crowd. When the bus stopped, everyone pushed their way on. It was so crowded you could feel people's breath in your face. The odor on the bus was horrific. Aaron told me it was the smell of kimchi.

I would find out that kimchi is the heart and soul of Korean cooking. Kimchi is fermented cabbage, kind of like sauerkraut, but with Korean flavors of garlic and Korean chilies. I would become fond of kimchi and would no longer be bothered by the smell.

We were packed in there like sardines. I asked Aaron if the bus ride was free because no one had paid, just pushed their way on. He told me it was not free, and someone would be collecting. A young Korean girl made her way through the bus and collected everyone's money. I did not know how she knew if she received bus fare from everyone, but obviously, she knew.

She was shaking people down who were trying not to pay, and it was not the soldiers. The bus was going so fast. There were no street signs that I could see, and he was taking corners like the bus was going to turn over. People were screaming and clutching on to each other for dear life. I was so happy to get off of that bus and refused to ride it for the next two weeks while we were going to be in country. Karmentrina and Keenan Wynn had told me about riding the screamer to and from work. Now I understood what they meant.

We walked off base to the markets, and there was so much to see. Street food, vintage clothing, oriental medicine, coffee, fruit and vegetable stands, T-shirts, sneakers, any brand for $10 to $15, poultry stands with chickens hanging from hooks, pig heads laid out on tables, little dogs in cages (which I heard was a delicacy), all kinds of fish and seafood, kimchi, a Korean dish of spicy pickled cabbage which I came to love with rice. Children and dogs were everywhere.

I observed little kids just pulling down their pants and squatting to have a bowel movement and or peeing whenever they needed to. No one paid any attention to them but me; even Aaron was acclimated to it and said nothing. It was strange hearing all the Korean nationals speaking their language in the open markets. Now I knew what it felt like when people could not understand me when they were not bilingual. We were definitely in the minority.

The markets became a daily thing for us. I loved going to them and soon went without Aaron. I shopped and purchased several pieces of Korean furniture because I knew the military was going to do a move back to the States for Aaron, so I had a ball.

Later on in the second week, we had dinner at the home of one of Aaron's military coworkers. He was from India. He was on a long tour, so his family was in country with him. We went to his home off base, not far from where Aaron was staying. We arrived and were greeted. All were very pleasant to us. They took our coats and escorted us to the room where dinner was going to be served.

Everyone had to sit on the floor cross-legged. The Indian tradition of this style of eating was to increase digestion. They felt one would have to bend down to eat his or her food and then sit up to chew and swallow. The constant back and forth movement of the head and chest would cause the muscles of the abdomen to increase stomach acid, making it much easier for one to digest their food.

There were several family members there, including the friend's wife, mother, father, and two children. The first to be served was what I thought was some kind of soup. The bowls were placed on the table that spun around. One would remove a bowl from the spinning turntable and place it in front of themselves. I looked up at the woman placing the food on the turntable and asked for a spoon and she said what for? I told her it was for my soup. Now I had an audience! She told me I was to drink from the bowl. It was mulligatawny (a spicy meat or chicken soup made in India), but I could have a spoon. Apparently, we were to drink from the bowl, but I was not feeling that. I started to dip my spoon into the soup, and I thought I saw an eyeball looking up at me. I nudged Aaron under the table and told him something was in my broth, and he told me it was octopus.

I never felt like Aaron had any taste buds, for he always liked everything. He slurped his right down, and as soon as he was done, I switched my bowl with his, and he slurped that down as well. Lord knows I would not have gotten past them eyeballs looking up at me.

Even though we had no utensils and had to eat the chicken curry, rice, and flatbread with our fingers, it was delicious. To go along with the meal, we had water and wine. It was a good experience; I now knew not to ask for a spoon at an Indian dinner.

Later on in the evening, we went to a club where many service members hung out with the Korean locals who were into the club life. It seemed like I had to pee as soon as we had arrived there. A Korean female friend of the group, Suki, showed me the way to the bathroom.

I was in culture shock when I walked into the bathroom. There were several open stalls with porcelain holes in the floor. Squatter toilets which were found in areas of Korea were not yet modernized. There was no toilet paper in sight; thank God I only had to pee. My problem was balancing myself over the hole in the floor in a squatting position, avoiding falling into it. There was cold running water to clean one's hands, but no soap in sight. I was so glad that there was a normal toilet that flushed at Aaron's apartment and a shower with a pull string to regulate the water.

The club DJ played all American music, and the owner, Mr. Kim had a down-home menu with collard greens, rice, and pig feet. His friends would find their way there to hang out with us until four in the morning. I was so tired, for I went to bed at nine o'clock back in the States whenever I was not working the night shift.

The two weeks were winding down, and it would be soon time for us to fly to the Philippines to visit some other military friends of ours, Kenny and Diane at Clark AFB. Just a day or so before we were to leave Korea, a male friend of ours whom we'd met in the USA through his wife, one of my nursing colleagues, came in from the USA. They were visiting family.

He got in touch with Aaron easily, for Seoul was his home. He took us downtown to a real Korean restaurant. It was beautiful. He ordered a spread of food for our table. I had some kind of kimchi with rice; I knew what that was. There was what I thought was a cake sitting on the table and I took a big slice. When I put that fork in my mouth with what I thought was cake, I wanted to spit, but I did not. Somehow, I swallowed it and let it sit there while we were all talking. Smart-ass Aaron asked me if I was finished and I said to both of them; "I don't know why I cut that cake, I am so full, I could not eat another bite of anything."

Aaron's friend started to laugh and said to us, "That is tofu."

I knew I would never touch that ever again. Of course, Aaron cut a piece and ate it, telling me it was something I would have to develop a taste for. I was thinking, *Not in this life!*

# Chapter Fifty: Hello Pampanga, Philippines

It was time to ride the bus from the base to the Korean airport to board our plane to the Philippines. I was ready to leave Korea, and I knew Aaron was as well. It would be a three hour and forty-five-minute flight compared to eighteen hours flying over international daylight to get to Korea.

Getting out of Korea was very different from my arrival in the country. They directed us to outgoing flights, checked and stamped our passports, and sent us on our way. There was no delay in getting our flight. We arrived on a beautiful day that was sunny and very hot. We cleared customs with no issues and took a bus to the terminal we needed to reach.

When we got off of the bus there were many people trying to take our suitcases from us, offering to carry them for money. Aaron kept telling them no. We finally entered the terminal, and it looked like we'd just stepped into another world. I had to go to the bathroom and spotted the sign *banyo* with a female picture on the door. Aaron reminded me to get the roll of toilet paper from my carry-on bag.

Once I entered, I knew why. There was no toilet paper to be found, but they had flushable toilets and trash cans next to the toilets to put toilet paper into after wiping. There was water and soap to clean one's hands.

We exited out of another door to catch a taxi to Clark AFB. Kenny and Diane gave us instructions on how to get to the base. Aaron told me to hold on to my purse and bags tightly because they could be snatched. There were cars, taxis and three-wheeler carts everywhere, available for transportation. Little kids were all over the place trying to peddle Juicy Fruit chewing gum and sodas or begging for pennies. Aaron told me not to reach to give or buy anything from them, for they would bombard us for money. We finally got into one of the taxis, which gave us a fifteen-dollar rate to get us to Clark, AFB. The streets were so crowded and narrow, it seemed like it took us forever to get to the base.

We finally made it to the gate and called Kenny, who came to pick us up. We had not seen each other for about two years, for they had gotten orders to Clark one year before Aaron got orders to Korea. It was nice to get to their quarters and just sit down and relax after such an ordeal. We just relaxed that day and evening and listened to the plans that they made for us. I was excited.

The next morning when we came out of our room, there was a woman in the kitchen cooking breakfast, and it was not Diane. Diane soon followed and entered the kitchen, telling us that the lady was their maid. Breakfast was made for all three of us, since Kenny had already left for work. Diane told Aaron that she would be taking me downtown to shop, and he was okay with it and said he would check out the base, for he had previously been there on a temporary assignment but never any long period of time.

Diane gave him a house key, and we left. It was a fun day seeing all of the shops and visiting the fresh air markets. Diane wanted to go to a shop where she had something on layaway, but it was a little too far to walk. So she hired a three-wheeler cart and told the driver where we were going and he told her it would be ten dollars. Along the way, she had him stop for a few minutes for something. We hopped back on and continued on our journey. When we got out of the cart, she gave the driver a US ten-dollar bill, and he told her she owed him five dollars more because she'd stopped along the way.

Diane refused to give him any more money, and they started to argue about it. She came out with her New York defensive bag.

A few minutes later, two Philippine police officers showed up to try to solve the issue. I was nervous and decided that I would give the man the five dollars, and all turned out okay. Diane told me that I should have not paid him, for he was getting nothing more than we agreed upon. I would find out later when we arrived back at her house that she had been in an argument before and ended up in a holding cell. Her husband's unit had to get her out. I was damn glad I paid the five dollars extra; Lord knows I would not have done well in a holding cell in that country or any other country.

We all went clubbing the next evening at the world-famous Nipa Hut, an icon of Philippine culture. I had never been in such a club before. We arrived to find several young boys standing on the outside of the club. They approached Kenny to tell him they would watch his car. He picked one of the boys and gave five dollars to him and told the boy he would give him another five dollars when we came out of the club. Kenny said that was a necessary cost because if you did not pay anyone to keep an eye on your car, it might not be there when you returned.

The club was packed. The windows were open; there was no air conditioning. The girls would dance on the bar with numbers attached to their bikinis. We found a table in the back of the room, and I found out rather quickly why that was the choice. The soldiers who sat at the bar were engaging in sexual acts in front of everyone. Others would choose the girl they wanted by the number and left out of the main room to somewhere else.

I asked Kenny, "What if someone's commander came into the club and saw that kind of behavior. What would happen?"

He said, "Nothing. There is my first sergeant sitting directly in the middle of the bar." He and Aaron just laughed and said, "Welcome to the Nipa Hut."

We stayed there for about one hour and a half and left the club to bar hop. We visited another club called Jacks. There were so many young girls and very few males. They did live shows and could imitate any singer in the US. They did Michael Jackson's "Thriller," and if I had not known they were imitators on stage, you could have fooled me. They imitated him and his dancers to perfection. One young lady imitated Janet Jackson; she even looked like her. It was an awesome show.

The next day we stayed on the base because I wanted to do our laundry, and they had a washer and dryer. When I woke up in the morning, the maid had already done our laundry that I put in the laundry room the night before. I told the maid she did not have to do that, and I offered her some money which she refused, telling me the laundry was her job.

I told Aaron we needed a maid when we returned home, and he responded, "You got jokes."

Aaron and I went shopping on the base two days before we left and purchased one large fish tank and one small fish tank that he had spotted earlier in the week. Kenny agreed to have it shipped back to the States for us. We would be leaving in a day, bound for Hawaii. Although I was not looking forward to the twelve-hour fight, we were both excited, for neither one of us had ever visited there before.

# Chapter Fifty-One: Hawaii Bound

Leaving the airport in the Philippines shocked us both. It was like there were two different worlds there. When we left the exit side, it was clean and modern with toilet paper in the bathrooms compared to the area where we entered the country. Getting through customs was a breeze. We flew out on a Korean airliner. They fed us well during the trip.

It was night when we arrived in Hawaii. We had reservations for seven days at the Hawaiian Hilton Village Hotel with a sprawling beach front, spa, restaurants, and other water activities. We were assigned to a suite on the fourteenth floor. That made me so nervous, for I am so afraid of heights.

The next morning, we went down to the front desk and asked for a suite on a lower floor and were offered one on the second floor. I was happy with that until we went to the newly assigned suite and looked out of the window. It seemed like it was still one hundred feet from the ground. It was all they had, and I would have to adjust.

We slept well that night and spent most of the next day on the beach in back of the hotel. Our hotel was right next to the Hale Koa military hotel, which is for military members and their dependents. We were not able to book in there, for they had no openings. However, because we were a military family, we could enter and enjoy the live bands and the restaurants, which were a little cheaper than the restaurants in the Hawaiian Hilton Village Hotel.

We spent time on the beach every evening. During the day hours, we visited places of interest and shopped. Aaron loved swimming. I kept him company and put my feet in the water a few times. Day two, we took a trip by taxi to Hickam Air Force Base, Honolulu, which was twelve miles from the hotel. We always made it a point to visit military installations whenever we were near one during our travels. On that same day, we visited Pearl Harbor, located on the island of Oahu, where 353 Japanese bombers attacked the United States naval base on the island waterway. Nineteen ships and 188 aircraft were destroyed, killing over 2000 Americans. The Japanese attacked the US early in the morning of December 1941, also hitting a mess hall during breakfast with a total loss of 121 men killed, 274 wounded, and 37 missing on the base. The United States was caught off guard, and military history tells us of the retaliation.

The USS Arizona Museum and the Pearl Harbor Aviation Museum were most interesting as well as all of the other museums there. There was so much history.

Day three, we spent the day shopping in Korean shops in Oahu. Koreans make up 1.6 percent of Hawaii's population. It felt like we were still in Korea. We entered a shop to look at what we thought were ivory statues. We knew we would not be able to afford them; however, we wanted to look at them close up.

To our surprise, when we entered the store to inquire about them, we were told by an elderly Korean man that the carvings were carved from whale bones and they were not expensive, so you know I had to have at least one of them, but the one I wanted came in a set, so I had to buy the set.

Aaron asked me to be careful with getting things to take home, for we may not be able to take them on the plane with us. I had forgotten about that and told him, no problem.

Day four, we went to the front desk of the hotel to find out where the post office was, so we could send some of our things home ahead of us. The postage cost almost as much as our items. That evening on the beach, I told Aaron I was homesick and wanted to go home. It had been almost a month since I'd left home to make the trip.

He looked at me and said, "No problem, babe. We can go to the airport and try to change our flights."

The next morning, day five, early in the morning, we took that trip to the airport to try to change our flights. We were in luck, somewhat. We could get out a day earlier but not on the same flight. One flight on United was leaving at ten o'clock in the morning going to Washington, DC, and one was leaving at two o'clock in the afternoon going to Baltimore.

We decided that I would leave on the early flight and Aaron would take the later one. We would be home a day earlier. It was a ten hour and forty-four-minute flight. We both agreed that I would pick him up in Baltimore since I would get there about four hours ahead of him. I was so happy to be going home early. I was exhausted from my travels. Day six, we were both home.

# Chapter Fifty-Two: Life Will Teach Your Children

It was February, and the weather was cold. I was now wishing for the warm sun in the Philippines and Hawaii. It was indeed a great vacation, and spending it with Aaron was like another honeymoon.

Karmentrina and some of her girlfriends had picked up jobs at the Jiffy Sub Shop across from Andrews. Kimmy Jo was back at college, and Kevin was jobless. He told me that he had been looking but could not find anything. His dad asked him if he had tried the fast-food restaurants, and he told him that he did not want that kind of job.

Aaron and I looked at each other, and I changed the subject to asking Keenan and Sean how school was going. They both said there were no problems in school. Sean was at Douglass Senior High School and Keenan at Croom Vocational High School. They would be out of school for the summer in about three and half months. Kevin obtained a few different jobs but did not hold on to any of them permanently.

Kimmy Jo called me and told me that some girl in York named Ruby Mitchell was pregnant by Keenan and that she was four years older than him. I was almost in shock, for Keenan was still in school and had no means to take care of a child.

I went up to Keenan's room to speak with him about it and indeed he said it was true and that the baby was due in May. I was livid! I always educated all of my children on the subject of drugs, sex, babies, and teenage parenthood. I asked him how in the hell did he have time to go to York to get some girl pregnant and he replied, "Kevin took me and Sean to York when he was taking the car."

I told Keenan that Dad and I would have to meet this girl, for we would have to help to support the baby until he would be able to contribute. That night at bedtime, I spilled the beans to Aaron.

He said thank God it was not one of our girls being pregnant. I reminded him that I did not want my sons to be teen fathers either, and they knew that I preached to them about teenage parenting. I called Mom and she told me that I should be grateful that he was not younger. He was eighteen and old enough to vote and buy cigarettes and pay taxes if he were to work. I agreed!

Things seemed to be falling into place when I received a call from Tracey asking me if she and Caprisha could come home for a while, and of course I could not say no to her. Aaron was assigned as planned to Andrews AFB, but attached to Bethesda at Uniformed Services University, Health Sciences Department, a special duty assignment. I started filling up my work schedule with agency nursing, which was easy, for there was a shortage of nurses in the area.

June was upon us, and both boys were promoted to the next grade. The kids were not really performing together at that time, but Kimmy Jo was active with her singing career. She showed up for the summer break May of 1987, but this time she told me that she was not returning back to college, and I asked her why? Miss thang told me that she did not need college to be a professional singer and to make it big out on the world stage as a prominent vocalist.

I am always thinking to myself! *No, she did not just say that to me, after all of the money I sent to that school for the past two years to keep her ass in college.* She soon moved into Amberwood Apartments with an old girlfriend from Andrews AFB, not too far from the house.

Soon after Kimmy Jo came home from college, Aaron's brother Michael (rest in peace) ,who was then in the Philippines, would notify him that he wanted to come to Maryland to find a job, for he was getting out of the military services. Their sister Helena told him he would easily find a job with his experiences in communication technology and his top-secret security clearance.

There was not enough room at Helena's house, and he thought we could accommodate them for a short period of time. How could I deny them when half of my family lived with us off and on? Michael would soon arrive with his wife and five children, one boy and four girls. They were beautiful children. All younger than our kids.

The only available space in our home at that time was Kimmy Jo's old room and the basement. They said they would make it work. Michael's wife Sung Nook (rest in peace) did not speak very much English; she was Thai. Aaron would go to the schools to assist Michael to register their kids. They completed the task.

About a week later, the youngest one would come home with a note from the school nurse telling Michael that she had head lice and would not be permitted back into school until she was free of them. I purchased the medicated shampoo and treated all of the children as a precaution. We had to cut the little ones' hair, for it was so long and thick. That was soon taken care of, and she went back to school.

Now we had to deal with his wife's addiction problem to cocaine. I did not know what to do for that, and Michael said that she would need a lot of Pepsi sodas. I did not know what that would do for her, but we purchased them.

Michael did not seem to have any money. I did not know why. Maybe he was waiting for his retirement to come through from the military. Aaron had told me that he was in for twenty years. I could hear them up all hours of the night and going in and out of the front door. I assumed she was dealing with withdrawal from the cocaine. There was a fishing lake close to us, and they spotted it one day. They started going fishing almost every day. Sung Nook would make the most delicious Thai dishes with fish cooked in so many different ways. She could take a small piece of beef and fish with rice and feed both families. We purchased Thai rice like Michael asked us to get.

About two months in, I had enough of the Thai dishes. Our entire house was smelling like fish each and every day. Kevin loved the food and would sometimes go fishing with them. Michael was looking for work, and I almost always had to drive him because Aaron was at work during the day.

I was sick of driving him. I agreed that he could use my gold Horizon. I only requested that he and his wife not to smoke in my car. That went right out of the window. About three months in, I saw two cigarette burns in my front car seat. I was so damn mad. I told Aaron that they had to leave; they were costing us so much money. Plus, their son kept taking things out of Keenan's room. Keenan wanted to kill him for taking his new sneakers and wearing them to school. The sneakers were way too big for him. I calmed Keenan down and told him that they did not have the things like he and Karmentrina had.

The older girls were taking things out of Karmen's room as well. One evening after school I caught Karmentrina interrogating the girls. I did not stop her, for the girls needed to know that stealing was not a good thing. Karmentrina got her things back. They never took anything from Kevin's room or our room. We had a lock on our door. The kids did not enter their room any more after the incidents had happened. Their dad had a talk with them.

Aaron and I discussed the cost of living with Michael, and he decided he most likely could not afford to live in the Washington, DC area. Michael decided to move the family to Pittsburg at the end of August with his sister Kaye (rest in peace).

On May the twenty-ninth, our first grandchild was born, a boy, named Keenan Wynn Kearse Jr. Keenan was in York with Ruby when the baby was born. I sent Karmentrina on a trip to York to make sure that the baby was Keenan's. When she called me, she told me to take a chill pill because that baby was surely Keenan's. "It's our baby, Mom!"

Oh! I felt some kind of happiness. I told Aaron and he said, "I guess we are grandparents."

I replied, "I guess so."

Aaron and I went to York to see the baby when he was about two weeks old. He was a spitting image of his father when he was a baby. He was certainly going to be spoiled. Keenan was in York just about every weekend because he was still in school. He was getting used to the idea that he was a dad, and we were getting used to the idea that we were grandparents as well as the kids being aunts and an uncle. The family would now be changed forever, in a good way. We now had Keej, the nickname I gave to Keenan's first-born son.

Kevin would now be twenty-one. He started trying to be the grown man again like when his dad was away on tours. He made the mistake of having a yelling at mom conversation, and Aaron heard him. Aaron approached Kevin and asked him who in the hell did he think he was talking to?

At this stage in Kevin's life, he was towering over Aaron. He looked at Aaron and said, "Dad, Mom is always in my business. She can't tell me what I can and cannot do."

Aaron walked away and went into the kitchen and pulled out some very large trash bags, then proceeded to enter Kevin's bedroom. He emptied all the dresser drawers, took everything of his out of the bathroom and his cologne from the top of the dresser, shoving everything into the trash bags. He dragged everything outside and placed it in the yard and said to Kevin, "Kevin you are right; your mom cannot tell you what to do or not to do in your house. This is not your house. Let us know your mailing address to forward your mail."

Aaron walked away to go back into the house, and I just stood there. Kevin would now start to crumble, whining, yelling to Aaron, "Dad, where am I supposed to go?"

Aaron did not even look back and said to Kevin, "Son, a grown-ass man would figure it out."

I was outside with Kevin, just looking at him with teary eyes. He was so not tough then, and all I saw was my little boy. I went into the house to talk with Aaron, and he would not bend and told me that he always supported my decisions when it came to the kids, but Kevin disrespecting not only his mom but his wife was not going to be tolerated. He also reminded me that he would never want to hurt Kevin and that was what it would come to if he caught Kevin verbally attacking me.

I asked him if Kevin could put his things in the shed and sleep in my car until he figured out what to do, and he agreed. It was hot outside, so I knew Kevin was uncomfortable during the night with that summer heat. I do not know where Kevin went for the day, but most likely with some of his neighborhood friends.

The next day, Aaron came home from work with a fifty-pound bag of white potatoes. He invited Kevin back into the house with his rules. #1. He could not have any friends in the house. #2. He could play his music loud enough to be heard only in his room. #3. He could only have water to drink and potatoes to eat. He was not permitted to cook or eat anything else in the house unless he purchased it. #4. Kevin was told not to let Aaron ever hear him yell at me again, because he would teach him what a man was.

Kevin would soon leave and go to York with his grandmom. Mom called me when he arrived and told me that he was there and that he would have to get a job. He would eventually meet a young Hispanic girl and connect with her. (They would become a permanent fixture.)

# Chapter Fifty-Three: Goodbye, Mr. Bill

Mr. Bill had been ill for about three months before retiring from the Pennsylvania Department of Transportation, PennDOT after sixteen years, on medical leave. He was diagnosed with chronic obstructive pulmonary disease (COPD), a group of lung conditions that causes breathing difficulties.

Being a registered nurse, I knew exactly what that meant. About two weeks before he passed, he was admitted to the York Osteopathic Hospital for breathing issues and a low blood iron level. Mom told me that he had been having rectal bleeding but elected not to tell her about it. He would have more hospital overnight visits. The last time Mom told me that Mr. Bill was in the hospital was July the tenth on a Friday afternoon. I told Mom that Aaron and I would drive up to the hospital to see him on Sunday, because I was scheduled to work on Saturday. She told me to make sure because she did not think Mr. Bill was going to be around much longer.

July twelfth, Mr. Bill passed. It was early on Sunday morning; Aaron and I were still in bed. The phone rang, and it was Tracey. She was at Mom's house. I could tell that she was crying, and she said, "Mom, Mr. Bill just died."

I was speechless and started to cry and told Tracey to let her grandmom know that I was on my way. The man who was there for me and my kids, for my sibling and our mom. The dad who taught me how to drive. I was really going to miss him so very much. As soon as I was off of the phone with Tracey, I phoned Bonita. She was as I was, beyond belief. Aaron and I got out of the house as quickly as possible to go over to pick up Bonita and her husband Mike, for she lived close. I did not think we both should take the drive. On our arrival, all of my siblings were there. Mom was in the dining room sitting at the table along with Mary. She looked so torn, for they had been together for so many years. She would tell us all that she felt that Bill was not going to make it. She told us that when she got the call from the hospital, she was not shocked to hear that he had died. She told us that he must have known also, for he told a nurse to give his wallet to his wife Dorothy, and when she went back to his bed, he had expired.

I would not be able to explain the pain I personally felt hearing of the loss. He was forever Dad to me and my siblings and granddad to our kids. Bonita, Mike, Aaron, and I stayed fairly late. Before we left, Mom and I had a chance to speak alone, and she told me that Mr. Bill did not have any life insurance. She was beside herself with worry. I sat next to my mom and hugged her and told her that she did not have to worry, for Aaron and I would pay for the funeral service, and we took care of it without asking for any help.

Mr. Bill had a yellow Cadillac, and Mom wanted me to take it and sell it for money towards the cost of the funeral. Mom would never learn to drive. We did do that and received enough money for half of the cost that we'd paid out. Aaron wanted to keep it, and I told him no way, for that would certainly cause friction among my siblings, especially Bucky. He understood.

Mr. Bill left behind to also mourn him four sisters in New Jersey, one sister in New York, two brothers, David in Philadelphia, Pennsylvania, and Frank in York, Pennsylvania. Our family would only ever meet Frank and his wife Leona, for they lived in York. Mom gave Mr. Bill an awesome readymade family. After all was over, Mom was home mostly alone because Bubbles was now older and spent most of his time with his girlfriend. I was worried about her, even though I knew all of my siblings were in York. It was not like someone being there all the time with Mom. Mary and her boyfriend

Pop would move in with her soon, as did Pokey for a while with her kids. So that helped me not to worry as much.

# Chapter Fifty-Four: Supporting and Accepting the Choices that the Children Made

Keej was now five months old, and Keenan asked if Ruby, her daughter Ashley, and the Keej could come to live with us because she was having problems with working and caring for the kids. Aaron and I agreed that they could come to live with us, but she and Keenan had to get jobs. I would work out my schedule to care for the two children.

The house was relatively quiet with only Karmentrina, Aaron, me, and our dog Sapphire. Bocious had run away some time ago. He kept scaling our six-foot fence and getting out of the yard. We would always find him at the entry to our development chained to a tree. The lady who lived there said that he always showed up there. And then one day he climbed the fence and we never saw him again.

The whole family fell in love with Ashley, and she was the first child to call us Grandma Sandi and Pop Pop. Things continued to move in a positive way.

I do not know what it was that kept my kids finding boyfriends and girlfriends in York, but Karmentrina told us that she met this fine Hispanic boy named Sergio Rodrigues in York and that he was going to move to Maryland to be with her. I asked her what was her plan, and she told me she was going to get an apartment where Kimmy Jo was living in Forestville, Maryland. She had a plan to pay for the apartment solo until Sergio could get a job. He arrived, and they got an apartment in one of the adult-only buildings. He would find a job working at a liquor store in Oxon Hill, Maryland soon after his arrival.

Early February, Karmentrina told me they were expecting and would have to move from the apartment to another building. They were worried about how they would afford this pregnancy and keep up with their bills. I told her not to get married for she was still her dad's military dependent, and she could go to Malcom Grow Medical Center for her prenatal care and birthing of the baby.

I spoke with Aaron about finding a place to put our mobile home that was sitting in storage at Linthicum, Maryland. We did our research and found a mobile home lot in Alexandria, Virginia at Audubon Estates. We would have them responsible for the lot rent of $275.00 a month and the electric bill. They were happy and so were we that we could help them out. The Air Force moved the mobile home at no cost to us.

Ashley was four years old when she came to Maryland, and it was time to be in preschool. I got her accepted into a half-day program, and I was the one doing the transportation. The first day I took her was hard for both of us. She cried and screamed as if someone was killing her. She was yelling, "Grandma Sandi, don't leave me."

The teacher told me to leave and that she would be okay. That was a reminder of when I dropped Kimmy Jo off at kindergarten back in Philadelphia many years ago. Ashley acclimated nicely and was always ready to leave for her preschool class.

Ruby got a job at the George Washington University Hospital in the central supply department on the day shift. Keenan, now out of high school, got a job working for the United moving company. They wanted to move out into their own apartment, so they too would move to Amberwood Apartments. Ruby was a determined young woman, and I felt that no matter what happened in her and Keenan's relationship, she would make sure to take care of her children. They did move out, and Aaron and I were alone for the first time in ages.

One day Ruby wanted to take Ashley to visit her dad in York. Karmentrina would drive Ruby and Ashley there. When they went back to retrieve Ashley, her father refused to give her back to Ruby. Well, when they came back, they came to my house first and told me what had happened. Ruby's eyes were red from crying, and Karmentrina was swearing like her mom.

I told Ruby to go and wash her face and she did. Then I came up with a plan that they were going to put into place for getting my granddaughter Ashley back. I called Pop, Mary's boyfriend and told him that I needed a bodyguard for Karmentrina and Ruby.

I explained to him about what was going on and he said, "I got you, Sandi." The plan was for Karmentrina to park a few doors down from Ashley's dad's house and Ruby was to go to see her and she was to come up with some kind of an excuse for him to walk back into the house. Once he did that, she was to grab Ashley and run to the car.

Pop was standing across the street just in case he came out and caught them. It went smoothly, they were back in Maryland the next two hours with me laughing and talking about how well my plan worked out.

Karmentrina teased Ruby, telling her, "I did not know your little skinny legs could run so fast."

About a year later, Ruby would decide to leave Maryland and go back to York because Keenan was not holding up his end of the bargain, and I understood just where she was coming from. Ruby and the kids would leave, and Keenan would follow her. Aaron and I knew that Keenan was not ready to be anyone's father. We just hoped that one day they would work things out.

# Chapter Fifty-Five: Welcome to the World, Joshua Stockton-Rodriguez

I was on the evening shift at Southern Maryland Hospital on November the nineteenth when I was called to the desk for a telephone call. It was Karmentrina, telling me that she was in labor and she felt the baby was coming. I told her not to worry for it was her first baby and that I would be off of my shift in a few hours. Tonya was with her, and I told her to drive Karmentrina to the hospital on Andrews AFB and that I would come straight there when I got off.

Another call came through and it was the nurse at Malcolm Grow Hospital. She told me the baby was not going to wait. I got someone to take over my shift, and I drove straight away to the hospital. When I arrived on the maternity ward, it was about eleven forty-five, and Tonya was in the room with Karmentrina. They told me that Sergio and Aaron were on their way. They both worked at Esquire Liquors. They would arrive about fifteen minutes after me.

We were all in the room encouraging Karmentrina to push that baby out, and every time she said, "I can't, Mom," I said, "You can. Relax your breathing and push when the doctor tells you to with all of your energy."

Finally, it was time for the baby to join us, and only one person could go into the delivery room with my baby girl and it was already decided by nonverbal communication that it would be me.

They hustled me to the delivery room with gown, head, and shoe covers. Joshua joined the group about one a.m. in the morning. They wrapped him up and laid him on Karmentrina's chest, and she said, "He is so wrinkled, Mom."

I kissed her on her forehead and said, "Congratulations, Mommy! He will grow, and the wrinkles will go away."

We would all leave soon and return the next day. I went back to visit my babygirl the next day alone, for I needed a long time with Karmentrina.

She was doing well. She was sitting on her bed. She got up, and we went to look at Joshua through the nursery window. When we got to the nursery and were looking through the window, a nurse came out and said to Karmentrina, "Your baby must be out getting weighed."

Karmentrina looked at her and pointed to her baby and said, "No, my baby is right there." She most likely thought that no way any of those white babies could be Karmentrina's.

She was so apologetic I said to the nurse, "You never know nowadays!"

Karmentrina and I smiled at each other. I did not stay long because I would have to return with Aaron and Sergio. There is a story about how Joshua's name came to be. I may write about that one day.

# Chapter Fifty-Six: Empty Nest Syndrome

Back in July when everyone had moved on with their lives and Aaron and I were living alone, I was getting glimpses of empty nest syndrome images in my head. I saw an ad in the Washington Post that the United States Army was actively looking for registered nurses due to a shortage in the nurse corps.

I answered the ad and met with a recruiter without Aaron ever knowing. I signed up and was ready to go in September of 1988, but I had to ask for an extension because Karmentrina demanded that I be there when she had her first baby. I knew that was the right thing to do. Mom was with me when I had Kimmy Jo, and I know how scared I was back then.

Now that Joshua Stockton Rodriguez was born, I could move on with my plans. I decided that I needed to let Aaron in on the news for I would be leaving for Officer Basic Training in San Antonio, Texas in April, which was four months away.

He was a little shook up but decided that he would support me with an active-duty nursing career if that was what I wanted to do. I was glad that he agreed because I was not going to change my mind.

I had never lived alone in my entire life for any period of time, and this was going to allow me to experience it, even if for only some time. It was time for Aaron to experience carrying the whole load as I always did when he was away on all of his many military tours. Of course, he would have it much better because all of the kids were grown and not living at home.

No sooner had I arrived in Texas than I received a call from Aaron. He was verbally stressing on the phone. I told him to calm down and tell me what was going on.

He started out by saying, "Tracey called!"

I stopped him and said, "Handle it, babe. See you when I complete my training course."

# Photos

*Sandra and Aaron Married February 24, 1973*

*Family Photo 1977*

*Aaron US Air Force*

Sandra US Army Nurse Corp

*Sandra's Children (dressed in white) Kevin Scott, Kimmy Jo, Karmentrina Schevelle, Keenan Wynn*

*Sandra and Mom Dot*

*Mom Dot and Mr. Bill Duncan*

# Reflections

**Denise Middle-Brown**
*Advanced Practice Registered Nurse*
*Board Certified Family Nurse Practitioner*

Autobiographies can be disengaged and predictable. However, Sandra L. Kearse-Stockton vividly captures her imaginable truth. If she were to tell of her journey regarding our paths crossing, it was instantaneous trust, love, and dedication. My superior at the 121 Evacuation Hospital in Seoul Korea. I needed a friend, big sister, and a confidant. She far exceeded my expectations by including me into the family. Professional, no nonsense, and able to stand up and hold her own when required. The beauty of it is, she never was intimidated by flesh. She intelligently spoke in a manner that captured audiences of various cultures. Her thoughts flowed from her mind, seemingly harsh at times, but undeniably the absolute truth. Then she too would live up to her own demands of excellence. Strongly defended the rights of her troops, civilian employees, Koran nationals, and ensured the team was continually cohesive. If not, she would pause to respond to the fallen, bruised, weak, abused, shattered, or whatever warranted her immediate attention. Even in Korea, she would travel via bus for hours, gather broken and wounded women. Me! It did not stop in Korea. Sandra has been there for me no matter where I was. When I would call, she would come.

I would be far removed if I did not marvel at her and her husband Aaron's service as foster parents to numerous children who return with their children to share her spirit of extending love and care.

Last but not limited to, Her 1st masterpiece, *480 Codorus Street*. Written in a cyclic upward spiraling direction with jagged edges. Whipping, jolting, humorous, and historically timely. I look wholeheartedly forward to the next winding twisting and totally unimaginable saga. The legacy of a true leader.

**Portia O. Perry**
*Sr. Writer, Communiqué Magazine*

In 1967 I met Sandra in Baltimore, Maryland. She had come to Baltimore to look for her mother, Ms. Dot. My mother, Bernice Owens, met and became good friends with a lady named Ms. Dorothy Smallwood (a.k.a. Dot) and her companion Mr. William Duncan (a.k.a. Mr. Bill). Ms. Dot lived across the street from us on Hollins Street with a neighbor whom my mother knew. Her young son Bucky lived with them also. At some point, things were not working out for Ms. Dot and she needed assistance. I did not know the specifics of what transpired, only that Ms. Dot needed support and my mother provided it. They met at a local cafe across the street from where I lived with my mother and brother, Jimmy. My mother always helped people. She believed that we all have a responsibility to help others when we are called upon. I was around 14, and my brother was 13. I did not think it was important for me to know the specifics. I knew if my mother felt Ms. Dot needed help, she would provide it if she could. Sandra was always so decisive about what she wanted to do with her life. I read her first novel, *480 Codorus Street*. It was so enjoyable and humorous, and I found myself laughing and remembering our teenage years. It brought back some great memories. Thank God she did not tell all of our secrets.

I learned that some of Ms. Dot's children would be coming to stay with us. The first people I met were her daughter Sandra and her two grandchildren, Kimmy Jo, age two and Kevin, age one. The family was likable enough, and Sandra and I became friends immediately. I fell in love with her and her children. Karmentrina and Keenan came later, and I fell in love with them also. Sandra became the big sister I always wanted. She was so grown up. I was the oldest child of my mom's (Bernice's) children. My father died from a stroke when Jimmy and I were around 8 and 9 years old, so it was just the three of us. Later, Jimmy and I had lots of sisters and an extra brother because our families blended well together. Subsequently, my sister Wendy was born and Sandra became a big sister to her as well. We would become lifelong friends / sisters. As did our mothers. Some of Sandra's siblings came to stay, and others just visited. Ms. Dot and Mr. Bill and Bucky would leave Baltimore soon and return to York, Pennsylvania, but Sandra stayed for two years and graduated high school. My mom became her legal guardian while she and her children lived with us. She would have a third child during her senior year, Karmentrina, she was so beautiful. Sandra did not miss a beat; she was determined to graduate to make her mother proud of her.

Sandra was easy to talk to and have fun with. I admired her because she was focused on what she wanted to achieve in life. Even though she had children, she wanted to complete school and move ahead. So I had my mother (a nurse) as a role model, but also a new big sister. I respected her motivation and ambition even though there were challenges in her life. She never complained and worked hard toward her achievements. In my mom's house, you could not take up company with a boy until age 16. However, I did sneak a telephone call now and then. Yes, Sandra protected me, and I appreciated her support and agreed I owed her for always covering for me. She never required me to pay her back, thank God.

I am proud of her military service. She and her husband Ace have a total of fifty years of military service between them, so proud of them and what they have contributed to this country. Although his perspective on the bus incident in *480 Codorus Street* Book One is different from mine, he is entitled. She has been successful in her career and marital choice. She has excelled in both, and I am glad that Ace and I are good friends. He ended up being a keeper and a nice guy for my big sister. Not too long ago, I advised Sandra that I was working part-time for someone who was helping others with their career choices. She was assisting a lot of people and especially people who were interested in becoming authors. I referred Sandra to her, and the rest is history, for I knew Sandra's desire was to write a book someday. I am so proud of Sandra for reaching for her dreams. Her fortitude in being a mother and pursuing her dreams during some very difficult times is commendable.

Sandra has been a good wife to Ace and a great mom to her children, and she has faced some incredible odds while transitioning through all of the adversities. She has gone through much and accomplished more. I could not be prouder of her and her success in life. Guess what? She is just beginning. I love her so much. I could not have asked for a better big sister than she is to me. I am looking forward to reading her next novel, *480 Codorus Street Book II: Trials and Tribulations.*

**Karla Graham**
*Case Manager, Access Housing Inc. Washington, DC*

Nurse Stockton, "Sandi" and I met back in 2017 when she began working as a part-time nurse consultant at Access Housing Inc., an organization dedicated to helping homeless veterans. I immediately loved working with Sandra. She is a no nonsense, take charge, straightforward person and has a desire to help others succeed. There were times when we thought that we had done all we could do for a veteran, but we would put our heads together and find a way out for that veteran. We were not only co-workers but soon became friends after meeting, sharing many hours discussing how we could best serve our veterans, but also laughing and having fun.

During our conversations, Sandi would drop tidbits of information about her life. You know how people say, if you look up "such and such" in the dictionary, you would see a picture of "so and so." Well, if you look up perseverance in the dictionary, there you would find Sandra's picture. The epitome of resilience. As a foster parent, the sheer number of lives she and her husband have touched attributes to the strong woman that she is. Her accomplishments, travels, and the fact that this retired lieutenant colonel still wasn't ready to pack up her boots and white coat. There was a book that took me through a full range of emotions and a bed and breakfast experience. After reading her book *480 Codorus Street: Surviving Unpredictability*, I now knew I really did not know her at all.

I must say truly, that I miss having her as my sounding board and voice of reason and insanity at times. I look forward to the next installment of her life.

**Debra P. Warner**
*Lifetime Family Friend, Maryland, USA*

I first met Sandi many years ago as mom to my childhood friend, Kimmy Jo Kearse. Even though I met Sandi many years ago as a child, I did not truly know her. In my mid-twenties, I got to know her in a different capacity, the mom/manager of my longtime friend Kimmy Jo Kearse and her singing group. She exhibited extraordinary skill as she managed Kimmy and her group members. She is the core of her family, not only to her biological children but to the masses as she is a mother to countless foster kids. Nothing like a woman exuding strength, wisdom, and power while giving of herself. If one did not have a voice, she would be the voice for them. She loves family and always displayed a hilarious side, especially when telling stories about her family.

In October 1997, Kimmy and her group were guest singers at the Million Women's March in Philadelphia. Sandi invited me to go along with her and the group, Johnita, LaVondra, and her daughter Karmentrina who took her new baby girl with us as well. We all loaded into a van to be a part of such an historic event. Sandi's manager partner was at the wheel. I thought it considerate of him to escort all of us females on this supposedly one-and-a-half-hour drive. We reached Philadelphia timely but didn't reach our final destination until

2 am. It was funny to watch her partner and Sandi have words back and forth on directions. We witnessed the militant Sandi come out of hiding. Sandi was right and always exhibited strength in her words. Her partner was in deep water with that conversation. It was comical at first, but the laughter ceased when we kept riding around with no end in sight. Her partner would not budge nor take Sandi's suggestions. In the end, we all just burst out in laughter. If only her partner had listened, an hour and a half drive would have not turned into a five-hour drive.

Whenever I recall this story of Sandi, I can't help but think of the lyrics to *"This is a Man's, Man's, Man's World, but it would be nothing without a woman or girl." James Brown, 1966*

## Karmentrina Schevelle Kearse
*Daughter*

My mother, **Sandra Lee Smallwood Kearse Stockton** will probably tell everyone how long it took me to write this reflection for her; especially since I am a classic procrastinator. But what she does not understand, outside of waiting for my creativity to kick in, we have had fifty-three years together. As with any relationship, there are a plethora of memories that are ingrained in my psyche. I will attempt to sum it up in this reflection, although it will merely be a glimpse into our past.

So my mother gave birth to me in Baltimore, Maryland during her senior high school year. I, Karmentrina Schevelle Kearse, was the only one of her children to be born with my eyes wide-open, fully alert, ready for the world. Not to mention it was 1968 during the Black Power Movement, and although I was rather light complected, make no mistake my afro spoke volumes. My earliest memory of my mother surrounded my bouts as an asthmatic.

At the age of two I was diagnosed with asthma. I was very sick during those years, but my mother always seemed to take it in stride. There were plenty of rides in ambulances to the Emergency Room, but what I remember most is all the appointments at York Hospital. We lived about five miles from the hospital, and since my mother did not have a car, we had to walk if she could not get a ride or pay for a taxi. We would start out toward the hospital, and my mother would tell me that if I got tired, she would carry me. Of course, I always got tired. She would not hesitate to hike me up on her shoulders or on her back. I liked it more on her shoulders because I would not forget to loosen my hands around her neck. I guess she did not like being choked! For years we would fight asthma together, and neither of us would allow it to dictate my life. My mother was very vested in her children having experiences that showed her love for us.

When we lived in the projects, she was a single mother with five children. But it did not stop her from working and spending a lot of time with us. My mother taught us how to jump rope, double-Dutch and jacks. She would really kick our butts at jacks. She was a pro in our eyes. Me, Kim and Tracey were pretty good, but Keenan and Kevin always had to throw the ball up with one hand and pick up the jacks in the other hand so they could catch the ball after it bounced. She would tell us spooky stories when it stormed outside to scare us, and only she could tickle me and make me laugh, but the most memorable fun-time was tag-team wrestling! It would be girls versus boys. It would be us, my mom and her friends. She was tough! Whenever I was getting beat, she would reach her hand out as far as she could until I could tag her in to rescue me. I knew that she would always be in reach when I needed her, but I did not realize how many parts of my life she would play.

My mom would be our protector preparing us for the real world. I can remember when I was really young my mom would tell me that I had pretty eyes and a beautiful smile. I was the only one with a gap in my teeth that I did not like so I could not see it at all, apparently, she could. She would tell me this so that I would not hear it for the first time from a boy. She was going to ensure that I did not fall for the bait. In seventh grade people would begin to tell me I had a pretty smile and I still get that, even from my dentist, so I guess she was right. This was the mom part, and trust me, by the time I was eighteen, the conversations became so much deeper. I was prepared and grateful I had a mother as open and honest as she was during those important conversations.

My mom taught me how to advocate for myself and be proud of who I am. She instilled in us a sense of pride and taught us that Black was most definitely Beautiful. She also warned us about how the world would perceive us based on the color of our skin which meant we had to work harder to get the same things. My father and her would work hard to have extra money to take us places to offer us the experiences that would help to broaden our horizons. Restaurants, dinner theaters, different genres of music and family vacations traveling to other places. Not to mention the summer me and Keenan had to go to Korea. Not so happy on the way there but very grateful for the experience afterwards.

One of the experiences that me and Mom did often was to look at big, expensive houses that we could not afford. Kim would never want to go because she thought it was boring. But Kim did not know what we did afterwards like the Dairy Queen banana splits we would share or the High's ice cream scoops! We would visit model homes on the weekend and while inside I would imagine a whole scenario of what it would be like if we lived there. She would also subscribe to magazines like Architectural Digest, Southern Living, and Homes and Gardens to name a few. She would say you have to think it before you can see it. She was right. My mother has always been the type that reaches for more. She is never stagnant. So writing is her new passion, and trust me she is not done.

I have loved my mom all my life, and like I always tell her, I chose her before I came to this world. Like all mothers and daughters, we had our times through those teen years. Sometimes I thought she was taking a slap class! She would give me several warnings literally. She would say, "Karmen, I'm about to slap you!" But my brain would not allow me to turn it off. I had to have the last word, and I knew no matter what she heard what I had to say. So yeah, I can definitely take a slap. I am laughing just thinking about it. Nevertheless, we continued to grow very close so much that it was difficult for me to understand how many people we are able to deeply love.

I can remember when I had my first child, I would be so stressed out about my love for my mom and Joshua. I would almost have nightmares about crossing the Woodrow Wilson bridge with both of them in the car thinking if we went over, I would not be able to save them both. One day I told my mom, and she just laughed and said, "You would save him. I've lived my life." I am certain instinctually I would, but I loved her so much I could not fathom it. I knew that the way I felt about my relationship with my mother, I had to have that for myself. My second child Kristian would be a boy and my last would be a girl, Sandra-Alexis! My daughter and I are definitely close, and thanks to my mom I had a good mother role-model.

In closing, I know you noticed my daughter's name is Sandra-Alexis, but she is not the only one of my children to bear my mother's name.

**Sandra**-Alexis Schevelle, Kristian **Leigh**, and Joshua **Stockton** Rodriguez!

Yep, all three! Sandra Lee Stockton had her way when my children were born.

Baby Girl

# Persons in My Life Who Have Influenced Me Tremendously

My Mother, Dorothy Mae Jackson -Smallwood (11/27/1927-2/01/1992), My Father, William Junior Smallwood (01/11/1921), My Sister, Dorothy Mae Smallwood-Stewart (Midget) (07/23/1951-02/01/1992), My Brother, Clifford Earl Smallwood "Bucky" (09/25/1955 – 03/22/2009), My Guardian Mother, Bernice Alene Owens (12/28/1928-10/30/1995), My Guardian Brother, James A. Owens (08/09/1954-11/25/2006), My Step-Father, William Henry Duncan (Mr. Bill – 04/01/1918 – 07/12/1987), My Paternal Grandmother, Mabel Paul-Smallwood (08/26/1902 – 07/10/1969), My Late Husband Joseph Kearse (04/10/1947 – 06/26/1968), My Sister-in-Law Cressie Kearse (08/10/1949-03/16/2004), My Maternal Grandmother, Margaret Ryan Jackson-McGee (08/08/1908-03/29/1966), My Maternal Grandfather, Charles Jackson (08/05/1902-06/14/1967), One of My Very Closest Girlfriends, Joanne Clayton-Borders (09/11/1945-09/24/2012), One of My Favorite First Cousins, William Lee Smallwood (07/02/1945-01/30/2019), and My Loving Aunt, Virgina Hawkins, AKA Aunt Ginny (07/04/1932 – 12/29/2010), My favorite Aunt Vera Horton-Smallwood (05/26/1926-03/21/2019). My Maternal Aunt Joanne McGee-Grant, My Paternal Aunt "Sis 'Lugenia Smallwood- Miller (04/28/2003 – 04/30/2003), Maternal Uncle Charles McGee, My Maternal Aunt Almeda Jackson (1924-1991), My Mother-In-Law, Katherine Stockton (07/13/1927 – 2/10/2011), My Sister -In-Law, Katherine Kaye Thompkins (02/13/1947 – 07/21/2007), and My husband, Aaron Edward Paul Stockton, whom I love and cherish so very much.

**Never underestimate your own ability to affect positive change in others. We are stronger together.**

Made in the USA
Middletown, DE
22 June 2023